Ethical Economics and the Faith Community

Ethical Economics
and the Faith Community
How We Can Have Work and Ownership for All

Stuart M. Speiser

MEYER
STONE
BOOKS

The cover photograph is a view of Trinity Church, Wall Street, New York.

Published in the United States by Meyer-Stone Books,
a division of Meyer, Stone, and Company, Inc.,
2014 South Yost Avenue, Bloomington, IN 47403
Telephone: 812-333-0313

Cover design: Terry Dugan Design

Typesetting output: TEXSource, Houston

Manufactured in the United States of America
93 92 91 90 89   5 4 3 2 1

Library of Congress Cataloging in Publication Data

Speiser, Stuart M.
    Ethical economics and the faith community.

    Bibliography: p.
    Includes index.
    1. Economics — Moral and ethical aspects.
2. Economics — Religious aspects — Catholic Church.
3. Stock ownership.   I. Title.
HB72.S63   1989   174   88-43052
ISBN 0-940989-22-0

Contents

Foreword

IN NOVEMBER 1986, the Catholic bishops of the United States issued an important document under the title "Economic Justice for All: Catholic Social Teaching and the U.S. Economy." A large portion of the unsolved remainder of the project that produced that document is the need to find creative yet practical ways of implementing the principles identified by the bishops as fundamental to a just economy. Among these are respect for human dignity, recognition of the value of human solidarity in the workplace, the opening up of economic activity and decision-making to broad participation, the granting of preferential protection to the poor, and an unwillingness to yield to higher levels of administration what can be managed effectively at levels closer to both process and product.

One of the participants in the policy debate the bishops quite openly hoped to stimulate is Stuart Speiser. His opening chapter describes his participation in hearings before the drafting committee of bishops as well as the evolution of his own thoughts regarding the promotion of social justice through broader ownership and increased employment. The bishops believe the most effective social welfare system is a full employment economy. Stuart Speiser suggests that the way to social justice in the economic order is a dramatic expansion of private participation in the ownership of productive wealth.

Earlier proposals of Employee Stock Ownership Plans did not satisfy Mr. Speiser. For one thing, they did nothing for really needy people. He projected the notion of Universal Stock Ownership, where even the poor and unemployed would have some ownership of corporations. This idea evolved into the Universal Share Ownership Plan, a device to spread ownership of the means of production to all of the people.

An explanation of how a policy bridge might be built from the more familiar "employee stock" arrangements (with full acknowledgment of their risks and weaknesses) to the unmapped territory of "universal shares" is best left to the author. He addresses that task in the chapters that follow. The traveler's advisory I would want to issue to the readers of this book is related not at all to Mr. Speiser's new idea, but to that all too familiar human tendency to dismiss a new idea prejudicially. Ideas must first be understood; they next need legs. Some readers who come to understand what Mr. Speiser is proposing will not like it and will be unwilling to enlist in the policy march. Others will agree with the direction of the argument offered in these pages; they will want to refine it and relate it to the modification of present arrangements. Some will enter into the policy debate and work for the revolutionary change envisioned by the author. All readers will benefit from the reflection on vitally important economic issues that Mr. Speiser provides.

WILLIAM J. BYRON, S.J., *President*
The Catholic University of America

Preface

I WISH TO THANK FATHER WILLIAM J. BYRON, S.J., for gracing this book with his foreword; John Eagleson, for applying his formidable editorial talents to what had been an unruly manuscript; and Shon Bearup, for his imaginative illustrations.

References in the text (e.g., "Friedman, 1962") are detailed in the Bibliography (see pp. 258ff., below).

In the spirit of Father Byron's plea that the reader resist the "all too familiar human tendency to dismiss a new plea prejudicially," I offer these words from the preface written in 1936 by John Maynard Keynes for his classic work, *The General Theory of Employment, Interest and Money:*

> The ideas which are here expressed so laboriously are extremely simple and should be obvious. The difficulty lies, not in the new ideas, but in escaping from the old ones, which ramify, for those brought up as most of us have been, into every corner of our minds.

Chapter 1

Personal Journey

MY SEARCH FOR A NEW PATH to social justice began in 1975. I am still searching, but along the way I have learned some things that I think are worth recording, particularly because I have sought specific tools and concrete remedies rather than abstract theories.

My knowledge of economics is a direct outgrowth of my legal practice, which involves accident cases where people are seriously injured or killed. In such cases, the loss of future wages suffered by accident victims and their families must be considered when compensation is calculated. This required me to project the earning power of accident victims twenty-five or more years into the future, which in turn led to my study of the likely structure of our future economy. I found it necessary to consider industry and company employment histories, earning levels likely to prevail in various jobs, and the effects of inflation. The end result was that I was virtually forced to immerse myself in economics and in the even more sophisticated field of econometrics: the statistical measurement of economic theories. Moreover, I did not have the luxury of remaining in the ivory tower of theoretical analysis. The rigid courtroom rules of evidence exclude speculation and restrict testimony to matters of relative certainty.

Along with other lawyers in this field, I helped to pioneer the practice of using economists as expert witnesses to prove in court the value of lost earnings. I wrote the first textbook on this subject, which has since been quoted by the United States

Supreme Court and many other courts throughout the country.

Through my legal work with economists, I began to notice flaws in the theory of capitalism — particularly the hybrid form of "welfare capitalism" now operative in the United States and other western democracies. I sensed that we had allowed our welfare capitalism to feed on itself and to evolve like a wild weed, without adequate nurture from such vital American values as democracy, fairness, ethics, and religious belief.

I classify myself as a frightened capitalist who believes that capitalism has enabled America to achieve much that would not have been possible under any other system. I organized my own law firm as well as other businesses, and once served as chairman of a company whose stock was publicly traded; I have also served as a trustee of pension and profit-sharing plans. I have achieved far greater success within the capitalist system than I ever dreamed I would, and I now have a respectable share of capital ownership I would like to retain. I believe our welfare capitalism is running down and has become a patchwork system that creates enough internal conflicts to threaten our living standards, our democratic institutions, and our moral values. With all our resources, I think that we should be able to come up with a system that is more logical and equitable than welfare capitalism — one that more clearly reflects the consensus of basic American values.

Kelso

My immersion in the vagaries of economics led me to search for improvements in American capitalism that would preserve our high hopes and ideals. I looked at many ideas and theories, and became especially interested in the works of Louis O. Kelso, a San Francisco lawyer who wrote a book called *The Capitalist Manifesto* with Mortimer Adler in 1958. I had read some articles about him and his appealing idea of universal capitalism — making all Americans owners of stock of our major successful corporations. My interest was piqued by his appearance on the television show "60 Minutes" in March of 1975. He was grilled by Mike Wallace and pitted against the guru of welfare capitalist economics, Professor Paul Samuelson of MIT, who quickly wrote Kelso off as an "amateur crank."

As I watched Kelso perform on "60 Minutes," I liked him instantly. He was a peppery, white-haired little fellow wearing a polka-dot bow tie, and he spoke with conviction and sincerity. He also seemed to be making some sense. His pixie-like appearance made me think of Edmund Gwenn playing Santa Claus in the film *A Miracle on 34th Street*. Indeed, his idea that capitalism should include everyone as owners sounded like it could come only from Santa Claus. I found myself starting to root for this feisty lawyer and his vision of a new age of universal affluence and equity. Maybe I was being selfish; he was a lawyer trying to do something good for everyone. After Watergate and the Nixon administration, we lawyers were sorely in need of a win.

Kelso held his own against the bulldozing Professor Samuelson. His performance so excited me that I decided to meet him and learn more about his plans for universal capitalism. A few weeks after his "60 Minutes" appearance, he was in New York on a business trip and he agreed to have lunch with me. During that meeting and several others in the spring of 1975, he brought me up to date on his activities. The more I heard, the more intrigued I became. I read his three books and transcripts of his testimony before congressional committees. I noticed that his theories were expressed almost entirely in words: there were no statistical projections or forecasts showing how they might work out in practice. I questioned him about this, and he said that he had tried to get such studies made, but found that they would be very expensive. Furthermore, he felt that because federal legislation would be required to implement his plans, the statistical studies should be done by the congressional committees that had the necessary facilities and funds.

Since I had worked with econometric forecasters, I offered to try to get such studies done privately, and Kelso eagerly accepted my offer. I thought that the best way to do this would be to write a book on Kelso's theories, backing them up with econometric projections. It was obvious that Kelso was *persona non grata* with the economics establishment, since his writings and theories attacked the very foundation on which conventional economics was built. I thought that I might be able to help him gain some support by inserting myself as a neutral third party. Kelso approved the idea of my writing such a book, and at my request he recommended a researcher: a University of California law student named Jeff Gates, who had written articles about Kelso's theories for his law school newspaper. Jeff Gates flew into New York in June 1975 and we made arrangements for him to work as my research assistant on the proposed book.

In reading Kelso's three books, I noted that his main idea for achieving universal capitalism was a program called the Financed Capitalist Plan (FCP), under which all Americans who did not have the savings to become capitalists would be enabled to buy shares in our major successful companies through credit arranged by the federal government. His books espousing the FCP were written in 1958, 1961, and 1967. By the time I met him in 1975, he was no longer talking about the FCP, but instead was championing ESOPs (Employee Stock Ownership Plans) as the key to universal capitalism. When I questioned him on this, he explained that he had spent more than fifteen years trying to stir up interest in the FCP, but found that it was too grandiose an idea to interest politicians, and so he had decided to start the capitalist revolution himself at the grassroots by designing and installing tax-advantaged plans that would enable workers to become shareholders of the enterprises that employed them. Kelso was so inventive a corporate and tax lawyer that he was actually able to install working models of employee share ownership even before the tax laws were amended to accommodate them.

Those tax law changes started in 1973 when Kelso met Senator Russell B. Long (Democrat, Louisiana), who was then the powerful chairman of the Senate Finance Committee. Senator Long, convinced that broadening stock ownership was the best way to ward off the threat of creeping socialism, used his great influence to enact legislation authorizing several types of Employee Stock Ownership Plans, which today exist in more than 7,000 American companies and cover about 7 million employees. Since my book was going to be devoted largely to ESOPs, and since I could not take the time away from law practice to study many ESOP companies, I assigned Jeff Gates to do the necessary traveling and interviewing.

Limitations of ESOP

Had I not undertaken the analysis necessary to write a book, I might have gone along with Kelso's 1975 position that ESOP was the way to universal capitalism. But in the process of thinking through the outline of the book I decided that this was not so. I still admired Kelso greatly for his pioneering books on universal capitalism and the Financed Capitalist Plan. And I could appreciate the practicality of his shifting to ESOP as a program that he could actually get going during his lifetime, one that would break the ice for the broadening of capital ownership and open the way for consideration of the more sweeping idea of universal capitalism. But I simply could not go along with the idea that employee ownership itself could bring about universal capitalism.

We will cover ESOP in more detail in Chapter Five. Here it is necessary only to note the main reasons why, unfortunately, it is not possible to spread capital ownership *broadly* among the people through employee ownership. While most Americans are employed, the great majority would not gain any benefits from holding shares in the enterprises for which they work. The relatively few companies that remain successful and whose shares retain market value over a working life span of forty years employ only a fraction of our population. Most of our people work for themselves, or for government agencies, or for entities that do not issue shares that are traded, or they do not work at all. Employee ownership brings no benefit to the unemployed, the very poor, and those who are not fortunate enough to be long-term employees of continuously successful companies. Furthermore, employee ownership has been facilitated by tax benefits, which amount to a tax subsidy to the most fortunate sector of our society, those who have steady employment with strong companies. To that extent, it decreases the funds available to help the disadvantaged sector: those who have the least desirable jobs or no jobs at all.

When I figured this out for myself, I was chagrined, and my first thought was to drop the book project. But then I read again through Kelso's earlier works on the Financed Capitalist Plan and decided that there he definitely had been on the right track. Therefore, I decided to write a book mainly about the FCP, giving Kelso full credit for his remarkable pioneering efforts and acknowledging the importance of ESOP as a step toward broadened stock ownership. I started writing in December 1975, seeking to stimulate discussion of universal capitalism in academic, government, and business circles. I dared to hope that this discussion might lead to legislative activity, perhaps even congressional support for a declaration of national economic policy in favor of making capitalism universal, and then a congressional search for the best way to do it. But I never dreamed that my efforts would contribute to such a declaration even before my book was published. That opportunity came when the Joint Economic Committee of Congress, then headed by Senator Hubert A. Humphrey (Democrat, Minnesota), announced public hearings on ESOP to be held in Washington on December 11 and 12, 1975.

The 1976 Joint Economic Report

I attended those hearings, along with Jeff Gates and Dr. Abel Beltran-del-Rio, an econometrician who worked with Professor Lawrence Klein, father of the econometric model, at Wharton Econometric Forecasting Associates (WEFA). Abel had long been a follower of Kelso's quest for universal capitalism, and he and I became friends when I arranged for WEFA to do some econometric studies for my book.

Kelso was the main witness in support of ESOP. His exuberant testimony created the impression that ESOP would lead us to the promised land of universal capitalism. Most of the other witnesses were opposed to expansion of the tax deductions supporting ESOP, and indeed many of them poked holes in Louis Kelso's theories. I was concerned that the staff and committee reports coming out of these hearings might set back the whole broadened ownership movement because of what the committee might consider an exaggeration of the usefulness of ESOPs. In an effort to head off such a disaster, I decided to meet and cultivate the Joint Economic Committee (JEC) staff member in charge of the hearings, knowing that he would be the one to draft the report. He turned out to be Robert Hamrin, a young Ph.D. who had taught economics at the University of Idaho and Hong Kong Baptist College, and who joined the committee as an economist in 1974. I found Bob Hamrin very receptive to ideas that went beyond ESOP. He said that one of his concerns about ESOP was that its benefits did not go to the really needy people. When I told him that I was writing a book on broader plans, he invited me and Jeff Gates to lunch in the Senate Dining Room. At the luncheon, I was all set to convince Hamrin that there was a lot more to Kelso's theories than ESOP, and that Kelso's ideas were too important to dismiss on account of ESOP's shortcomings. But I found that Hamrin already knew this. He had focused the hearings on ESOPs only because Senator Humphrey was specifically interested in examining those plans. Hamrin was most desirous of including in the hearing record evidence of broader plans that could actually lead to universal capitalism. He eagerly agreed to publish in the hearing record a four-page statement that I submitted, covering broader plans such as the FCP that should be considered as the potential basis for a new national policy. I suggested that the Joint Economic Committee should not limit its study to the known limitations of ESOP but should address these wider questions: What can the United States accomplish by adopting as national policies the broadening of employee share ownership and the diffusion of newly created capital throughout our population? What are the best instruments for achieving such a national policy?

The first fruits of this effort appeared on March 10, 1976, in the *1976 Joint Economic Report,* which included a three-page section entitled "Broadening the Ownership of New Capital." The Employment Act of 1946 requires the JEC to issue the *Joint Economic Report* each year as the congressional reaction to the president's annual *Economic Report.* It is usually the most important economic report issued by any committee of Congress. The 1976 report recited statistics about the overconcentration of wealth, pointing out that the last comprehensive effort by the federal government to measure wealth concentration was made by the Federal Reserve Board in 1962. That 1962 study estimated that more than three-quarters of the country's total wealth was owned by less than one-fifth of the people, and more than one-quarter of the total was owned by the top one-half percent.

The *1976 Joint Economic Report* said that the ownership of corporate stock was particularly overconcentrated, even more so than total wealth, with the top 1 percent of the people owning 51 percent of individually owned corporate stock. It also described the present system of corporate capital expansion in these terms:

> Meanwhile, the new capital assets generated by business, which in recent years have averaged well over $100 billion annually, redound largely to the benefit of these persons who already have great wealth.

Then came the punchlines, words that I had never expected to see in the *1976 Joint Economic Report*:

> To begin to diffuse the ownership of capital and to provide an opportunity for citizens of moderate incomes to become owners of capital rather than relying solely on their labor as a source of income and security, the *Committee recommends the adoption of a national policy to foster the goal of broadened ownership.* [Italics added]

The report did not recommend any particular method of broadening capital ownership. It concluded:

> Whatever the means used, a basic objective should be to distribute newly created capital broadly among the population. Such a policy would redress a major imbalance in our society and has the potential for strengthening future business growth.
>
> To provide a realistic opportunity for more U.S. citizens to become owners of capital, and to provide an expanded source of equity financing for corporations, it should be made national policy to pursue the goal of broadened capital ownership.
>
> (Joint Economic Committee, 1976, pp. 98–100)

Coming within three months of the nearly disastrous ESOP hearings, here was a declaration of the Joint Economic Committee that broadened capital ownership should be made a national goal and a new economic policy of the United States. Furthermore, that declaration was adopted unanimously by the entire

JEC, even though other parts of the *Joint Economic Report* contained divergent partisan positions. I learned that Bob Hamrin had done most of the drafting of that statement. Now I had some hope that his report on the ESOP hearings would help open the way to universal capitalism.

Following the JEC's stirring call for a new national economic policy, the Hamrin staff study, issued on June 17, 1976, was almost an anticlimax. But for those interested in implementing the broad mandate of the *Joint Economic Report,* the staff study was a gold mine of specific information. It went way beyond ESOP and analyzed broader plans, including the FCP. It even suggested modifications of the FCP that might make it a feasible starting point (Hamrin, 1976).

Since I had undertaken to call the Financed Capitalist Plan to the attention of the JEC and had suggested the need for an urgent federal search for the best means of achieving a national economic policy of broad capital diffusion, I felt personal satisfaction with the Hamrin report's conclusions and details. I don't want to exaggerate my limited role, however. Hamrin and the JEC staff didn't need any help from me to decide that we needed a plan broader than ESOP. But the Hamrin report — and the ground-breaking declaration of national policy in the *Joint Economic Report* — demonstrated to me that anyone who has researched the existing plans for broadened capital ownership can make a contribution to the important debates that lie ahead, because there has been so little discussion of this subject.

Keynes on Broadened Ownership

It took me the rest of 1976 to finish writing the book. During that time, I met and interviewed Senator Russell Long, and on a trip to England I also interviewed Maurice MacMillan, son of former Prime Minister Harold MacMillan and a member of parliament and cabinet minister himself. Maurice MacMillan had participated in the organization of the Wider Share Ownership Council (WSOC) in London in 1958. The WSOC from its beginning has been a nonpartisan organization, with financial support from British businesses and banks. As they put it, their purpose was "encouragement of share ownership by more people."

I also interviewed Nicholas Davenport, a financier, writer, and former close associate of John Maynard Keynes. Davenport himself had written two books in which he supported the idea of universal capitalism through means other than employee ownership (Davenport, 1964 and 1974). I was anxious to learn what Davenport thought Keynes would have done today, if he hadn't died in 1946. The interview went like this:

> SPEISER: Do you think that when Keynes wrote the *General Theory,* he was handing down a permanent structure, carved in stone? Or do you think that he was just improvising something to get out of the Depression as quickly as possible?
>
> DAVENPORT: Of course he wasn't setting up a permanent structure. We had a frightful world Depression and millions of unemployed. He tried to find a way in which we could employ people with deficit spending. He wrote under that awful condition. If he had lived on into the boom years you can be sure that he would have shifted quickly to concentrate on the need for spreading the benefits of capital growth.
>
> SPEISER: Do you think that if he were alive today, he would be in favor of a broad-based plan to make capital ownership available to everyone?
>
> DAVENPORT: Of course he would. In fact, he started working on such a plan during the war.

This was a reference to Keynes's 1940 pamphlet, *How to Pay for the War,* in which he proposed a radical plan of forced savings that would bring about the broadening of capital ownership. He foresaw that wartime conditions would put upward pressure on wages, and he concluded:

> We cannot reward the worker in this way and an attempt to do so will merely set in motion the inflationary process. But we can reward him by giving him a share in the claims on the future which would belong otherwise to the entrepreneurs. (Keynes, 1940)

Keynes said that this plan would bring "an advance towards economic equality greater than any which we have made in recent times."

A Piece of the Action

My book was published in June of 1977, under the title *A Piece of the Action* (Speiser, 1977). The first effect of the book was to terminate my friendship with Louis Kelso. Although the book constitutes the first (and to date the only) biography of Louis Kelso and his crusade, and although it was so complimentary to Kelso that my publisher complained, nevertheless Kelso himself was infuriated. He did not agree with my conclusion that ESOP would not lead to universal capitalism. And he vehemently objected to Chapter Five, which was entitled "Kelso's One Mistake: The Two-Factor Theory."

In his own writings, Kelso insisted that traditional economists completely overlook capital as a factor in production and that they claim that goods and services are produced only by labor. But in reality, traditional economists *do* recognize capital as a factor in production. Indeed, most elementary economics books refer to *three* factors of production: land, labor, and capital. The Two-Factor Theory has led Kelso to advocate measurement of the relative contributions of capital and labor, which would ultimately require reduction of the wages of labor. In an attempt to build a bridge between Kelso and traditional economists, I went to great lengths to explain that Kelso's Two-Factor Theory is not a necessary part of his theory of universal capitalism. But I succeeded only in alienating Kelso. My claim that Kelso is mistaken on the Two-Factor Theory led him to break off communications with me, and he has not spoken to me since publication of the 1977 book. I regret this estrangement, since I consider him a great hero who is entitled to tremendous credit for pioneering ESOPs and for making thousands of people open their minds to the concept of universal capitalism.

A Piece of the Action was the first book that I had written for the general public. It was a heady experience. It got some favorable reviews, causing the publisher to order a second printing even before the publication date. It earned me the privilege of writing a full-page article for the business section of the *New York Sunday Times* on June 5, 1977, an article that brought more than a hundred responses to me and to the newspaper. And it propelled me into a nationwide tour of fourteen major cities, where I found myself discussing universal capitalism on radio, television, and in interviews with journalists.

From this experience, I learned two important facts about universal capitalism. First, there is a very strong appetite among the American people for a fairer system of capitalism under which all of us could become capitalists, even if only in a modest way. Second, there is a fairly high degree of comprehension of the complicated system of capital ownership and how it can be changed. This comprehension was a pleasant surprise, as I struggled to explain the Financed Capitalist Plan over the radio in such places as Detroit, Houston, and San Francisco. It was much easier to do on television, where I had the help of props and flowcharts that illustrated the capital ownership system. But the people from all walks of life who called in to the radio shows demonstrated that they understood the FCP, even though their total exposure to it was a four-minute oral explanation sandwiched in between commercials. Most callers were enthusiastic about the idea of becoming capitalists, but on almost every show there were people who picked up the weaknesses of the FCP, such as the possibility that it would increase inflation or inhibit the work ethic. My overall impression from the tour was that most Americans have a strong yearning for an economic system that is more consistent with our political democracy, and that they would support a practical plan to achieve universal capitalism.

Senator Gravel and "Full Return Stock"

Shortly after publication of the book in June 1977, I received a telephone call from Senator Mike Gravel (Democrat, Alaska). He was a member of the Senate Finance Committee, serving under Senator Russell Long, and had been given the job of finding a better way to pay for welfare and other government transfers. He had read the *1976 Joint Economic Report* and also the Hamrin report on the ESOP hearings and had been struck by the possibility that the Financed Capitalist Plan, or some form of broad stock distribution not based on employment, might serve as a substitute for some government transfer payments such as

Social Security and welfare benefits. He had also read my book, and he invited me to Washington to meet with him and his staff to discuss how the FCP could be tested through federal legislation.

I was elated by the apparent ease with which this revolution was gathering momentum. In a matter of a few months, the Joint Economic Committee had called for universal capitalism as a new national economic policy, and an influential senator was taking on the job of making this a reality.

I found Senator Gravel to be an engaging fellow, full of enthusiasm for this project. He assigned his top staff members to the job and brought in more than a dozen outside consultants as voluntary advisers. These included other Senate staff members, bankers, financiers, and economists, notably Professor Lawrence Klein and Dr. Abel Beltran-del-Rio, my friends from Wharton Econometric Forecasting Associates (WEFA). With their help, Senator Gravel developed the *Full Return Stock Plan,* the name being based on the feature that would require corporations to pay out as dividends the entire earnings (full return) of a special class of stock. To discuss and refine the plan, he convened "The Seminar on Policies for Capital Diffusion Through Expanded Equity Ownership," at the Brookings Institution in Washington on September 30, 1977. At the seminar, he described the plan as follows:

> I propose a new approach to capital expansion which would diffuse ownership of new capital to those who have not previously reaped the benefits of capital ownership. In simple outline the plan would guarantee private loans to purchase corporate stock, with the new capital being used by the corporation to pay for the expansion of plant and equipment. The stock would be held as security for the loan, and dividends used for repayment. After the loan is fully or partially retired, the investor would receive dividend income. The plan provides investment capital for industry while developing an alternate source of income for those who historically have depended on their labor income alone. The plan would not transfer existing wealth from the rich to the poor, but rather allow the poor to obtain a share of the new wealth generated by our capital expansion....

The plan should be tested on a limited scale to determine its effect on individuals, corporations, government and the economy as a whole. In each of five consecutive years $800 million in private, federally guaranteed loans could be made available to participants in amounts of $20,000 per family unit.... The test program would involve about 40,000 participants per year for five years for a total of 200,000 participants. This would give a sufficiently large and representative sample for analytical purposes....

The proposal contemplates the creation of a new class of corporate stock. The stock, referred to as Full Return Stock, would be preferred as to dividends and have its share of corporate earnings distributed quarterly....

Participants would be drawn from a cross section of American society. They would be chosen at random from four target groups: the blind and disabled, low-income working poor, middle income taxpayers, and Social Security recipients.

The meeting was chaired by Professor Lawrence Klein. He and others present concluded that such a plan, with some modifications, would be feasible. Senator Gravel issued a new draft in December 1977, which included some of the refinements developed at the Brookings seminar (Speiser, 1986, pp. 133–135).

Senator Gravel and his staff amassed hundreds of pages of studies, projections, and opinions about the feasibility of the Full Return Stock Plan. Unfortunately, however, before Senator Gravel could get his plan into legislation, he was defeated in the 1980 Democratic Primary. Since that time, no senator or member of Congress has resumed work on the promising start that he made toward universal capitalism.

The Need for Grassroots Support

The Gravel experience was a sobering one for me. It made me realize that changing the economic system through legislation alone is like punching a giant sponge. It is easy to make some apparent headway at first, but in the end nothing really happens until new tactics are brought to bear — in this case it is necessary that there be a strong grassroots movement that forces our legislators out of their natural mode of compromise. But that is not to say that such revolutions are impossible. Nobody gave tax reform a chance before 1984, but its overwhelming logic and fairness finally overcame the natural inertia of the legislature, and it quickly became a consensus steamroller that nothing could stop.

Going back to the drawing board, I realized that universal capitalism would need more discussion and background support in the academic and professional economics establishments before it made any progress toward legislation. While most senators and congressional representatives prefer to ignore economists, when legislators are faced with the prospect of initiating or supporting proposals of structural change in economic theory, they naturally reach for words of support from economic gurus. At the very least, they want to be sure that the change being proposed is not ridiculous or self-destructive, or something that was used a hundred years ago with disastrous results. Such reassurance was not forthcoming in the case of universal capitalism, largely because Louis Kelso, its earliest proponent, had estranged himself from the economics establishment by insisting that his Two-Factor Theory was an essential part of universal capitalism. As we have seen, that theory accused the economics establishment (unjustly) of ignoring capital as a factor in production. I resolved to try to overcome this obstacle by getting professional recognition of the theory of universal capitalism.

Fortunately, I had been appointed to the honorary board of editors of a new publication, the *Journal of Post Keynesian Economics*. The board was headed by John Kenneth Galbraith, and the working editors were Professor Sidney Weintraub of the Wharton School and Professor Paul Davidson of Rutgers University. I was able to convince them that universal capitalism merited a hearing, and so in the spring of 1979 the *Journal of Post Keynesian Economics* published the first article on universal capitalism in an economics journal, "Increasing Capitalism's Capitalists — A Challenge for Economists," which was written by Abel Beltran-del-Rio, Robert Hamrin, and myself. I can't say that there was an electrifying response to the article, but at least we could point to publication of the theory in a reputable economics journal.

Soon after publication of *A Piece of the Action,* I received a call from Franklin R. Stewart, a career State Department official. He had read the book and it had rekindled his long-time interest in Kelso's theories of universal capitalism. He invited me to Washington, where he arranged a luncheon at the State Department attended by other government and foundation officials. Frank Stewart wanted to make universal capitalism a political issue, even if it meant organizing a new political party for that purpose. Frank and I became good friends, and we tried to interest all the presidential candidates in the 1980 and 1984 elections in universal capitalism as a campaign issue. We were not successful, but we opened the minds of several candidates (or at least members of their staffs) to the possibilities of such a plan.

I was still quite busy in law practice, but I found the time to write more books and articles about universal capitalism. In 1982, I wrote a novel called *SuperStock,* a fictionalized version of the quest for universal capitalism. I coined the term "SuperStock" for a modified version of Kelso's Financed Capitalist Plan. I felt that a new name was needed because the plan departed materially from Kelso's original version. I hoped that the public would grasp a name like SuperStock more readily than a more technical description. Although the jacket of *SuperStock* carried complimentary blurbs from Gay Talese, Jane Bryant Quinn, Professor Sidney Weintraub, and Joseph F. Cullman, III (then the chairman of Philip Morris, Inc.), all of them valiant friends who were pressed into service in the cause of universal capitalism, I can't say that *SuperStock* was the rage of the bookstores. In fact, it received rather rude treatment at the hands of some reviewers who felt that I had tricked them into ingesting a lesson in economics under the guise of an international espionage-murder mystery. While not an artistic success, the novel did manage to carry the message of universal capitalism to a few thousand people who would not otherwise have read a book about economic theory.

By popular demand, I went back to writing non-fiction. In 1984, I wrote *How to End the Nuclear Nightmare.* That immodest title was designed to attract the attention of the millions of people concerned about the runaway nuclear arms race. In that book, I attempted to relate the nuclear arms problem to economics. I tried to demonstrate that of all the factors underlying Soviet-American enmity (nationalism, lust for power, differences in political system, and differences in ideology) only the latter, the differences between capitalism and communism, could be removed. I pointed out that while all the other differences *might* cause enmity, they did not *compel* us to be enemies, because we were friendly with some nations that had different political systems and with many nations whose leaders were driven by nationalism and lust for power. It was only the natural enmity between capitalism and communism that compelled us to be enemies of the Soviet Union, I claimed. The solution I proposed was the installation of universal capitalism (which I then called SuperStock) in the United States, thus removing from this enmity Marx's main objection to capitalism: exploitation of the nonowners by the owners of capital. This, in my opinion, would remove the main ideological barrier to world peace and nuclear disarmament. This rather simplistic analysis of the gravest problem ever to confront humankind infuriated some reviewers and readers, but by and large the book was favorably received. Many readers felt that I had reached out too far in attempting to solve the nuclear arms crisis through installation of SuperStock, but at least their minds were opened to the possibilities of SuperStock itself as an economic remedy for the United States, regardless of whether it could reduce Soviet-American enmity.

Nuclear Nightmare brought some important breakthroughs. In conjunction with the book, I sponsored an essay contest to spur worldwide discussion of SuperStock and its chances of lessening Soviet-American tensions. Ward Morehouse, president of the Council on International and Public Affairs, agreed to have his organization administer the contest, for which I donated a $10,000 prize. In September 1984 we launched the *Nuclear Nightmare* book and the essay contest in a seminar sponsored by the Council on International and Public Affairs held in the United Nations community. Ward Morehouse served as moderator, and the other panel members were the renowned liberal economist Robert Lekachman, Distinguished Professor of Economics at the City University of New York; and Admiral Noel Gayler, former director of the National Security Agency and one of the leading advocates of a sane nuclear weapons policy. We had an excellent turnout, including members of the press, econo-

mists, clergy, and anti-nuclear activists. The most lasting contribution of the seminar was the presentation by Professor Lekachman, who stated unequivocally that he thought SuperStock was
entirely feasible and indeed was a mainstream conservative idea
that should fit in very well with the prevailing American consensus under Ronald Reagan. He himself preferred to stand by
his dedication to democratic socialist remedies, but his complimentary remarks about SuperStock constituted an important
breakthrough. His seminar speech, as well as a similar contribution by Professor Paul Davidson, were reprinted in the *Journal
of Post Keynesian Economics* in the spring of 1985 (Davidson,
1985b; Lekachman, 1985).

The *Nuclear Nightmare* book also gave me the opportunity
to lecture and participate in seminars on college campuses, since
nuclear disarmament was a much more compelling topic than
economic theory. Most of the remarks hurled at me by the
audiences indicated great resistance to the idea that the nuclear nightmare could be avoided by taking the exploitation out
of American capitalism. But again, thousands of minds were
opened to the idea of SuperStock, and many people asked me
why I didn't drop the nuclear argument and simply promote
SuperStock on its own. I explained that I had been promoting
SuperStock as an economic theory for at least eight years, but
had not been able to arouse as much public discussion as occurred when I dared to propose it as a solution to the nuclear
nightmare.

The Winning Essays

The most important after-effects of *Nuclear Nightmare* came
from the essay contest. I had a half-hour segment on Dennis
Wholey's wonderful talk show, "Late Night America," which
is broadcast from Detroit to many public television stations
throughout the United States and Canada. As a result, the Council on International and Public Affairs received more than four
hundred requests for essay contest entry forms. The contest
itself, which closed on December 31, 1985, brought hundreds
of entries from all parts of the United States and many foreign countries. The eventual winner was Jon Wisman, Professor
of Economics at the American University in Washington, D.C.

(Wisman, 1986). At the presentation ceremony hosted by the Council, the principal speaker was the Rt. Hon. David Howell, Conservative Member of Parliament and formerly a minister of the Thatcher cabinet, who has written and lectured widely on the need for the broadening of both work and ownership. The overall quality of the entries was so high that the Council decided to publish a collection of the papers, edited by Kenneth B. Taylor, Professor of Economics at Villanova University (Taylor, 1987). But one of the entries that did *not* win the contest made an even stronger impression on me. That essay, entitled "Modified SuperStock, Full Employment and Elimination of the Federal Debt," was submitted by John A. Sedlak, a Roman Catholic priest from Greensburg, Pennsylvania, who wrote:

> [Speiser's concept of universal stock ownership] would seem to have several significant weaknesses which need to be addressed. The first and most important is that it does not take into account the value of work beyond financial remuneration, and it might reduce the incentive to work, with adverse social consequences. It should be plain that work has a value that goes beyond distributing the wealth derived from the means of production, thus sustaining workers and their families. Society depends on and benefits from the products and services of human labor, and the worker would seem to gain in self-discipline and self-esteem from productive participation in society.

Father Sedlak went on to document this point by references to the history of the Works Progress Administration (WPA), demonstrating the rise in self-esteem among people who moved off welfare into a WPA public service job. Father Sedlak continued:

> From my religious-moral perspective, it can be added that human work is, by God's design, a sharing in His creative activity, and therefore, is integral to man's nature and well being. From this point of view could come the conclusion that along with other economic rights, such as to adequate food, housing, and health care, man also has a need and a right to work.

Here Father Sedlak cited sections 18 and 25 of *Laborem Exercens*, the 1981 encyclical of Pope John Paul II, and also passages from the second draft of the Catholic Bishops' pastoral on the American economic system. Father Sedlak went on to modify the SuperStock plan by devoting a substantial portion of it to creating employment rather than making us a nation of coupon-clippers. His paper convinced me that I had fallen into the trap of becoming a one-issue person, carried away by the magic dream of universal capitalism: an age of leisure and affluence that would make work less important in our society. I had ignored the non-monetary rewards of work and had written off the concept of full employment as unnecessary and unattainable, since the capitalist income from stock ownership would take the place of some or all employment for millions of Americans. While my work had demonstrated that this was mathematically and economically feasible, I had overlooked the important human element that Father Sedlak's essay brought home to me. I learned from his essay that social justice could not be achieved through universal stock ownership alone. We would also have to provide for meaningful participation by all those able to work.

A starting point would be to restudy the history of Franklin Roosevelt's New Deal agencies that created public service jobs: the Public Works Administration, the Works Progress Administration, and the Civilian Conservation Corps, which operated between 1933 and 1941. While it has become unfashionable to pay for such work from the public treasury, the addition of the ownership factor, and the dividends that could be paid to all citizens through universal share ownership, might make it possible to build on the New Deal foundation a permanent system of public service employment.

The Bishops' Pastoral

In 1982, I learned that the National Conference of Catholic Bishops was drafting a pastoral letter on Christianity and capitalism, an idea suggested by Auxiliary Bishop Peter A. Rosazza of Hartford, Connecticut. The pastoral committee of five Bishops, led by Archbishop Rembert G. Weakland of Milwaukee, was holding hearings throughout the country to receive the views of people from many walks of life on how American capitalism could be made into a more moral system, more consistent with Catholic social teaching. I managed to wangle an invitation to appear before the committee, and in September of 1982 they listened politely as I addressed them at the headquarters of the U.S. Catholic Conference in Washington.

At that time, many people feared that the forthcoming pastoral would be a denunciation of capitalism as an inherently immoral system and that it would advocate a change to democratic socialism. In my presentation, I pointed out that despite the moral shortcomings of capitalism, capitalist nations generally are more democratic and offer a greater degree of religious and social freedom and a higher standard of living than do Marxist nations. I tried to convince them that there is a way to make American capitalism a morally just system. I called their attention to the *1976 Joint Economic Report of Congress,* which urged a national policy of distributing the ownership of newly created capital broadly throughout society. I suggested that they include that section of the *Joint Economic Report* in their pastoral letter, also pointing out that American companies are creating new capital (plants, equipment, computers, etc.) at the rate of more than $300 billion per year, and that if the ownership of this new capital were shared by the 50 million American families who do not own significant amounts of capital now, we could actually provide capital ownership of $100,000 to each of those 50 million disadvantaged families. I suggested that such a wide diffusion of capital ownership would move us much closer to social justice and would make American capitalism more consistent with Catholic social teaching, as well as removing the principal cause of ideological conflict between capitalism and Marxism.

I eagerly awaited publication of the first draft of the pastoral, which came in November 1984. While the Bishops declared the need for new experiments to make capitalism a more just system and cited expansion of employee stock ownership as one promising tool, they did not mention the broader concept of SuperStock or the ownership of shares by people other than employees. Since this was only a first draft, which was thrown open for comments, I took it upon myself to convince the Bishops that they should include the SuperStock (or universal capitalism) concept in the list of experiments to be tried in an effort to make our economic system consistent with our political democracy. I tried to explain, in a written submission to the Bishops, that while employee share ownership was a very important and positive step, it would do nothing for the poor, who were supposed to be the main concern of the pastoral. Apparently the message got through, despite the tens of thousands of pages of comments received by the Bishops, because the second draft included a recommendation for research and experimentation with profit sharing, employee ownership, cooperative ownership of firms by all who work within them (all of which had been in the original draft), and "schemes for enabling a much larger number of Americans, regardless of their employment status, to become shareholders in successful corporations." The new provision was the embodiment of SuperStock. My prayers had been answered.

I feel reasonably certain that the idea for those four lines came from me, since a footnote in that section refers to my 1985 article on SuperStock in the *Journal of Post Keynesian Economics* (Speiser, 1985). I also believe that the Bishops' decision to include the universal stock ownership language was influenced by my calling to their attention the article by the eminent Robert Lekachman in the same issue of the *Journal of Post Keynesian Economics,* "SuperStock: A Conservative Alternative to the Welfare State" (Lekachman, 1985).

I waited impatiently through the year that transpired between the second draft and the adoption of the final pastoral in November 1986, hoping that the precious four lines that had cost me four years of labor would not wind up on the cutting room floor. But the Bishops saw fit to leave those four lines in, even improving them by changing the word "schemes" to "programs." Of course, the Bishops did not recommend the installation of SuperStock, but only continued research and experimentation with it, along with a number of other proposals for greater economic democracy.

Continuing the Essay Contests

In the meantime, the results of the 1985 essay contest were so exciting that I decided to continue the experiment in 1986. This time I omitted the focus on the nuclear nightmare and confined the subject to universal share ownership. I decided to sponsor concurrent contests in the United States and Great Britain. I had established a strong friendship with Harry Ball-Wilson, a former Royal Air Force pilot of roughly my vintage who had served in the Battle of Britain and the even more perilous mission of the "Hurricats," those intrepid fighter pilots who fought off the Nazi submarine menace by being catapulted from the decks of freighters without landing gear, hoping to return safely by landing their Hurricanes (land-based fighter planes) in the water near enough to the freighter to be fished out by a derrick. Harry was one of the British pioneers of wider share ownership and has been active in the field since 1950, when he first became Parliamentary Liberal candidate for Bermondsey. He has long been a director of the Wider Share Ownership Council in Great Britain, and he was kind enough to introduce me to that organization, which agreed to administer the British essay competition.

The Anglo-American essay contests were open for the calendar year 1986, and the assignment for both was: "In 5,000 words or less, devise a plan for spreading ownership of America's [or Britain's] productive assets broadly among the people, and reviving the economy, without confiscation or increased taxation." Again, the results were startling. We received marvelous essays from all parts of the United States and the United Kingdom. Leading essays from both contests were published by the Council on International and Public Affairs (Speiser, 1988). I will describe some of the new ideas gleaned from these essays at relevant places later in this book. They demonstrate the important contributions that individuals, as well as religious organizations, can make in the search for a new path to social justice.

In connection with the 1986 essay contests, I wrote *The USOP Handbook: A Guide to Designing Universal Share Ownership Plans for the United States and Great Britain* (Speiser, 1986a). My years of fruitless quest for legislation embodying the SuperStock principle had caused me to abandon that rather expansive term. A new term, USOP — Universal Share Ownership Plan — was suggested by my son, Jim Speiser, who feels that it is a complete description of the concept.

Facing the Political Realities

Throughout these literary endeavors, I was still trying to promote political interest in SuperStock-USOP. The Council on International and Public Affairs established a subsidiary organization known as the Center for Study of Expanded Capital Ownership, which had its headquarters at the Washington office of my law firm. Ward Morehouse and I donated our services, along with Frank Stewart as director and Bob Hamrin as chief economist, with the unofficial assistance of Jeff Gates, who had become counsel (and resident ESOP expert) to the Senate Finance Committee, working directly under Senator Russell Long. We thought that we had hit paydirt when Bob Hamrin became economic consultant to Senator Gary Hart's 1984 presidential campaign. But despite Senator Hart's claim that he was the new ideas candidate, he did not embrace USOP, although he did support expansion of employee share ownership. Frank Stewart and I had several interesting meetings with campaign aides of other 1984 candidates, but again we struck out. Despite our enthusiasm, we began to realize that a step as revolutionary as universal share ownership was going to take a lot more spade work before it could become part of a major party's platform.

This message was brought home in a meeting with Senator Russell Long just after he had announced his retirement from the Senate in 1986. He told me that he appreciated the research and writing that I had done and that he was sympathetic to the idea of expanding the ESOP concept beyond employees to needier people, but he did not believe this could become a practical legislative program unless the recipients of shares could *earn* their stock. He did not think the American people would support a handout of permanent property ownership evidenced by stock certificates. I had been gradually coming to that conclusion myself, and I was further moved to connect universal stock ownership with employment, or earning of the shares, through Father Sedlak's 1985 essay.

That gives you a brief outline of more than ten years of work on the concept of universal share ownership.

The following Ten Principles summarize what I have learned about using job creation, broadened ownership, and action by religious organizations to achieve greater social justice. (Please note that I do not claim they will lead us to complete social justice or an ideal society — the claim is merely *greater* social justice.)

The first five principles are accepted by most Americans, and therefore can be called *consensus* principles. Principles Six through Ten (which I call *complementary* principles) are less familiar to most Americans. The main mission of this book is to convince you that individuals and religious organizations can use these principles to design and create new structures, thereby taking important steps toward greater social justice. If these new structures are built from the consensus building blocks, they will represent a *practical* approach to social justice because they will attract wide public support.

TEN PRINCIPLES FOR A PRACTICAL RELIGIOUS APPROACH TO SOCIAL JUSTICE

Consensus Principles

- *First:* Capitalism, despite its faults, is the economic system supported by most Americans.

- *Second:* Structural changes can make capitalism more just.

- *Third:* People who want to work should be able to work.

- *Fourth:* When the private sector is unable to provide sufficient employment, public service jobs are an effective way to put people to work, provided the cost is reasonable.

- *Fifth:* The ownership of corporate stock is too highly concentrated.

Complementary Principles

- *Sixth:* Decisions regarding changes in the economic system should be made at the lowest possible level.

- *Seventh:* The feasibility of economic policies is determined in large part by trial and error.

- *Eighth:* Experiments seeking more economical methods of paying for public service employment should include use of stock ownership.

- *Ninth:* Distribution of income and distribution of ownership are value judgments and therefore are just as much religious issues as they are political and economic issues.

- *Tenth:* Religious organizations have a crucial role to play in making capitalism more just.

These principles constitute the opening statement of my case. Judges admonish jurors that the lawyer's statements are not evidence, and that they are to decide the case only on the evidence. So, you need not accept these principles without concrete evidence of their validity. In the following chapters I shall present the evidence to you, through such witnesses as Ronald Reagan, Hubert Humphrey, Henry Kissinger, Paul Samuelson, Jack Kemp, Lawrence Klein, John Maynard Keynes, Milton Friedman, and many others. I hope to convince you, as a juror, that all ten principles belong within the mainstream American consensus and that they can be molded into a force that our religious organizations can use to help bring about greater social justice. I cannot hope for a unanimous jury verdict, as is required to convict someone of a crime. But I am not trying to convict anyone of a crime. This is a civil matter that involves money, and in such cases the law, in its wisdom, does not require a unanimous verdict. In New York, a verdict of ten to two is sufficient, and in California it is nine to three. I believe my case is convincing enough to merit such a majority vote.

Since I cannot avoid thinking like a lawyer, this book will reflect some of the lawyer's methods of reasoning. We are trained to separate fact from opinion, and the relevant from the irrelevant. We try to line up the evidence in a cause-and-effect sequence, searching for what the courts call "causation." We are accustomed to dealing with opinions of technical experts who differ sharply in their conclusions. We are experienced in striving to reach consensus on complicated financial transactions, including multi-million dollar lawsuits involving hundreds of contending parties and factions. We are particularly trained to distinguish *substance* from *procedure,* because different rules of law govern these two factors. So much for lawyer's palaver. Let's get on with the evidence.

Chapter 2

The Supporting Evidence

IN THIS CHAPTER, I shall examine the evidence supporting the Ten Principles mentioned in Chapter One. Since all of these principles are matters of opinion on which reasonable people may differ, it would be unreasonable to expect this evidence to be conclusive. I shall try to demonstrate that the first five (consensus) principles are accepted by most Americans, and I shall present whatever facts I have been able to marshall to persuade you that all ten are worthy of your support. Specific plans that might achieve the goals of these principles will be discussed in later chapters.

Before considering each principle separately, it is worth noting that according to the most popular textbook on economics, most of the major goals underlying our first eight principles are widely (though not universally) accepted in American society. In his introductory section, University of Nebraska Professor Campbell R. McConnell, whose text recently dropped Paul Samuelson's to second place, lists these consensus goals: economic growth, full employment, economic freedom, an equitable distribution of income, economic security for those needing help, and improvement of the physical environment (McConnell, 1987, pp. 9–10).

A Word about Social Justice

Before we discuss the Ten Principles that may lead to greater social justice, it is necessary to note that not everyone accepts

28

the legitimacy of that term. For centuries, philosophers have used the word "justice" to describe humane economic measures. The term "social justice" itself dates back to the eighteenth century (Godwin, 1793), but some conservatives, such as Milton Friedman, simply ignore the term, although they do not necessarily ignore the need for humane efforts to improve income distribution. As Thomas Sowell points out in *A Conflict of Visions,* Friedman himself has proposed schemes of income transfer to the poor (Sowell, 1987, p. 192). Sowell goes on to analyze the writings of one conservative who does discuss social justice: Friedrich A. Hayek. Hayek believes that the term is empty of meaning, if not dishonest. However, it is clear from Sowell's analysis that "Hayek's objections are to the *process*" by which specific social results are sought (Sowell, 1987, pp. 194–198). Thus, Hayek's views create a mere procedural disagreement that can be resolved by trial and error. If we accepted Hayek's position, which Sowell calls the "constrained" vision — one that considers it beyond the capability of decision makers to achieve social results — we would have to ignore such advances as the abolition of slavery, the outlawing of child labor, and the establishment of Social Security.

If you share Hayek's aversion to the word "social," you may be more comfortable with "economic justice" or just plain "justice." Indeed, you might equate "justice" with "fairness," as John Rawls does in his famous thesis, *A Theory of Justice* (Rawls, 1971).

Evidence for the First Principle: American Support of Capitalism

Fortunately, we do not have to guess at the current American consensus on capitalism versus the alternative, socialism. In 1984, Harvard University Press published *The American Ethos: Public Attitudes Toward Capitalism and Democracy,* written by University of California Professor Herbert McClosky and Princeton Professor John Zaller, and sponsored by the Twentieth Century Fund. *American Ethos* is based on more than eight years of expert public opinion surveys, and draws upon similar surveys done by the Gallup and Louis Harris polling organizations. *American Ethos* found that 89 percent of the American public, and 96 percent of influential Americans (those in a position to affect public opinion), were opposed to socialism (McClosky and Zaller, 1984, p. 135). By margins of better than 80 percent, the general public and the influentials supported the propositions that "the free enterprise system is necessary for free government to survive," and "our freedom depends on the free enterprise system" (ibid., p. 110). This led the authors to conclude that capitalist values have been so deeply etched into the national consciousness that they must be considered one of the two major strands of thought that compose the American ethos, the other being democracy (ibid., p. 101).

Some may assume that in order to achieve a morally just system, we have to discard capitalism altogether because it is inherently immoral. On paper, socialism may appear theoretically to be a more moral and just system than capitalism, but it will not produce a concrete plan for achieving greater social justice within the mainstream American consensus. Socialism as such has never had much of a following in the United States, the high point having been reached in 1912 when labor union pioneer Eugene Debs polled 6 percent of the popular vote as the presidential candidate of the Socialist Party. Socialism has failed to make much of an impact here mainly because labor has been able to attain a comparatively high standard of living and has been relatively free to move into the capitalist class. Those nations that have installed socialism have generally been unable to sustain the incentives that fuel successful economies.

Socialism in the form of government ownership of the means of production is not a viable alternative in the United States today, simply because it hasn't worked. The Socialist International, a descendant of Marx's First International, no longer advocates government ownership. But other forms of socialization are now integral parts of welfare capitalism. The platforms of the Republican Party in the United States and the Conservative Party in Great Britain are loaded with social welfare measures that could not be dropped without bringing on disaster for the party in question.

Indeed, the labels of "capitalism"' and "socialism" have become less useful as the two systems converge, probably because the persistent problems of both have produced a natural flow toward accommodation. For the past fifty years, we have been trying to combine the best features of capitalism with useful facets of socialism, producing today's patchwork system of welfare capitalism. The choice is not between pure socialism and pure capitalism, because pure forms do not exist today. Rather, we now choose between socialist and capitalist *solutions* to social and economic problems.

Even in the business world, there is convergence from the right and left. Lee Iacocca, chairman of Chrysler, probably is the most prominent success symbol of American capitalism. But Iacocca headed Chrysler when it failed, and under the rules of capitalism it should have gone out of business. Instead, the government bailed it out with the most massive intervention into private business in our history, and then it protected Chrysler from foreign competition by imposing import quotas. Iacocca's autobiography advocates trade protection through tariffs and a national industrial policy that would make the government a partner of business and labor. Government money and services have supported American free enterprise throughout its history, from the time when the cavalry protected the westward expansion of the railroads to today's business tax benefits, research subsidies, loan guarantees, and outright grants to new business operations. Practically every business receives important benefits from public expenditures on highways, transportation, public health, and education.

The convergence of capitalism and socialism has been dramatized recently by movement toward more free enterprise in the bastions of Marxism, the Soviet Union and the People's Republic of China. Lenin himself sanctioned private enterprise in a mixed economy in 1921 under his New Economic Policy, largely because the Soviet economy was near collapse and he wished to restore trade with capitalist nations. The Lenin mixed economy disappeared with the adoption of central government planning and the collectivization of agriculture under Stalin, but it seems to be coming back under Gorbachev, who has grasped the reality that some of the incentives of private enterprise are needed to bring the Soviet Union into the computer age. The success of market economies in Hungary and Yugoslavia led to demands for experiments with free enterprise in China and the Soviet Union, which are unfolding in the late 1980s.

Gorbachev's book, *Perestroika,* contains some remarkably candid insights on the stagnation and lack of incentives inherent in a socialist system. Gorbachev describes these negative factors as "a kind of braking mechanism" that prevents economic progress:

> It became typical of many of our economic executives to think not of how to build up the national asset, but of how to put more material, labor and working time into an item to sell it at a higher price. Consequently, for all "gross output," there was a shortage of goods. We spent, in fact we are still spending, far more on raw materials, energy and other resources per unit of output than other developed nations.... Parasitical attitudes were on the rise, the prestige of conscientious and high-quality labor began to diminish and a "wage-leveling" mentality was becoming widespread. The imbalance between the measure of work and the measure of consumption, which had become something like the linchpin of the braking mechanism, not only obstructed the growth of labor productivity, but led to the distortion of the principle of social justice.... Our rockets can find Halley's comet and fly to Venus with amazing accuracy, but side by side with these scientific and technological triumphs is an obvious lack of efficiency in using scientific achievements for economic needs, and many Soviet household appliances are of poor quality. This, unfortunately, is not all. A gradual erosion of the ideological and moral values of our people began.
>
> (Gorbachev, 1987, pp. 19–21)

Evidence for the Second Principle: Changes Can Make Capitalism More Just

Although most of my friends and business associates are dedicated to free-enterprise market capitalism, I don't know anybody who thinks American capitalism — or any other brand of capitalism — is perfect. Most economics professors agree that in order to survive, capitalism needs repeated injections of social welfare medicine, particularly in a representative democracy. As David Stockman puts it, the American electorate does not want pure capitalism but "a moderate social democracy to shield it from capitalism's rougher edges." But we do not have to become engulfed by the question that has plagued western civilization for centuries: *Is capitalism inherently an immoral system?* Instead we can address a much more precise and practical question: *How can we build on the existing consensus to bring American capitalism closer to the kind of moral system that will bring out the best in all of us?*

Until recent years, many (probably the majority) felt that economic growth would take care of most of our problems, including the justice issue. As John Kenneth Galbraith put it:

> The twenty years from 1948 through 1967 may well be celebrated by historians as the most benign era in the history of the industrial economy, as also of economics. The two decades were without panic, crisis, depression or more than minor recession.... It was a very difficult time for critics of the capitalist system. (Galbraith, 1975, p. 253)

This cornucopia was based on growth, a rising tide that appeared to be lifting all boats. Hope for continuing growth is still strong. Robert Lekachman says of the "neo-liberals" that they, along with conservative supporters of the "supply-side" school of economics,

> ... have convinced themselves that lower tax rates promote growth, and growth is the best assurance that free markets will lift the poor out of their poverty and provide resources for government to alleviate the plight of the shrinking minority still below the poverty line.
>
>   (Lekachman, 1987, p. 179)

But in recent years it has become apparent that growth probably will not continue to supply the required lifting force. This view is held on both the left and the right. Michael Harrington, Chairman of the Democratic Socialists of America, writes in *The Next Left*:

> *The fact is, the nature of economic growth has changed.* Investment can now create more national product but not

more jobs, or at least not more jobs of the kind essential
to upward mobility for the great mass of the people.
                                              (Harrington, 1987, p. 6)

At the other end of the spectrum, a special report by *Business
Week* (April 20, 1987) titled "Can America Compete?" pointed
out that "our competitive drop is really a growth crisis." The
report says that as economies mature, it is natural for growth
to slow down, and in today's worldwide competition, America
faces a real decline in living standards unless we take dramatic
steps to recapture our ability to compete. The key statistic is
U.S. economic growth, which has slipped from the 4 percent
annual rate of the 1960s to "a sluggish 2.4 percent" in 1986.
The article concludes:

> Long-term growth has slowed to a crawl, and without a
> rapidly growing economic pie, America just isn't the same.
> Both personal and national agendas that were once unques-
> tioned suddenly seem too expensive. For individuals, that
> might mean a delay in buying a home or even getting mar-
> ried. For the nation, the list includes the programs that
> burgeoned in the 1960s and 1970s to care for the poor and
> the elderly, the projection of U.S. power overseas, and the
> pushes for safer workplaces and a cleaner environment.
> Which do we give up?

Despite these doubts about future growth, it is difficult to make
structural changes when the majority of American voters believe
themselves to be well off. Voting statistics reveal a number of
facts relevant to our discussion of structural change: a disproportionate number of disadvantaged people do not vote; only
about half the total of eligible voters go the polls in each election — in other worlds, 26 percent of the electorate can control
our political system; of that 26 percent that can control political
power, a disproportionate number are relatively affluent. Thus
structural changes through proposed legislation must appeal to
the self-interest of people who are relatively well off, and their
self-interest requires that changes leave intact such existing features as personal incentives, growth, efficiency, high living standards, and individual freedom. It is necessary to design care-

fully legislation to address these self-interests not only because this influential segment of the population plays a large role in controlling politics, but also because they play a significant role in bringing about structural changes in the private sector; this type of legislation is often necessary because such changes in the private sector usually will not be forthcoming unless there is a threat of legislation.

While self-interest is an obstacle to structural change, it need not be narrowly defined as something that directly benefits only the person in question. It is in the best interests of self-sufficient people to have *everyone* working at a satisfying job and a decent wage, with as many people as possible sharing in ownership. The alternative is increased pressure on the welfare system, which turns the underclass into a ticking time bomb — a threat to the self-interest of the rich and satisfied Americans. In order to open the way for structural change, we must avoid ideas that require extensive government funding and redistribution of wealth or income, and instead look to a trait of human nature that is not as attractive as altruism but is infinitely more reliable: self-interest. We must be imaginative enough to create programs that, while primarily intended to benefit the disadvantaged, will also have demonstrable benefits for the more fortunate Americans.

The ultimate economic problem is how to have economic growth and fairness at the same time. This is sometimes expressed as efficiency versus equity. But I suggest that growth and fairness (or efficiency and equity) need not be trade-offs, since they are not necessarily opposites of each other. Indeed, each can nurture the other. Adam Smith himself recognized this in *The Wealth of Nations*:

> Servants, labourers, and workmen of different kinds, make up the far greater part of every great political society. But what improves the circumstances of the greater part can never be regarded as an inconveniency to the whole. No society can surely be flourishing and happy, of which the far greater part of the members are poor and miserable. It is but equity, besides, that they who feed, clothe, and lodge the whole body of the people, should have such a share of the produce of their own labour as to be themselves tolerably well fed, clothed, and lodged. (Smith, 1776, I, 8)

36

A case in point is the well-known story of Henry Ford and his Model T. When he introduced the Model T in 1908, it sold for $950, well beyond the means of the average factory worker, who then made no more than $250 per year — less than a dollar a day. As Ford created a revolutionary increase in efficiency by introducing the mass production assembly line in 1913, he also increased wages to the then astronomical level of $5 per day, while cutting work time from nine to eight hours and reducing the price of the car itself to the range where his own workers could begin to dream of owning one. By 1927, the Model T cost only $290, and most of America's factory workers could afford automobiles. It was this dynamic combination of efficiency and equity — creating the mass purchasing power required to consume vastly expanded production — that made the United States a great industrial power.

We cannot, of course, rest on the laurels of Henry Ford's Model T. As writers in *Business Week* and many other journals have pointed out, we have put ourselves in a hole by failing to keep pace with the rest of the world in growth. Therefore, we must constantly seek adjustments in our economic system to sustain growth. But in doing so, we need not leave our sense of justice behind us. History tells us that we *can* develop programs leading to growth with fairness, efficiency with equity, through trial and error, using the moral input of religious organizations as a creative force.

Most people will agree that self-interest is the central force of American capitalism. As mainstream economist Campbell R. McConnell puts it:

> ...capitalism presumes self-interest as the fundamental *modus operandi* for the various economic units as they express their free choices.... Altruistic motives are part of the makeup of economic units. Yet, self-interest is the best single statement of how economic units actually behave.
> (McConnell, 1987, pp. 38–39)

As we seek a religious path to social justice, must we reject capitalism as immoral because it is based on self-interest — or can we progress toward greater social justice by trying to *enlighten* self-interest with moral principles? It seems clear that if we are to make any real progress, we must work within self-interest and try to temper it as much as possible with altruism and morality, so that it does not degrade into mere selfishness or greed.

This process was well described by Professors Prentiss Pemberton and Daniel Rush Finn in *Toward a Christian Economic Ethic*:

> The Christian tradition has always recognized the excesses of sin. But where capitalism counts on competition from other self-interested persons to hold self-interest in check, Christianity has always held out two additional prescriptions: a personal change of heart, and institutionalized requirements and restrictions. The individual can be exhorted to a less selfish way of living, and the structures of the community can be molded so that the basic needs of all persons are met and the self-interest of individuals corresponds more closely with the common good.
>
> (Pemberton and Finn, 1985, p. 135)

Thus, in using self-interest as a cornerstone of our consensus program of social justice, we are not abandoning moral principle. We need not adopt Ayn Rand's Objectivist philosophy of self-interest, which to many seems a glorification of greed. We are simply accepting the fact of economic life that capitalism based on *enlightened* self-interest is best able to secure justice for the greatest number of Americans, and that *effective* concern for the poor requires a degree of economic success that today can be delivered only by capitalism.

Some of the specific structural changes that can make American capitalism more just are discussed below, especially under the Fourth, Fifth, and Eighth Principles.

Workplace Democracy Excluded

In our search for a social justice consensus, unfortunately we must put aside some seemingly attractive programs that will not achieve majority support and that may be counterproductive to the effort to broaden employment and ownership. One such issue is *workplace democracy*, or automatic worker participation in decisions affecting the workplace. Many people feel that this is an essential part of any moral economic system. Definitive texts on this subject are *Working Together* (Simmons and Mares, 1983), and *Workplace Democracy and Productivity* (Frieden, 1980). I do not question its place in an ideal world, but I do not include it in our Ten Principles because it is inherently controversial. The public opinion surveys in *American Ethos* showed that less than one-third of the public supports increases in the decision-making power of workers (McClosky and Zaller, 1984, p. 155).

No doubt we are moving toward more workplace democracy, but I choose not to make it a part of the consensus we are seeking here because I do not believe we need it in order to make the first important steps toward a more moral economic system. Those vital first steps are the broadening of access to meaningful work and ownership. The decisional process at the workplace, while important, is not vital enough to add as excess baggage to the already heavy burden carried by those seeking to broaden work and ownership. The problem here is trying to pull off too many revolutions at once. Also, within the framework of expanded stock ownership, workers could achieve voting rights that would open the way for their participation in decisions affecting the workplace.

I wholeheartedly support further experiments in workplace democracy. The question is whether it can be implemented without creating intractable problems. For instance, take the experience in Yugoslavia, the leading situs of experimentation in workplace democracy. A *Wall Street Journal* report from Belgrade in 1987 reached the conclusion that workplace democracy and worker self-management have wrecked the Yugoslavian economy, according to the workers themselves, who are in the process of reducing self-management in order to regain economic efficiency. Some of the nightmares that can result from workplace democracy are described in the article, focusing on one of the largest factories in Yugoslavia, the Rakovica Motor Works. The article describes various factions within the factory, each of which elects a council and sends delegates to a central council:

> The general manager presents the central council with a budget. The council amends it and sends it to each of the

other ten councils. When all the councils have passed it, the budget goes to a vote of the entire work force. The process is only slightly more involved than amending the U.S. Constitution.

Any one of the 10 councils can veto the budget. Each can veto a project to build a new model or to buy new machinery. And for every variation of every product, each council negotiates a joint-venture deal with all the other councils. Rakovica has 78 of those. The meetings take up 18,000 man hours a year, when they go smoothly. But they don't always go that way. That is why Rakovica workers strike about once a year. (Newman, 1987)

To achieve the required consensus, we must stick to plans that don't seek radical changes in human nature. The drive for workplace democracy runs counter to some important human tendencies toward power, authority, and hierarchy. On the other hand, the broadening of employment and ownership do not necessarily run counter to these major tendencies, especially if we can design them to coincide with the self-interest of the middle-class majority.

Despite all the foregoing arguments, some supporters of our Ten Principles will remain convinced that workplace democracy is indispensable for a practical religious approach to social justice. Of course, they are free to disagree with me, and they can add workplace democracy as an Eleventh Principle, or consider it a part of our Second Principle.

Evidence for the Third Principle: Everyone Should be Able to Work

As previously noted, it is to the advantage of the wealthy and comfortable Americans that everyone who wants to work be given a fair opportunity to do so. Full employment, or anything approaching it, obviously would reduce the need for transfer payments and thus alleviate the pressures for higher taxes and other changes that might disturb the comfortable class. And paychecks in every household would assure the growth of the economy and a ready market for the services and products of American business.

There has never been any question about the preference of practically all Americans for a fair opportunity for everyone to have a decent job — provided that there is no costly government subsidy involved. This is borne out by the public opinion surveys in *American Ethos,* which found that close to 80 percent of Americans believe that "most of the poor and needy could contribute something valuable to society if given the chance" (McClosky and Zaller, 1984, p. 66); but the majority felt that in order to improve their conditions, the poor should help themselves rather than receiving special government help (ibid., p. 92).

These surveys reflect the American consensus for blending the right to work with the obligation to work. *American Ethos* includes many polls on government welfare programs. The authors summarized the results:

> By margins that are sometimes very large, Americans support welfare programs that require recipients to perform useful work in order to receive aid.
> (McClosky and Zaller, 1984, p. 275)

This conclusion is borne out by the very strong consensus reflected in welfare reform proposals endorsed by both parties and many political leaders in 1987. Thus, on February 25, 1987, the *New York Times* reported:

> With only one dissenting vote, the nation's governors today approved an ambitious plan to overhaul the largest welfare program and require every able-bodied recipient to work or get training. The governors said they had the assurances of President Reagan and Congressional leaders that they would cooperate with the states to put the plan into effect. (Herbers, 1987)

This reflects the experiments undertaken by thirty-nine states to include a workfare or training component in state welfare programs.

Evidence for the Fourth Principle:
Putting People to Work Through Public Service Jobs

There is a great deal of work needed to rebuild our infrastructure and improve the quality of life — work that is not now organized as paid occupations (public service work, which we shall call "the work of humanity"). Few would disagree with the conclusions of Pat Choate, Director of the Office of Policy Analysis for TRW, Inc., and one of the nation's most respected idea men:

> Today, America's public infrastructure is wearing out faster than it is being repaired, replaced, and rehabilitated. This deterioration is found in every part of the country. As a result, half to two-thirds of U.S. communities cannot support expansion of their economies. Their basic public facilities are simply obsolete. (Choate and Linger, 1986, p. 162)

Choate's earlier book, *America in Ruins* (Choate and Walter, 1983), inspired a report in *Time* magazine (April 27, 1981), which pointed out that the percentage of Gross National Product devoted to investment in public works dropped from 3.6 percent in 1965 to 1.7 percent in 1980, and concluded:

> From the rusting spans of its once proud bridges to the leaking sewers beneath its streets, America is structurally unsound. Highways are crumbling. Avenues are cracking. Trains jump their worn-out tracks. Coal ships languish outside overburdened ports. While the U.S. has the technological prowess to blast a magnificent space shuttle into orbit and land it gently back on earth, it has failed to care properly for its most important public works.

A year and a half later, a *Newsweek* cover story ("The Decaying of America," *Newsweek,* August 2, 1982) reported that of the estimated $3 *trillion* in needed repairs, $33 billion would be required for the interstate highway system; $47.6 billion for repair of the nation's 248,500 structurally deficient or obsolete bridges; and $75–110 billion for maintenance of water systems in 756 major urban areas over the next twenty years.

In addition, some one-third of 9,000 dams inspected have been found unsafe; public buildings are rapidly deteriorating; many mass transit systems across the country are in bad shape; and many city streets are in an alarming state of disrepair. In addition to infrastructure repair, there are, of course, crying needs for low-income housing construction and repair; services for the elderly and the handicapped; and environmental protection, all of which we shall discuss in detail in Chapters Four and Five when we get down to the question of how to pay for the work of humanity. Here we are concerned only with demonstrating the consensus that the work needs to be done and cannot be handled through the regular channels of paid employment. Without getting into the question of funding, *American Ethos* surveys found that 89 percent of Americans favor the creation of public service jobs such as "helping out in hospitals and cleaning parks" as well as youth programs similar to the Civilian Conservation Corps of the 1930s (McClosky and Zaller, 1984, pp. 272, 276).

Evidence for the Fifth Principle: Overconcentration of Stock Ownership

Americans obtain their financial support in four ways: by working for it (wages); by receiving government checks (welfare); by cheating (crime, welfare fraud, etc.); and by receiving the return on invested capital (capitalist income). The first three methods have been used throughout the world for centuries and have often been fostered by government policies. The fourth, return on invested capital, has never been used as a method of creating an equitable distribution of income. It has remained the sole province of the rich — the "capitalists" who have the savings or credit power to buy corporate shares and other forms of income-producing capital.

Wages are obviously the ideal method of supporting people, and as long as our traditional capitalism was able to create enough decent jobs for those who wanted them, it was acceptable to most of us. But in an increasingly automated era, it has become apparent that no economic system and no government — regardless of political bent — can create enough above-poverty-level jobs to support everyone through wages. The attempt to create equitable income distribution solely through wages, while the machines and computers produced by industrialization actually destroy or degrade jobs, causes a basic contradiction in industrial societies. Indeed, welfare capitalism is a system at war with itself.

The first three methods of support — wages, welfare, and cheating — are used in virtually all economic systems. Only the fourth method is unique to capitalism, and thus far the politicians in capitalist nations have allowed capitalist income to be restricted to a very small class at the pinnacle of the economic structure.

In Chapter Five, we shall consider some specific ideas for fashioning capitalist income into a new tool to solve economic and social problems. Here, we are concerned with the consensus for the broadening of capital ownership. As early as 1776, it was recognized that individual ownership could help preserve democracy and control government tyranny. In those days, when America was yet to be industrialized and land was the principal form of capital, John Adams wrote:

The only possible way, then, of preserving the balance of power on the side of equal liberty and public virtue, is to make the acquisition of land easy to every member of society ... so that the multitude may be possessed of landed estates. If the multitude is possessed of the balance of real estate, the multitude will have the balance of power, and in that case the multitude will take care of the liberty, virtue and interest of the multitude in all acts of government.
(R. Taylor, ed., 1979, p. 210)

That was the Federalist (conservative) viewpoint. The Anti-Federalist (liberal) stand was identical, as best expressed by Thomas Jefferson:

Whenever there is in any country, uncultivated lands and unemployed poor, it is clear that the laws of property have been so far extended as to violate natural right. The earth is given as a common stock for man to labour and live on. If for the encouragement of industry we allow it to be

appropriated, we must take care that other employment be
provided to those excluded from the appropriation.

(Boyd, ed., 1953, vol. 8, p. 682)

Jefferson was U.S. Ambassador to France in 1785, when he was
inspired to write those words in a famous letter to James Madison because he had been struck by "that unequal division of
property which occasions the numberless instances of wretched-
ness which I had observed in [France] and is to be observed all
over Europe." Jefferson was determined to avoid that fate for
his own country, and in his home state of Virginia he fought
for and won abolition of the laws of primogeniture and entail,
which contributed to overconcentration of property ownership.

In the bipartisan tradition of Adams and Jefferson, Ronald
Reagan took up the fight for broadened capital ownership. In
1975, when he was a privately employed radio commentator,
Reagan said in a broadcast:

> Capitalism hasn't used the best tool of all in its struggle
> against socialism — and that's capitalism itself. Roughly
> 94 percent of the people in capitalist America make their
> living from wages or salaries. Only 6 percent are true capi-
> talists in the sense of deriving their income from ownership
> of the means of production.

And in a July 1974 address to the Young Americans for Freedom, Reagan said:

> Over 100 years ago, Abraham Lincoln signed the Home-
> stead Act.... It set the pattern for the American capitalist
> system. We need an industrial homestead act.... It is time
> to formulate a plan to accelerate economic growth and pro-
> duction and at the same time broaden the ownership of
> productive capital. The American dream has always been
> to have a piece of the action.

The consensus of politicians in favor of broadened capital ownership is clearly stated in the *1976 Joint Economic Report*,
adopted unanimously by the Joint Economic Committee of Congress. As we saw in Chapter One, that report recommended

that "it should be made national policy to pursue the goal of broadened capital ownership." This broad consensus is also reflected in the congressional votes on the major pieces of ESOP legislation enacted by Congress between 1973 and 1987. They received overwhelming bipartisan support, many of them passing by margins of ten to one. And Robert Lekachman said of a specific plan for universal share ownership:

> From a political standpoint, it goes very much with the grain of American faith in market capitalism. It is an extension of the idea of property ownership.
>
> (Lekachman, 1985, p. 440)

Now we shall consider the complementary principles.

Evidence for the Sixth Principle: Changes Should be Made at the Lowest Possible Level

The mood of the country in the 1980s is to distrust government and to favor private sector solutions over legislation. The successful 1976 campaign of Jimmy Carter against the Washington politicians and the Reagan crusade against big government clearly demonstrate this. Even when there is a strong consensus for change, such as workfare or training requirements for welfare recipients, state and local programs are favored over sweeping federal plans that concentrate power in the federal bureaucracy. As Robert Lekachman points out in his book on the prospects for the 1988 election, this preference for market solutions, with federal legislation as the last resort, is not exclusively a conservative or Republican position. It is shared equally by "neolib politicians and their gurus" (Lekachman, 1987, p. 184).

American Ethos observes that "Americans, though skeptical of unrestrained capitalism, still seem to maintain a distinct preference for private management of the economy — unless, in their opinion, private mechanisms fall short and public remedies appear to be the only effective alternatives" (McClosky and Zaller, 1984, p. 151). It also describes the American penchant for equal distrust of big business and big government:

> ...popular distrust of the motives of business has usually
> been matched — both historically and in modern survey
> data — by high levels of distrust toward government. In
> assessing the likelihood that antibusiness feeling will lead
> to pressure for a government takeover of the private econ-
> omy, one would do well to recall Ralph Nader's remark
> that Americans think "the only thing worse than having
> a car built by General Motors is to have one built by the
> government." (McClosky and Zaller, 1984, p. 158)

This concept has been a part of Roman Catholic social teaching
since 1931, under the name of "subsidiarity," which we shall
consider in more detail in the next chapter. Under subsidiarity,
solutions must be sought at the lowest possible level, so that
if legislation is found necessary, it should be tried at the local
or state level, if possible, to demonstrate its feasibility before
federal legislation is attempted.

While there is general agreement regarding the goals of increasing employment (Fourth Principle) and broadening ownership (Fifth Principle), opinion on how to achieve these goals
is sharply divided. Most of the major disagreements among
economists, politicians, and religious commentators concerning
changes in the American economy revolve around the appropriate degree of government intervention in the free market system. The overwhelming majority of liberals and conservatives
want a fair system based on capitalism. They differ only on
the choice of procedures required to achieve that common goal.
Some professional economists who have devoted their careers
to one procedure or another are inclined to either advocate or
reject government intervention dogmatically, and in their eyes
they may perceive this to be a matter of principle. But for our
purposes, we can disregard the battle royal that would occur if
we locked these economists up in the same room, and focus on
the area in which their principles coincide. There is ample evidence that this consensus is wide enough and strong enough
to serve as a foundation for a moral restructuring of capitalism.

This consensus was described by Anthony Solomon, former
Under Secretary of the Treasury and President of the Federal
Reserve Bank of New York:

My own judgment is that, over a reasonable amount of time, given the kind of economy we have and the kind of financial system we have that weaves the total structure together, the guts of economic policy (that is, fiscal, monetary, and exchange-rate policy) will always have to come around to a commonsensical, centrist, and pragmatic approach. I believe that this will be true whether we have Democratic or Republican administrations.

(Solomon, 1986, p. 15)

The consensus is evident from discussion of the critical question of what policies will restore vigor to American industry, given the setbacks caused by declining productivity and loss of markets to Japan, Germany, and Third World nations. During the 1984 presidential campaign, Senator Gary Hart and the eventual Democratic candidate, Walter Mondale, pushed various versions of a new industrial policy which called for a business-government-labor partnership to increase the productivity and competitiveness of American industry. The idea of establishing such a business-labor-government partnership to restore the work ethic, improve education, and move away from the welfare syndrome was championed by liberal MIT Professor Lester Thurow under the label of "industrial policy" (Thurow, 1985). But the same concept is also advocated by staunch conservatives such as Henry Kissinger, who called for adaptation of the Japanese-style partnership to the American economy (Kissinger, 1983); Kevin P. Phillips, a leading conservative Republican spokesman, who labeled this partnership an "enterprise-oriented industrial competitiveness strategy" (Phillips, 1986); and conservative Georgia Congressman Newt Gingrich, who called his version of that partnership the "conservative opportunity society" (Gingrich, 1984).

The "industrial policy" label was dropped after the 1984 campaign. Democrats now call it "rebuilding America," while Republicans are more likely to refer to it as "competitiveness." Spurred by some successful state government initiatives to promote industry, Ronald Reagan's White House advisors built the competitiveness strategy into his 1987 State of the Union message:

The Congress will soon receive my comprehensive proposals to enhance our competitiveness, including new science
and technology centers and strong new funding for basic
research.

Competitiveness strategy does not differ substantially from industrial policy, and is as strongly backed by conservatives as
by liberals. For example, the Defense Science Board, a high-
level advisory committee to the Secretary of Defense, working
closely with the semiconductor industry's main trade group, recommended in February 1987 that the federal government provide $1 billion and special anti-trust exemptions to launch a con-
sortium of computer companies and chip manufacturers, with
another $1 billion for laboratory semiconductor research to be
allocated over five years; the purpose of these governmental actions would be to enable our private semiconductor industry to
compete with Japan. And conservative Republican Jack Kemp,
interviewed in *Business Week* of April 13, 1987, stated his position on government intervention: "I still believe a rising tide
lifts all boats, but where boats need repair, I'd be willing to use
the government" (p. 92).
    This willingness of conservatives to use the government was
dramatized during the October 1987 stock market crash, when
John J. Phelan, chairman of the New York Stock Exchange,
pleaded for government intervention to lower interest rates and
thereby rescue the stock market, which he said had moved away
from its main function of raising capital for industry. In an interview published in the *New York Times* on October 27, 1987,
Phelan said:

If we destroy the markets by too much volatility, too much
professional trading, too much leverage, we ruin their cred-
ibility and we ruin the function for which they are supposed to exist.

In *American Ethos,* the authors conclude:

Americans favor most of the specific programs associated
with welfare capitalism. Study after study has shown that

while Americans continue to express distaste for big government, they nonetheless repeatedly call upon government to alleviate the problems that arise when capitalism is left to operate on its own.

(McClosky and Zaller, 1984, pp. 301–302)

Their surveys also found very strong support for existing federal regulation of business as a necessary brake on free-wheeling laissez-faire (ibid., p. 146). Indeed, the dean of free-market libertarians, Milton Friedman, states in his classic *Capitalism and Freedom*:

There is no avoiding the need for some measure of paternalism.... There is no formula that can tell us where to stop.... We must put our faith, here as elsewhere, in a consensus reached by imperfect and biased men through free discussion and trial and error. (Friedman, 1962, p. 34)

Evidence for the Seventh Principle: Testing Economic Policies by Trial and Error

The above quotation from Milton Friedman is as important for the principle of trial and error as it is for his acceptance of the inevitability of some degree of government intervention. History demonstrates that trial and error is the basic method of economic innovation.

Thus, in 1933 when Franklin Roosevelt decided to fight the Depression by setting up a vast public works program, he had no economics handbook to turn to for guidance. He simply decided to start a transfusion of income flowing to millions of Americans who were out of work and hope. He put Harry Hopkins on a train, and in a matter of a few weeks Hopkins established from scratch the foundation for the Works Progress Administration (WPA) and other agencies which eventually employed millions of Americans in public works projects such as the building of thousands of bridges, court houses, and post offices.

In his book, *The Coming of the New Deal,* Arthur M. Schlesinger, Jr., describes the early days of what was originally called the Civil Works Administration (CWA). On November 15, 1933,

Hopkins announced that his objective was to employ four million people by December 15th, even though he had no planning staff and no formulated program. An Army officer assigned to study CWA for the War Department reported in amazement that despite Hopkins's lack of an organization, he employed in two months nearly as many people as were enlisted in the U.S. Army during World War I, and in that time pushed his program into every county and town in the United States despite one of the most severe winters on record (Schlesinger, 1958, pp. 270–271).

Trial and error is also a basic principle of business. Sales executives test new products and selling programs wherever possible by marketing in small quantities and isolated areas before committing their resources. There is a great deal of guesswork in business as well as in government. In his study of the most successful American companies, *In Search of Excellence,* Tom Peters points out that the winning companies are strong on experimentation, innovation, and structural change. Modifying the usual procedure, the motto is: READY-FIRE-AIM! (Peters and Waterman, 1982, p. 134). Thus, even at the highest and most successful levels, innovation is largely a game of trial and error.

Thus, there are no economic principles that prevent us from achieving greater social justice through increased employment, broader ownership, or both. The feasibility of economic policies has always been determined largely by trial and error, and any program for broadening employment or ownership that carefully considers past experience is appropriate for such experimentation.

Evidence for the Eighth Principle: Paying for Public Service Work with Stock Ownership

Even though the Full Employment and Balanced Growth Act (Humphrey-Hawkins) has been on the books since 1978, we have been unable to attain its targets: A 4 percent unemployment rate along with a 3 percent inflation rate. As Paul Samuelson said of these goals:

The goals were *too* precise. Moreover, they were wildly ambitious. The U.S. economy has not come near to these goals since the 1960s. Being so unrealistic, they in reality offer no guidance for policy makers. And, in the end, the 1978 act created no new policy instruments that would enable the nation to attain these goals.... In the early versions of the bill, there were provisions that established the federal government as an "employer of last resort" and that set up a large "planning" apparatus. These two new instruments were unacceptable to economic moderates and conservatives. After these were stripped from the bill, nothing remained but the unattainable targets.

(Samuelson and Nordhaus, 1985, p. 86)

We have observed the consensus for doing the work of humanity (Fourth Principle) provided that a way can be found to pay for it other than by tax funds. We have seen what was accomplished by the Works Progress Administration of the 1930s. In summary, during the eight years of its existence this one agency

> [built] 651,087 miles of highways, worked on 124,087 bridges, and constructed 125,110 public structures, 8,192 parks, and 853 airports. It operated community centers, carried out numerous surveys of federal, state, and local archives, and through various theater, dance, art, music, and writing projects supplied jobs to thousands. When it ended in June 1943, the WPA had employed more than 8,500,000 people on 1,410,000 projects, costing about $11 billion, and had left a permanent imprint on American life.

(Louchheim, 1983, p. 177)

We have even more vital work that needs doing now, and with a surplus of workers, it is ridiculous not to get these jobs done. Present experiments with welfare reform and other employment programs are designed to produce minimum wage jobs, and most require government funding which in today's political climate is difficult to sustain. You have only to look at the help wanted ads of fast food restaurants and supermarkets desperately seeking employees at $5 to $6 an hour (well above the minimum wage) to realize that wage incentives alone are not sufficient to motivate many of the unemployed to take such jobs. We must create an additional incentive, and the only possibility I can envision is stock ownership: creating jobs for the unemployed with compensation to include shares of stock in new companies formed to employ them, and possibly shares of stock in major successful companies that do not employ them — all provided that the shares are *earned* by useful services.

While there is no existing consensus for combining the work of humanity with broader stock ownership, there is certainly no conceptual objection to it. The idea simply has never been discussed or undertaken as an experimental project. Certainly most people would favor small-scale experiments of this type if they were based on careful planning and drew upon our best minds and resources. As always, we adhere to the requirement that to attain consensus, such programs must appeal to the self-interest of the governing middle class. We shall discuss specific plans combining stock ownership and the work of humanity in Chapters Four and Five. Here we are concerned only with developing the consensus for experimenting with such initiatives.

The need for such innovation becomes clearer when we consider the paucity of other ideas that might accomplish the work of humanity through the other two possible methods: wages and welfare. For example, in his 1987 book *Let's Put America Back to Work,* Senator Paul Simon (Democrat, Illinois) outlines a plan to create public service employment for approximately 3 million workers, at a net cost of $8 billion per year in tax funds. Simon's plan is very carefully thought out, and draws upon the successes of the New Deal public works agencies. Yet, even at the annual cost of $8 billion, his program does not offer much incentive for people to perform these low-level jobs, because wages are limited to 10 percent above welfare or unemployment compensation, whichever is greater. Simon feels that this 10 percent margin would be sufficient incentive for people to work rather than to receive welfare or unemployment compensation, but many would disagree. In any event, even at that low level, Simon concedes that the plan falls far short of consensus support:

If the Guaranteed Job Opportunity Program were brought to the floor of the Senate and House in the fall of 1986,

probably one-third of the members would vote for it.
(Simon, 1987, p. 183)

Using stock ownership as a work incentive would be an improvement over the present system, which offers most of those at the bottom of the ladder a choice of either a poorly paid dead-end job or welfare.

David Howell, a Conservative Member of Parliament and a former member of the Thatcher cabinet, advocates broadened stock ownership linked to the work of humanity. In his book, *Blind Victory,* he speaks of "a fully occupied society" instead of "full employment." By opening stock ownership to everyone, he sees the basis for accomplishment of the work of humanity:

> As capital ownership widens, so does the scope for voluntary work either for free or on a pin-money basis. A vast new network of voluntary endeavor is already springing up, ready to support and substitute for the personal social services, and to do so on a far more flexible and intimate basis. (Howell, 1986, p. 178)

Evidence for the Ninth Principle: Distribution of Income and Distribution of Wealth Are Religious Issues

The crucial social justice question for most Americans is: How much income and ownership will each of us receive through the economic system? Economists call these factors *income distribution* and *wealth distribution.* While other phases of economics, such as the monetary and banking systems, are so complicated that most of us must throw up our hands and leave them to the economists and the politicians, this is not true of income and wealth distribution. From the very beginning of economics, income and wealth distribution have been classified as value judgments or political questions rather than scientific issues. John Stuart Mill, in his classic *Principles of Political Economy*, stated it this way:

> The distribution of wealth, therefore, depends on the laws and customs of society. The rules by which it is determined

> are what the opinions and feelings of the ruling portion of
> the community make them, and are very different in differ-
> ent ages and countries; and might be still more different, if
> mankind so chose.... Society can subject the distribution
> of wealth to whatever rules it thinks best.
>
> (Mill, 1848, pp. 200–201)

In our time, the famous textbook by Paul Samuelson, used by
millions of Americans to gain their first knowledge of economics,
puts it this way:

> Whether incomes should be completely determined by a
> competitive struggle — the survival of the survivors — is
> an ethical question that goes beyond the mere mechanics
> of economics. (Samuelson, 1980, p. 42)

The same principle was enunciated by Professors Robert Heilbroner and Lester Thurow in their handy guide, *Economics Explained*:

> Economics is the language we use to talk about the work-
> ings and options of our system, but it is not the language in
> which we appraise the value of the system or decide what
> elements in it to preserve or change. Politics and moral-
> ity — our collective wills and our private value systems —
> remain the bedrock of society.
>
> (Heilbroner and Thurow, 1982, p. 240)

Our opinions and feelings as individuals and as members of
religious organizations are entitled to at least as much weight
as the opinions of economists, business executives, and government officials when it comes to formulating the rules for income
and wealth distribution. Technicalities like monetarism, Keyne-
sianism, and supply-side economics need not block out moral
principles in making the value judgments that govern distribution of income and wealth.

And so the good news is that income and wealth distribution
are political questions that lie within the proper scope of our
scrutiny. The bad news is that there has been very little research
on how we can actually achieve equitable distribution without

threatening growth, freedom, and other advantages of capitalism. For 200 years, these value judgments have been largely
made for us by Adam Smith, Karl Marx, or their disciples of
various shadings, without substantial religious input.

We have left this up to the economists and politicians for
too long. We expect too little of our politicians when it comes
to economics, because we have not explored the potential of
capitalism to bring us a democratic and moral economy. We
see little difference in the party platforms, and we accept those
platform statements as the only possibilities, without trying to
develop economic policies that are moral and equitable according to our standards. There is no need for any of us to say, "I
don't know anything about economics," when considering how
to achieve equitable distribution of wealth and income. It is up
to us to apply the moral standards that we bring from our own
experience and our religious teaching.

To bolster our confidence, it is only necessary to look at what
some leading economists say about the ability of economists and
politicians to scientifically design the economy. Herbert Stein is
one of our most prestigious economists. Now a Senior Fellow
of the American Enterprise Institute in Washington, D.C., and
editor of *The AEI Economist,* he served as chairman of the President's Council of Economic Advisors for Richard Nixon and
Gerald Ford and has been a consultant to the Reagan administration. In the preface to his latest book, Professor Stein begins
his story:

> The essays included in this volume are the reflections of an
> economist who has spent almost 50 years in Washington
> as a bureaucrat, researcher, presidential adviser, observer,
> and commentator. Two main lessons derived from this
> experience are the themes of these essays:
>
> 1. Economists do not know very much.
>
> 2. Other people, including the politicians who make
>   economic policy, know even less about economics
>   than economists do.
>
> (Stein, 1986, p. xi)

In *The High-Flex Society,* Pat Choate writes:

> The more economists learn about the economy, the less
> certain they are about what this knowledge means for eco-
> nomic policy. For example, there is widespread disagree-
> ment about whether cutting taxes will increase capital in-
> vestment, whether industrial policy is the key to Japan's
> economic success, or whether automation will increase or
> decrease the total number of jobs.
>
> (Choate and Linger, 1986, p. 156)

Choate's appraisal was validated by the frenzied calls for raising
taxes and reducing the budget deficit after the 1987 stock market
crash — medicine hauntingly reminiscent of Herbert Hoover's
disastrous reactions to the 1929 crash. As Peter Kilborn reported in the *New York Times* of October 24, 1987:

> Despite today's cheery report of 3.8 percent economic
> growth in the third quarter and declining inflation, so lit-
> tle is known about prospects for the economy that the
> confidence-building measures that the White House and
> Congress may ultimately agree upon stand as great a
> chance of doing harm to the economy as good.... "Is it
> obvious that we should raise taxes to reduce the deficit?"
> asks Thomas A. Lawler, chief economist at the Federal Na-
> tional Mortgage Association. "Is that really inherently an
> obvious solution? Ten years from now will textbooks say,
> 'Unbelievably, they raised taxes as the economy was about
> to go into a recession'?"

That is not to say that we should disregard economists in seeking
equitable income and wealth distribution. They are the first to
admit that we are dealing with a value judgment. But they have
something to contribute, as stated by Professor Samuelson:

> In the modern mixed economy, the electorate insists on
> providing minimum standards when the market fails to do
> so. Economics teaches how interventions can be accom-
> plished at least cost in terms of inefficiency; and it shows

how inept intervention may fail to achieve either equity or efficiency. (Samuelson, 1980, p. 42)

Again, we are dealing with a procedural problem that can be worked out by trial and error, using the recorded experience of various types of intervention as a guideline, but not necessarily as a barrier to trying old ideas again at a different time and in a different way.

Evidence for the Tenth Principle: The Crucial Role of Religious Organizations

Much of the work of humanity is now accomplished through religious organizations, some of which have had centuries of experience in organizing it. Seventy percent of American charitable donations goes to religious organizations. They are a prime source of the expertise needed to shape experiments that may lead to broadening employment and ownership.

Despite the logic and consensus that support the need for structural change, the inertia of our economic and political systems is overwhelming. Even though all the necessary pieces exist, solving the puzzle of social justice through secular organizations appears ultimately to be impossible. It is my thesis (which I will develop more fully in the next chapter) that religious activity in economics is not only appropriate but is a prerequisite for the structural changes needed to make capitalism a more moral system. Religious groups can bring a consensus, a reconciliation, that is difficult to achieve in a field as confused and contentious as economics. The ability of people to react to religious and moral stimuli is almost limitless — much stronger than their response to political, economic, or social stimuli.

The required response is something on the order of a tidal wave — a massive galvanizing force strong enough to overcome the great inertia of our economic and political systems. Such a tidal wave can be built by harnessing the moral forces inherent in our religious organizations.

Professor Robert Lekachman, in his preview of the 1988 election, despairs of progress toward social justice through political parties, unions, and even universities. Instead, he pins his main hopes on religious groups and devotes a large segment of the book to the importance of the 1986 Catholic Bishops' pastoral and similar religious statements (Lekachman, 1987, Chapter 7, "New Wars of Religion," pp. 205–253).

This quest will require us to give capitalism a thorough trial for the first time. We capitalists have been too cynical to open capitalism to everyone, lest we lose the leverage that keeps us in a pinnacle class. Most of us have disdained to search for the inner energy of capitalism, fearing that we would find only exploitation and greed at its core. Experiments driven by the quest for a moral capitalism might disclose that there is something more to that core: a force that can be used to build a better life for all Americans and that can be shared equitably by all of us.

If you doubt the need for a religious quest for social justice, then ask yourself: What other force in our society can create a tidal wave strong enough to make the required structural changes in our economic system? And if you question the expenditure of religious energy required in such a quest, ask again: What greater opportunity or higher adventure awaits religious organizations than the chance to morally reshape the economic system?

Indeed, as we shall now see, the Judeo-Christian tradition teaches that when we observe social outcomes contradicting religious values, correcting these injustices becomes a moral imperative.

Chapter 3

The Religious Quest
for Social Justice

RELIGIOUS ACTIVITY IN SEARCH OF SOCIAL JUSTICE has a long history. We'll examine it here through the work of the major American religious groups: Jewish, Catholic, and Protestant. As before, we shall focus on the principal theme of our Ten Principles: the attempt to broaden work and ownership.

Judaism

The three major American religious groups have a common foundation in the Old Testament, and it is there that we find the first recorded attempts to achieve social justice through religious activity. The English Catholic commentator Paul Johnson concluded in his *A History of the Jews*:

> To [the Jewish people] we owe the idea of equality before the law, both divine and human; of the sanctity of life and the dignity of the human person; of the individual conscience and so of social responsibility; of peace as an abstract ideal and love as the foundation of justice, and many other items which constitute the basic moral furniture of the human mind. (Johnson, 1987, p. 585)

The major Old Testament social justice statements have been collected by Professor Ronald Green, Chairman of the Department of Religion at Dartmouth College (Green, 1987, pp. 88–90). Green concludes:

> The emphasis on social justice is, of course, a hallmark of prophetic faith. The beginnings of Israel as a nation stem from a battle against economic oppression at the hands of Egyptian masters, and the memory of this is reflected in the many specific covenantal requirements of justice imposed on the nation. Under the constant reminder that they were once themselves bondsmen in Egypt (Exod. 23:9; Deut. 15:15, 16:12), the Israelites were required to show special solicitude for the economically and socially "marginalized" in their midst: the poor, the slave, the orphans, the widow and the sojourner. (Green, 1987, p. 88)

These requirements were promulgated in a series of commandments of Jewish law, including cancellation of debts, return of transferred property, and emancipation of slaves in the Jubilee year; the Sabbatical year, during which fields and gardens were to be left for the poor to harvest; the tithe of produce every third year, turning one-tenth of it over to the needy; and the requirement that at every harvest, a corner of all grain fields (one-sixtieth of the crop) and the gleanings of other fields and orchards be left to the poor and the stranger. (Summaries of important Old Testament social justice references will be found in the Appendix.)

The Hebrew Bible also gave us the principle of stewardship. As Green states:

> Human owners are regarded as holding their possessions in trust and subject to the conditions of righteous stewardship.... Within this context, assistance to the poor and the marginal is not requested or encouraged, but is required.
>   (Green, 1987, p. 89)

This tradition was maintained after the biblical period, as reflected in the writings of Moses Maimonides and other great medieval codifiers, and, as Green puts it, "was expressed in the daily practice and institutions of Jewish communities over many centuries" (ibid., p. 87). The Jewish communities of the Diaspora constructed an elaborate social welfare network, based on two forms of support for the needy: *Zedakah* (justice, or required giving) and *Gemilut Hasadim* (voluntary service and giving). The mandatory *Zedakah* was firmly embodied in Jewish law and rabbinic rulings, with officials designated to collect the compulsory levy and act as trustees for the needy, without pay. Any Jews in these communities who failed or refused to pay their legally mandated minimum contribution to the community fund could be compelled to do so by the rabbinical courts, which had the power to seize property for this purpose. Usually the required contribution was at least 10 percent of annual income.

Given our interest in broadening employment and ownership, we should take particular note of the manner in which this help was given. Human dignity and self-respect were prized above personal comfort, and great care was taken to avoid humiliation of the recipients. Loans and offers of employment were prized above outright gifts. Thus, when Maimonides codified his famous eight degrees of charity, the highest degree was that which enabled poor persons to earn their own way, or to go into partnership with the donor. Work was prized for its own sake, to avoid dependency. The father who failed to teach his son a trade was regarded as making that son a thief (Green, 1987, pp. 92–94).

The nineteenth and twentieth centuries brought emancipation to most Jews, and with it came termination of the self-governing Jewish communities that enforced mandatory giving to the needy. But voluntary communal responsibility remains strong and has actually been broadened to include support from abroad for the State of Israel, as noted by Meir Tamari, Chief Economist for the Bank of Israel:

> The massive financial aid channeled by world Jewry to the State of Israel for humanitarian purposes could never have been raised were it not for this tradition of communal responsibility. And this tradition has extended to host societies as well. Every country in Western Europe and in the Americas bears physical evidence of Jewish philanthropy's financing of health services, social amenities, and educational facilities for the benefit of the general public.
>
> (Tamari, 1987, p. 79)

Although today's world is very different from that of Maimonides, many of the medieval traditions survive in updated forms. Jewish administration of direct aid to the disadvantaged became highly specialized, with separate organizations established to offer such services as free medical care, orphanages, homes for the aged, and burial. The commitment is particularly evident in the work of the United Jewish Appeal and the Jewish federation movements, which have raised and distributed billions of dollars throughout the world to alleviate the suffering of Jews and non-Jews alike. And the Torah's requirement of the Sabbatical year is still observed by Israeli farmers. As the *New York Times* reported on June 11, 1987, "Not only will observant Jews not farm their land during the Sabbatical year; they also will not eat food grown on Jewish-owned land."

Strong American social justice programs are implemented annually by the National Jewish Community Relations Advisory Council, whose eleven constituent organizations include the American Jewish Committee, the Anti-Defamation League, Hadassah, and other major groups. For example, the 1986–1987 Joint Program Plan for Jewish Community Relations, in addition to covering matters of special concern to Jewish groups, has a large section on "social and economic justice" devoted to a "society committed to equal rights, justice, and opportunity." The program plan contains a long list of social justice projects, and calls upon Jewish organizations to:

- promote the development of a coherent national domestic social agenda that places its highest priority on meeting human needs and achieving equality of opportunity....

- urge Congress to launch a comprehensive national attack on unemployment and underemployment, as reflected in the Emergency Jobs Program of the Full Employment Action Council (See 1984–1985 Joint Program Plan, page 37)....

- encourage greater utilization of collaborative partnerships by private industry and public-sector agencies, as provided by the Job Training Partnerships Act, to provide training and permanent job opportunities in the private sector....

- forge coalitions to secure these goals. (p. 47)

The Roman Catholic Church

The New Testament picked up where the Old left off, with Jesus devoting his ministry to the poor and humble while seeking universal justice and love. (The Appendix contains summaries of many New Testament references to justice and sharing with the poor.) Particularly pertinent is the passage in the Acts of the Apostles: "And all that believed were together, and had all things in common; And sold their possessions and goods, and parted them to all men, as every man had need" (Acts 2:44–45).

The Catholic Tradition

An excellent overview of Catholic social thought from biblical times through 1984 will be found in *Justice in the Marketplace* (Byers, ed., 1985). In the introduction, John T. Pawlikowski summarizes:

> Catholic social thought has taken multiple turns since biblical times. For many centuries, however, the theological vision articulated by St. Thomas Aquinas shaped the Church's approach to social questions. Aquinas primarily emphasized the duties a responsible Christian is required to carry out in the social sphere.... Hence there existed little or no basis for claims against society except in those instances where the state might prevent someone from fulfilling socially assigned duties.... These premodern ecclesial attitudes helped explain Catholicism's somewhat tardy entry into the struggle for economic rights. The medieval vision died slowly and grudgingly. (Ibid., p. 3)

Father Pawlikowski goes on to say that the rise of Marxism and socialism in the late nineteenth and early twentieth centuries gave working-class Europeans a much greater sense of personal dignity and led some to question or abandon their faith, which was largely Catholic. The Church's response to this threat was the social encyclicals, beginning with Pope Leo XIII's *Rerum Novarum* in 1891. Father Pawlikowski continues:

> The first social encyclicals had a profound impact in the United States. They enabled the American Catholic leadership firmly to support workers' rights and unionization. This little-known support represents one of American Catholicism's brightest moments. Through official statements and at times even through prophetic witness, Church leaders stood up for the workers in the factories and the miners in the coal fields. Some historians attribute the American labor movement's relative immunity to Marxist sympathizers to the influence of Catholicism on trade unionism. (Ibid., p. 4)

In the 1891 encyclical, *Rerum Novarum* (*The Condition Of Labor*), Pope Leo XIII underscored the importance of private ownership (Nos. 4–5) and rejected socialism (Nos. 11–12). He drew on scriptural sources to affirm the dignity of labor (Nos. 20–21). He proclaimed that the Church and the state must work for justice toward all people (Nos. 23–27), and made very clear the type of justice he was referring to:

> Among the many and grave duties of rulers who would do their best for their people, the first and chief is to act with strict justice — with that justice which is called in the schools *distributive* — toward each and every class.
>
> (No. 27)

He went on to deal with the right to organize labor unions and such reforms as humane hours of labor, elimination of child labor, and just wages (Nos. 31–38). And, of particular interest to us, he made the first encyclical statement on the sharing of capital ownership:

> The law, therefore, should favor ownership and its policy should be to induce as many people as possible to become owners.

Many excellent results will follow from this; and first of all, property will certainly become more equitably divided. (No. 35)

These principles were reaffirmed by succeeding Popes, most dramatically in Pope John XXIII's 1961 encyclical, *Mater et Magistra* (*Christianity and Social Progress*):

It is not enough, then, to assert that man has from nature the right of privately possessing goods as his own, including those of productive character, unless at the same time, a continuing effort is made to spread the use of this right through all ranks of the citizenry. (No. 113)

Pope John XXIII also put his great prestige behind the broadening of work and ownership in his 1963 encyclical, *Pacem in Terris* (*Peace on Earth*). In an oft-quoted section entitled "Rights Pertaining to Economic Life," he declared that "human beings have the natural right to free initiative in the economic field, and the right to work" (No. 18). He carried this a step further: "From the dignity of the human person, there also arises the right to carry on economic activities according to the degree of responsibility of which one is capable" (No. 20). And he moved from work to ownership in the next section: "The right to private property, even of productive goods, also derives from the nature of man" (No. 21).

In 1981, on the ninetieth anniversary of Pope Leo's *Rerum Novarum*, Pope John Paul II issued an encyclical entitled *Laborem Exercens* (*On Human Work*). In it, he renewed the Church's commitment to broader ownership of the means of production, and he distinguished it very sharply from Marxism:

Merely taking these means of production (capital) out of the hands of their private owners is not enough to ensure their satisfactory socialization.... We can speak of socializing only when... on the basis of his work each person is fully entitled to consider himself a part-owner of the great workbench at which he is working with everyone else. A way towards that goal could be found by associating labour with the ownership of capital, as far as possible.... (No. 14)

For our purposes, *Laborem Exercens* is critically important, since it is the first religious document that clearly unites the principles of universal work and ownership. Indeed, the section quoted from above, No. 14, is entitled "Work and Ownership."

In No. 2 of *Laborem Exercens,* Pope John Paul II calls for a new definition of work and the formulation of new tasks for the whole human race and the Church itself, thus providing a religious foundation for our discussion of the work of humanity. The biblical basis for *Laborem Exercens* is the Old Testament injunction, "Be fruitful and multiply, and fill the earth and subdue it" (Gen. 1:28). In No. 9, "Work and Personal Dignity," the Pope cites Genesis 1:28 as an expression of the will of the Creator that work should enable human beings to achieve proper dominion in the visible world. Despite the burden of toil, work is good for human beings. It is useful and enjoyable and worthy in the sense that it corresponds to human dignity, expresses that dignity, and increases it. "Through work man not only transforms nature, adapting it to his own needs, but he also achieves fulfillment as a human being and indeed in a sense becomes more a human being" (No. 9).

In Part III of *Laborem Exercens,* entitled "Conflict Between Labor and Capital," the Pope shows how capital and labor grew apart in the age of industrialization and became conflicting forces. In No. 13 he demonstrates how labor is treated as a commodity today, and he calls for changes based on the primacy of the person over things. Throughout the encyclical he makes the major point that persons are the subjects of work rather than mere instruments of production, and that work is essential to our nature, our self-esteem, and our well-being, because it enables us to share in God's creative activity.

No. 14, "Work and Ownership," contains a formula for reconciling capital and labor. There the Pope says that behind both of these abstract concepts are *people* — and that ownership of property plays a key role in reconciliation of the basic conflict of interest between capital and labor.

The portion of No. 14 quoted above is probably the most important concrete proposal of *Laborem Exercens*: the concept of the Great Workbench that will be owned by everyone. Earlier in that section, the Pope used the metaphor of the Great Workbench to describe the means of production. He advocates private ownership shared by everyone, in the form of the Great Workbench principle. Since there is no blueprint for such a workbench, he makes some suggestions:

> ... proposals for joint ownership of the means of work, sharing by the workers in the management and/or profits of businesses, so-called shareholding by labor, etc. Whether these various proposals can or cannot be applied concretely, it is clear that recognition of the proper position of labor and the worker in the production process demands various adaptations in the sphere of the right to ownership of the means of production. (No. 14)

Thus, in referring to employee ownership, he expresses some doubt as to whether the past proposals can be applied concretely, but he urges us to develop such a plan in order to solve the age-old conflict between capital and labor. I take this section of No. 14 as a challenge to all of us to find a plan that will make the Great Workbench a reality. The "various adaptations" demanded in No. 14 above are the very subject of our inquiry, because our trial-and-error search for an ideal consensus plan of social justice requires such adaptations in the systems of work and ownership.

In seeking a concrete proposal, John Paul limits himself to worker ownership because that was the only concept available for discussion in 1981. As we have seen, worker ownership unfortunately will not produce the degree of broadened ownership required to achieve social justice, and so we must push our search beyond the employment relationship.

Commenting on the philosophy of Pope John Paul II as expressed in *Laborem Exercens,* Robert Suro observed in his major article for the *Sunday New York Times* Business Section of September 7, 1986:

> Building on work done before he became Pope in 1978, John Paul has developed a theological view of work as an essential part of man's spiritual mission. He places questions of work and ownership at the heart of most social issues.... Ultimately, John Paul's economic thinking comes down to faith and hope. He deeply believes humanity is

capable of moral enlightenment and he is convinced that spiritual awakening is the one sure answer to social injustice.

The Pope's view is consistent with our Tenth Principle concerning the importance of religious activity in achieving social justice.

John Paul II continued to express this theological view of work and ownership in his 1988 encyclical, *Sollicitudo Rei Socialis* (*The Social Concerns of the Church*). In defining the scope of "the option or love of preference for the poor," he said that it included the "decisions to be made concerning the ownership and use of goods" (No. 42). He went on to proclaim the doctrine of the Social Mortgage:

> The goods of this world are originally meant for all. ... Private property, in fact, is under a "social mortgage," which means that it has an intrinsically social function, based upon and justified precisely by the principle of the universal destination of goods. (No. 42)

In the footnotes to this section, John Paul traces the Social Mortgage principle back to St. Thomas Aquinas (*Summa Theol.,* IIa, IIae, q. 66, art. 2).

As the Vatican took up the social justice issue, the American Bishops began their own campaign. In a farsighted 1919 document entitled "Program of Social Reconstruction," the Administrative Committee of the National Catholic War Council laid out a groundbreaking program of social justice (Byers, ed., 1985, pp. 367–383). In addition to proclaiming the need for jobs and maintaining the dignity of work, the Program stated that social justice will not be attained "so long as the majority of the workers remain mere wage earners. The majority must *somehow* become owners, or at least in part, of the instruments of production" (No. 35; emphasis added).

That poignant word "somehow" corresponds to the demand in *Laborem Exercens* for adaptations in ownership of the means of production to apply the Great Workbench principle concretely. The ideal of shared and democratic ownership is there, but when it came to a concrete plan, in 1919 and again in 1981, the Catholic Church had to settle for "somehow." It is our job to turn "somehow" into concrete plans that can realize the Great Workbench through trial and error.

Gaudium et Spes, the Pastoral Constitution on the Church in the Modern World adopted at the Second Vatican Council in 1965, contains some important social policy statements, especially in Chapter 3, "Economic and Social Life." These provisions, as well as five Depression-era statements of the National Catholic Welfare Conference and other pre-1986 statements of the U.S. Catholic Bishops, are reprinted in *Justice in the Marketplace* (Byers, ed., 1985).

In 1969, the American Bishops decided to make a direct response to the social justice problem. They created an important social action arm called the Campaign for Human Development (CHD), which is struggling to find a way to make structural changes in capitalism. As the Bishops stated in their November 1970 resolution on the CHD:

> In our time, however, it has become apparent that merely to alleviate the suffering of the poor, while essential, is not enough. Determined efforts are needed, as His Holiness Pope Paul VI has said, to "break the hellish circle of poverty" — to eradicate the conditions which impose poverty and trap generation after generation in an agonizing cycle of dependency and despair. In our time the legitimate aspirations of the poor for self-determination cannot be ignored. (Byers, ed., 1985, p. 467)

Since its inception, the CHD has distributed more than $100 million to groups of poor people who are trying to help themselves by eliminating the cause of their poverty. CHD is the largest national funding program for self-help projects of poor and low-income groups struggling for social change, and it is one of the largest national funding programs for low-income, worker-owned, worker-managed business ventures. In its first fifteen years of operation, CHD awarded over 2,500 self-help grants in 175 dioceses.

Most of this money has gone to social development projects, usually grassroots community organizations that challenge the policies of public and private authorities. The CHD also sponsors economic development projects, some of which involve the acquisition of businesses by employees. All of CHD's funds are allocated to projects that enable the poor to develop a means of self-support, rather than to charity handouts. In fact, CHD's basic aim is to distribute property ownership largely to those who own nothing.

During the past half-century, Catholic social teaching codified the principle of *subsidiarity,* which is embodied in our Sixth Principle that decisions should be made at the lowest possible levels. Pope Pius XI enunciated it in his 1931 encyclical *Quadragesimo Anno* (*Reconstructing the Social Order*):

> 79.... it is a fundamental principle of social philosophy, fixed and unchangeable, that one should not withdraw from individuals and commit to the community what they can accomplish by their own enterprise and industry. So, too, it is an injustice and at the same time a grave evil and a disturbance of right order, to transfer to the larger and higher collectivity functions which can be performed and provided for by lesser and subordinate bodies....
>
> 80. The state authorities should leave to other bodies the care and expediting of business and activities of lesser moment, which otherwise become for it a source of great distraction. It then will perform with greater freedom, vigor and effectiveness, the tasks belonging properly to it, and which it alone can accomplish.... Let those in power, therefore, be convinced that the more faithfully this principle of "subsidiarity" is followed and a hierarchical order prevails among the various organizations, the more excellent will be the authority and efficiency of society, and the happier and more prosperous the condition of the commonwealth.

Although this was the first mention of subsidiarity by name, the doctrine itself was enunciated by St. Thomas Aquinas and was at least implied in the 1891 encyclical of Leo XIII, *Rerum Novarum.* Subsequently, Pope John XXIII quoted Pius XI's subsidiarity statement with strong approval in his 1961 encyclical *Mater et Magistra* (*Christianity and Social Progress*), No. 53.

Pope John XXIII went on to spell out the practical application of subsidiarity:

56. Furthermore, the course of events thus far makes it clear that there cannot be a prosperous and well-ordered society unless both private citizens and public authorities work together in economic affairs....

57. Experience, in fact, shows that where private initiative of individuals is lacking, political tyranny prevails....

58. Where, on the other hand, appropriate activity of the State is lacking or defective, commonwealths are apt to experience incurable disorders, and there occurs exploitation of the weak by the unscrupulous strong, who flourish, unfortunately, like cockle among the wheat, in all times and places.

Pope John's formulation is consistent with the Latin source of the English word "subsidiarity": *subsidium,* which means "help." The subsidiarity principle is a key element of social justice consensus, because it can unite people with common goals who differ only on the appropriate degree of government intervention to provide help to those who need it. We will return to this vital point in our discussion of the 1986 Pastoral.

The 1986 Catholic Bishops' Pastoral

On November 13, 1986, the National Conference of Catholic Bishops adopted the Pastoral Letter, "Economic Justice for All: Catholic Social Teaching and the U.S. Economy," by a vote of 225 to 9. The 1986 Pastoral is a landmark in the religious search for social justice, as much because of the process by which it was drafted as for its substance. It went through three versions: the first draft, released in November 1984; the extensively revised second draft, October 1985; and the third draft, June 5, 1986, which was adopted with minor changes (National Conference of Catholic Bishops, 1986).

Throughout this drafting process, the committee of five Bishops charged with developing the Pastoral (Archbishop Rembert Weakland, O.S.B., chairman, Milwaukee; Archbishop Thomas Donnellan, Atlanta; Bishop William Weigand, Salt Lake City;

Bishop George Speltz, St. Cloud, Minn.; and Auxiliary Bishop Peter Rosazza, Hartford) held public sessions across the nation and solicited presentations from hundreds of economists, sociologists, and others deemed qualified to make a contribution. These witnesses came from all major religions and walks of life and covered the entire spectrum of political, social, and economic opinion. More than 10,000 pages of written presentations were received and processed by the Bishops, and the extensive annotation of the Pastoral shows that many of these ideas were incorporated into the final text. Thus, the 1986 Pastoral is the result of an open debate that was both democratic and ecumenical; it was given very careful consideration through the more than four years of the drafting process; and, of equal importance, it does not rely upon idealistic hopes and theoretical reforms, but it actually tackles specific problem areas and proposes specific solutions. Moreover, it has received extensive nationwide examination and criticism in the media, and it is supported by a substantial Catholic financial commitment to future implementation.

While some of the media criticism alleged that the Pastoral suffers from the incompetence of the Bishops in economic science, I have not seen any documentation of that charge. The following overall appraisal was made by Wharton School Professor Lawrence R. Klein, a Nobel prize winner in economics:

> Above all, the pastoral letter is a scholarly document that relates modern economic ideas and practices to the ancient scriptures. The economic analysis is very professional.... (Klein, 1987, p. 7)

The Pastoral itself is a book-length document that I do not have the space to discuss in detail. I am concerned mainly with the manner in which the Pastoral treats work and ownership, and how it might facilitate the trial-and-error process of our Ten Principles. No doubt many books will be written about the Pastoral itself. Three excellent collections of essays have already appeared: *The Deeper Meaning of Economic Life* (Douglass, ed., 1986); *The Catholic Challenge to the American Economy* (Gannon, ed., 1987); and *Economic Justice* (Pawlikowski and Senior, ed., 1988).

Before examining its treatment of our Ten Principles, it is worth noting that the main themes of the Pastoral are human dignity, the right of all people to participate in the economic life of society, and the special obligation of all members of society to the poor and vulnerable. The Bishops conclude that "basic justice demands the establishment of minimum levels of participation in the life of the human community for all persons" (No. 77) and that every economic system must be judged by three criteria: what it does *for* people, what it does *to* people, and how people participate in it.

In a short Pastoral Message accompanying the final letter, the Bishops made clear what the Pastoral is *not:*

> The Pastoral letter is not a blueprint for the American economy. It does not embrace any particular theory of how the economy works, nor does it attempt to resolve the disputes between different schools of economic thought. Instead our letter turns to Scripture and to the social teachings of the Church. There we discover what our economic life must serve, what standards it must meet.
>
> (Pastoral Message, No. 12)

Despite this disclaimer, the Pastoral is not limited to lofty platitudes. It considers some nuts-and-bolts solutions to economic problems, particularly in the areas of work and ownership.

The scriptural foundation of the Pastoral is laid down in Chapter II, entitled "The Christian Vision of Economic Life." (The most important scriptural references are summarized in the Appendix of this book.)

The importance of human dignity is proclaimed throughout the Pastoral. For example, at the start of Chapter II, the Bishops say:

> The dignity of the human person, realized in community with others, is the criterion against which all aspects of economic life must be measured. (No. 28)

Participation is also a basic and recurrent theme. For example:

> Social justice implies that persons have an obligation to
> be active and productive participants in the life of society
> and that society has a duty to enable them to participate
> in this way. (No. 71)

The Pastoral's dedication to the poor is proclaimed throughout
the text, starting with the scriptural references to the life of Jesus
and his ministry to the poor. Under "Moral Priorities for the
Nation," the Bishops say:

> The obligation to provide justice for all means that the
> poor have the single most urgent economic claim on the
> conscience of the nation. (No. 86)

Those ideals have been expressed before. The special importance of the Pastoral is that it goes on to attempt some specific
applications of these principles to the American economy. Let
us consider now how the Pastoral relates to our Ten Principles.

Capitalism: Structural Changes and Self-Interest

The Pastoral does not endorse any particular system of economics (No. 129) but it does mention the claim "that an un-
fettered free-market economy, where owners, workers, and consumers pursue their enlightened self-interest, provides the greatest possible liberty, material welfare, and equity" (No. 128).
While the Pastoral does not embrace that claim or the counter-
argument that capitalism is inherently inequitable and immoral,
it does acknowledge the positive values of capitalism (Nos. 6,
8, 110, 114, 117–118). The overall thrust of the Pastoral is to
accept the enlightened self-interest of American capitalism as a
starting point from which structural changes can bring us closer
to social justice (cf. our First and Second Principles). This was
acknowledged by the most prolific critic of the Pastoral, Michael
Novak, in the Lay Commission Report which we shall discuss
in detail below.

Some critics of the Pastoral decry its failure to engage in
"class analysis," apparently assuming that the best way to change
the unjust structures of American capitalism is to discard the
entire system, good and bad elements alike. Instead, the Bishops
chose to preserve the freedoms and productivity of capitalism,

but this did not prevent them from attacking the structures that bar millions of Americans from participation in the economy through work, ownership, or both.

By tackling specific economic structures, the Pastoral goes beyond past Church efforts to achieve social justice, such as symbolic attacks on capitalist ideology, or works (such as those of Mother Teresa) that are inspirational in their compassion but do not address structural roadblocks. The Bishops' insistence that economic justice requires participation by all Americans in work and ownership (Nos. 91b, 114, 200c) in itself mandates significant structural change, as we shall see.

Employment and the Work of Humanity

The Pastoral is clearly consistent with our principles of the right to a work opportunity and the opportunity to achieve the work of humanity (Third and Fourth Principles).

The right of every person to an opportunity to earn a living is reaffirmed in No. 80 of the Pastoral, which is based on human rights and the requirements of human dignity as outlined by Pope John XXIII in *Pacem In Terris,* Nos. 8–27, as well as on Pope John Paul II's encyclical, *Laborem Exercens,* Nos. 18–19.

There are many other statements in support of broadened work opportunity throughout the Pastoral. In Nos. 102–103, the right to work is discussed in the framework of labor unions, with workers to be treated as persons rather than simply as a factor of production. Again, the Bishops rely on *Laborem Exercens,* Nos. 16 and 19.

The Bishops become even more specific in Chapter III when they discuss employment as one of four selected economic problems:

> 151. We recommend that the nation make a major new commitment to achieve full employment. . . . The country is doing far less than it might to generate employment.
>
> 152. . . . Although we recognize the complexities and trade-offs involved in reducing unemployment, we believe that 6 percent to 7 percent unemployment is neither inevitable nor acceptable. . . . The acceptance of present unemployment rates would have been unthinkable 20 years ago. It should be regarded as intolerable today.

> 153. We must first establish a consensus that every-
> one has a right to employment.... We must work for the
> formation of a new national consensus and mobilize the
> necessary political will at all levels to make the goal of full
> employment a reality.

The Bishops make it clear that the subsidiarity principle must be
applied to this search for full employment, with the private sector to account for most of the new jobs (No. 154). They go on
to recommend further experiments with targeted employment
programs, including job-training and apprenticeship programs
in the private sector (No. 159), and direct job-creation programs
for the long-term unemployed and those with special needs, including both direct public-service employment and public subsidies for employment in the private sector (No. 162). Again,
they follow subsidiarity by calling for "increased collaboration
and fresh alliances between the private and public sectors at all
levels" (No. 166).

Welfare reform, implicit in our Third and Fourth principles,
is clearly endorsed by the Bishops:

> 210.G. A thorough reform of the nation's welfare and
> income-support programs should be undertaken.
> 211. (1) Public-assistance programs should be designed
> to assist recipients, wherever possible, to become self-
> sufficient through gainful employment. Individuals should
> be no worse off economically when they get jobs than when
> they rely only on public ass:stance.... To help recipients
> become self-sufficient and reduce dependency on welfare,
> public assistance programs should work in tandem with
> job-creation programs that include provisions for training,
> counseling, placement and child care. Jobs for recipients
> of public assistance should be fairly compensated so that
> workers receive the full benefits and status associated with
> gainful employment.

In the section of the Pastoral dealing with direct job creation
programs, the Bishops dramatically state the need for the work
of humanity:

165. Jobs that are created should produce goods and services needed and valued by society. It is both good common sense and sound economics to create jobs directly for the purpose of meeting society's unmet needs. Across the nation, in every state and locality, there is ample evidence of social needs that are going unmet. [Specific examples of parks, recreation facilities, bridges, highways, and low-income housing are cited, as well as defects in the educational systems, day-care services, senior-citizen services and other community programs.] At the same time, there are more than 8 million Americans looking for productive and useful work. Surely we have the capacity to match these needs by giving Americans who are anxious to work a chance for productive employment in jobs that are waiting to be done. The overriding moral value of enabling jobless persons to achieve a new sense of dignity and personal worth through employment also recommends these programs.

Broadened Ownership

The Pastoral contains several general statements on the importance of ownership, which are relevant to our Fifth principle:

91. Basic justice calls for more than providing help to the poor and other vulnerable members of society. It recognizes the priority of policies and programs that support family life and enhance economic participation through employment and widespread ownership of property.

114. Widespread distribution of property can help avoid excessive concentration of economic and political power. For these reasons ownership should be made possible for a broad sector of our population.

200.C. Self-help efforts among the poor should be fostered by programs and policies in both the private and public sectors.... Efforts that enable the poor to participate in the ownership and control of economic resources are especially important.

In Chapter IV, "A New American Experiment: Partnership for the Public Good," broadened ownership is given special emphasis, notably in No. 300, which mentions some specific arrangements that should be the subject of further study:

> 300. . . . Several arrangements are gaining increasing support in the United States: profit sharing by the workers in a firm; enabling employees to become company stockholders; granting employees greater participation in determining the conditions of work; cooperative ownership of the firm by all who work within it; and programs for enabling a much larger number of Americans, regardless of their employment status, to become shareholders in successful corporations.

While the Bishops do not give a blanket endorsement to any of these arrangements, they say that continued research and experimentation is justified (No. 301).

Subsidiarity and Government Intervention

The Pastoral repeatedly reaffirms the Catholic principle of subsidiarity — that social functions should be assigned to the smallest effective unit (cf. our Sixth Principle). The Bishops quote Pope Leo XIII's 1931 formulation of the subsidiarity principle, and go on to say that it guarantees institutional pluralism, providing space for freedom, initiative, and creativity on the part of many social agents (Nos. 99–101). In the section dealing with government intervention they again rely on subsidiarity:

> 124. The primary norm for determining the scope and limits of governmental intervention is the "principle of subsidiarity" cited above. . . . The precise form of government involvement in this process cannot be determined in the abstract. It will depend on an assessment of specific needs and the most effective ways to address them.

In Chapter IV, where the Bishops get into specific details of the proposed "New American Experiment in Partnership for the Public Good," they reiterate their reliance on subsidiarity (Nos. 297, 308, 314, 323). Thus, by their reaffirmation of subsidiarity in the Pastoral, the Bishops hold that every action should be taken at the lowest possible level, starting with the individual, the family, the private sector, and the local church, rather than through governmental or hierarchical intervention.

The subsidiarity principle is quite appropriate for religious organizations, structured as they are with a national or international hierarchy, with regional supervision by Bishops and many units at the local or diocesan level. There is a great reservoir of energy and good will at the local level that can be tapped through subsidiarity.

The procedural nature of the quarrel over the degree of government intervention also comes into play here. Despite the repeated reaffirmation of subsidiarity in the Pastoral, press coverage immediately after its adoption centered on the question of government intervention, because many of the specific remedies and experiments suggested by the Bishops involved government participation. Thus, in the *New York Times* of November 29, 1986, E. J. Dionne, Jr., wrote:

> The debate, then, is largely over how much government should intervene in the economy, the balance between market forces and the power of government.

And Leonard Silk, the chief economics correspondent for the *New York Times,* wrote on November 14, 1986:

> This report cannot by any means be called a radical document. It urges rather the continuation of the "mixed economy," with both private enterprise and government having important roles to play.... The Pastoral letter is likely to play a significant role in the debate on United States economic policy in the post-Reagan era.

Obviously, a great deal of government intervention exists, and some of it (like Social Security) is permanent. Therefore, one cannot discuss improvement of the economic system without touching on existing and proposed government participation.

As we have seen, even the conservative gurus are urging increased government intervention in the form of "industrial policy" or "competitiveness policy." Unfortunately, there is no scoreboard or checklist showing what proposed solutions are available short of government intervention, and which problems are falling between the tables. As Harvard political economist Robert B. Reich observed:

> Business has no clear mandate of stewardship for the development and employment of our workers; government alone lacks the competence to take on the task.
>
> (Reich, 1987, p. 251)

Perhaps religious groups should create such a *Subsidiarity Scoreboard*. It could list major problems like unemployment and inequitable wealth distribution, and then enumerate proposed solutions at all levels, starting with the lowest: the individual, the family, individual businesses, local business associations, etc., working up to national organizations of the private sector. If the scoreboard shows that these solutions are working or promising to work, we need not go any further up the subsidiarity ladder. But if the lower orders are not doing the job, then — and only then — the scoreboard would list governmental solutions, beginning with local government, and working up to the state and national levels if necessary. By dramatizing subsidiarity through such a scoreboard, religious organizations could demonstrate that they are dedicated to solving these problems at the lowest possible level, rather than automatically advocating government intervention.

The Subsidiarity Scoreboard would be a challenge to the private sector to develop specific programs which would make government intervention unnecessary. Religious organizations could also form coalitions with business to develop yardsticks measuring the effectiveness of nongovernmental initiatives. Or religious organizations could themselves set standards for measuring the effectiveness of private sector remedies, and join in coalitions with business to make private remedies work. Once there are clear standards for the scoreboard, a much stronger popular consensus can be developed for legislative remedies in cases where there are no effective private solutions.

Trial and Error

It is clear from the title of Chapter IV of the Pastoral ("A New American Experiment") that the Bishops are aware of the trial-and-error nature of most economic innovation (cf. our Seventh Principle). The Bishops realize that no economic principles prevent us from achieving greater social justice through increased employment, broader ownership, or both. Throughout Chapters III and IV, they call for experiments that will bring us closer to full employment and will broaden ownership throughout society. Wherever the Bishops are specific on policy changes and innovation, they do not stumble over any supposed theoretical obstacles, nor do they hesitate to recommend experimentation.

Combining Public Service Employment with Stock Ownership

As we have seen, the Bishops define participation in economic life as a basic level of access to wealth and income that is required by justice. That participation must include both employment and ownership (No. 91).

While the Bishops have specifically recommended broadening of employment (as in our Third Principle) and ownership (as in our Fifth Principle) they have not combined these two elements to advocate public service employment combined with stock ownership as in our Eighth Principle. Nevertheless, all the policy recommendations of the Pastoral are consistent with our Eighth Principle. Indeed, at my urging, the Bishops inserted in No. 300, as one of the plans that are gaining increasing support, "programs for enabling a much larger number of Americans, regardless of their employment status, to become shareholders in successful corporations." This is one of the experimental tools of our Eighth Principle — the idea of creating public service employment through which the newly employed worker receives shares in major successful companies even though not employed by them. In Chapter Five we shall discuss methods of breathing life into this concept.

Income and Wealth Distribution as Value Judgments

Throughout the Pastoral Letter, the Bishops demonstrate their awareness that income distribution and wealth distribution are value judgments or political questions rather then scientific issues (cf. our Ninth Principle). Repeatedly (especially in Chapters III and IV) they call for more equitable income and wealth distribution, without deference to any barriers of economic science. As leaders of a religious organization, they do not hesitate to make value judgments regarding more equitable income and wealth distribution.

The Crucial Role of Religious Organizations

As we have seen, more than 70 percent of charitable donations in the United States go to religious organizations, which are charged with the duty of delivering help to millions of needy people. This has given religious organizations hands-on experience with soup kitchens, shelters for the homeless, and other forms of direct emergency assistance. Beyond that, many religious organizations have conducted their own campaigns for social justice and for improvements in the economic system. Another strong reason for religious input is the natural inclination of individuals to depend upon their religious organizations for moral guidance. Few individuals consider themselves qualified to judge the need for moral input in our economic system. Most throw up their hands at the arcane jargon of economics, and the task is not made any easier when questions of theology are inserted. Therefore, religious organizations need to formulate moral economic positions for their followers to consider. No blind acceptance is required, but most religious people will follow their leaders in this respect.

This moral consensus is one of the key elements of the Pastoral. As Georgetown Professor Diane Yeager stated:

> The legitimacy and success of the letter ought to be evaluated in terms of this larger project of establishing a moral consensus that will command the respect, allegiance, and energy not simply of Roman Catholics, and not even simply of Christians, but of an entire diverse nation.
>
> (Douglass, ed., 1986, p. 188)

Along with the Pastoral, the Bishops adopted and funded a three-year plan for follow-up and implementation. The plan has an ecumenical tone, for it welcomes "the valuable support and participation of other religious organizations," and seeks "op-

portunities to work on an ecumenical basis with other religious
organizations and with other groups in the secular community
in joint efforts to pursue the moral vision of the Pastoral Letter."

The plan will attempt to establish "an ongoing mechanism
for stimulating research and public policy debate grounded in
the moral vision of the Pastoral." Some of the suggestions for
the follow-up program include a Catholic institute for ongoing
research and public policy analysis; a series of commissioned
policy papers to examine specific issues; and invitations to Catholic colleges, universities, and research groups to examine ways
of implementing the Pastoral.

The Pastoral itself called for broad application of the resources of the church to implement its recommendations, including the following steps:

> 360. Renewed emphasis on Catholic social teaching
> in our schools, colleges and universities; special seminars
> with corporate officials, union leaders, legislators, bankers
> and the like; the organization of small groups composed
> of people from different ways of life to meditate together
> on the Gospel and ethical norms; speakers' bureaus; fam-
> ily programs; clearinghouses of available material; pulpit
> aids for priests; diocesan television and radio programs;
> research projects in our universities — all of these are ap-
> propriate means for continued discussion and action.

The first offshoot of the Pastoral came quickly from the Maryland Catholic Conference, which issued its own statement to
the laity on December 6, 1986, along with a formal set of policy
recommendations on the state and local levels and in the private sector to promote economic justice in accordance with the
mandate of the Pastoral. Their recommendations covered four
areas: taxes, unemployment, poverty and hunger, and shelter.
Of these, the recommendations on unemployment are of most
interest to us. They include support for "a statewide consensus
that every Marylander who can work should have an opportunity to work," and "substantial new state investment in direct
job-creation programs."

The Maryland plan includes specific recommendations to

the state legislature and a special appeal to the business community on taxes, unemployment, hunger, and shelter. Ronald Kreitemeyer, chief staff member of the Bishops' Committee that drafted the Pastoral, was particularly pleased with the way the Maryland Bishops extended the agenda of the Pastoral by focusing on the specific problems of that state. He noted that housing, which was not given detailed treatment in the Pastoral, nevertheless is an important part of the Maryland program, so that the Pastoral was quickly adapted to meet local social and economic problems.

Soon after the Maryland statement came a pastoral letter entitled "Justice for All" issued jointly by the Episcopal Bishop of West Virginia and the Roman Catholic Bishop of Wheeling-Charleston, W. Va. The letter is in the form of a beautifully illustrated twelve-page booklet, with poetic statements summarizing principles of social justice. The joint statement is in the ecumenical spirit of the 1986 Pastoral, which seeks the cooperation and support of all, regardless of religion or tradition (No. 27).

The Third World and Liberation Theology

The Pastoral devotes considerable attention to international and Third World social justice problems. In No. 77, it includes people of the less developed countries in the group that must be allowed to participate in economic growth: "Acquiescence in [these patterns of exclusion] or failure to correct them when it is possible to do so is a sinful dereliction of Christian duty." An entire section of Chapter III is entitled: "The U.S. Economy and the Developing Nations: Complexity, Challenge, and Choices" (Nos. 251–292), concluding with a call for "a U.S. international economic policy designed to empower people everywhere and enable them to continue to develop a sense of their own worth, improve the quality of their lives, and ensure that the benefits of economic growth are shared equitably" (No. 292).

At the end of Chapter IV, which deals with a New American Experiment, there is a section on "Cooperation at the International Level." It echoes the treatment of the international issue in Chapter III:

322. If our country is to guide its international economic relationships by policies that serve human dignity

and justice, we must expand our understanding of the moral responsibility of citizens to serve the common good of the entire planet. Cooperation is not limited to the local, regional, or national level. Economic policy can no longer be governed by national goals alone.... The unfinished business of the American experiment includes the formation of new international partnerships, especially with the developing countries, based on mutual respect, cooperation, and a dedication to fundamental justice.

The Pastoral's discussion of international and Third World problems is not couched in terms of liberation theology. Instead it stresses the duty of Americans to care for all the disadvantaged peoples of the world. Given all of the problems of implementing the Pastoral in the United States and carrying out its international mandates, apparently the Bishops felt no need to confront the controversies of liberation theology. But those people interested in liberation theology will find much comfort in the specific policy recommendations of the Pastoral for the disadvantaged people of the Third World, where the liberation theology movement has taken root.

We shall discuss the international situation in more detail in Chapter Seven.

The Lay Commission Report

To put the Pastoral in proper perspective, it is useful to examine its most detailed criticism: the *Report on the U.S. Catholic Bishops' Pastoral Letter on the American Economy*, published by the Lay Commission on Catholic Social Teaching and the U.S. Economy on November 5, 1986, and written by William E. Simon and Michael Novak, co-chairmen of the Commission. The Commission was organized in 1984 by prominent conservative Catholic lay people, after the Bishops announced their intention to publish a Pastoral Letter on the U.S. economy. The Lay Commission's first statement, a 120-page booklet entitled *Toward the Future,* was published even before the Bishops released the first draft of their letter in 1984. It was a ringing defense of capitalism, apparently written in anticipation of a Pastoral that would condemn capitalism on moral grounds and possibly advocate democratic socialism.

The Lay Commission's second (and presumably final) report was issued November 5, 1986, a few days before the Bishops' Pastoral was actually released. The Lay Commission's comments are based upon the third draft of the Pastoral, which is practically identical in substance to the final Pastoral, so that we can consider the Lay Commission's 1986 report as their definitive criticism of the Pastoral. Since the Lay Commission's report was written largely by Michael Novak, we shall refer to it as the Novak report (Novak, 1986).

The Lay Commission membership consists of twenty-nine American Catholics from the fields of public service, business, education, labor, law, and journalism. It includes such leading conservatives and political pragmatists as William E. Simon, Alexander M. Haig, and Clare Boothe Luce, who recognize that today's capitalism must be tempered by some government intervention.

The Novak report agrees wholeheartedly with the Bishops' dedication of the Pastoral to the poor:

> We especially commend their emphasis on helping the poor. (Novak, 1986, executive summary, p. 1)

> We think it admirable that our Bishops placed stress on lifting the poor out of poverty. (Ibid., p. 2)

> We share with our Bishops the full intention of raising up every single poor person on earth from the tyranny of poverty. (Novak, 1986, p. 4)

> What the final draft has done well, we admire. We welcome especially its emphasis on lifting up the poor. (Ibid., p. 23)

While questioning the Pastoral's interpretation of papal teaching on economic rights, the Novak report agrees that:

> Economic rights in papal thought include rights to initiative, to physically and morally healthful working conditions (with special rights for women, wives and mothers), to opportunity to achieve responsibilities compatible with talents, to work that provides a decent standard of living

for one's family, and to private property and its inherent social duties. (Ibid., p. 10)

Novak goes on to distinguish "economic rights" from "welfare rights," and argues that the Pastoral has somewhat confused these two. Nevertheless, for our purposes, the above statement is an endorsement of the right to work as proclaimed by Pope John XXIII in *Peace on Earth* and as reaffirmed by the 1986 Pastoral in the sections previously discussed (Nos. 80 and 153).

The Novak report also supports the welfare state:

> We are very much in favor of a disciplined and realistic welfare state that, while encouraging independence and self-reliance, provides assistance to those who cannot rely on themselves. (Ibid., p. 11)

And on welfare reform, the Lay Commission's position is very close to that of the 1986 Pastoral:

> [Our] theory turns to empirical research in order to discern the most effective means for providing welfare benefits that strengthen habits of self-reliance and personal autonomy. Such a theory notes, with Pope John Paul II, that among those able to work, human dignity is rooted in work. Several passages in the final draft commendably recognize this point. (Novak, 1986, p. 12)

> Welfare programs should be designed to inspire self reliance, autonomy, fruitful and lasting marriages, and a sense of personal dignity based upon achievement. If human dignity is rooted in work, welfare should also include a component of work, for those who can work.... In addition, welfare policy in the U.S. is probably well served by having the different states try different experiments, so as to learn from each other. (Ibid., p. 20)

In that one section, the Lay Commission endorsed the principles of trial and error, human dignity rooted in work, and work opportunities for welfare recipients, just as did the 1986 Pastoral.

In listing the institutions deemed crucial for the early development of the United States, the Novak report mentions "the Homestead Act, favoring a multiplicity of owners rather than a few large land owners" (ibid., p. 7), thus endorsing the principle of broadening capital ownership through appropriate government intervention.

In discussing government intervention, the Novak report defines free markets:

> When one speaks of "free markets," one does not mean that there are no interventions from the political system. Rather, one means such interventions are prudent and confined to cases in which markets are failing or in which market performance can be improved. (Ibid., p. 9)

Surely this definition of free markets, with its support of government intervention when it can improve market performance, falls within the American consensus and is consistent with the 1986 Pastoral's discussion of work and ownership.

The Lay Commission does not attempt to portray American capitalism as a perfect system:

> There are particular evils, weaknesses, and flaws in our economic structures. The Bishops do well to note them and to assert the need to remedy them.
> (Novak, 1986, executive summary, p. 4)

The Novak report goes on to note (with an almost perceptible sigh of relief) that the Pastoral is a pro-capitalist document:

> In some ways, the final draft includes stronger statements in favor of a capitalist economy, such as that of the United States, than are to be found in any other document of the tradition of Catholic social thought. They have mentioned the crucial role of creativity and invention, the role of enterprise, the importance of economic growth and job creation and other institutions of the free society. For this we commend them. (Novak, 1986, p. 3)

> To be sure, the Bishops have written a pro-capitalist, not a socialist, document. Nevertheless, they turn too readily to

the state to "direct" economic activism, to create jobs, to
determine foreign aid assistance.
(Ibid., executive summary, p. 3)

The state must be active; but excessive state entanglement
raises barriers. To repeat, we are not opposed to an activist
state, but wise activism means counting costs as well as
benefits. (Ibid., p. 8)

Here the Novak report overlooks the Bishops' repeated reaffirmation of *subsidiarity*, which prescribes government intervention only when the other elements of society fail to do the job.
(The Novak report does not mention subsidiarity.) As we have
seen in the discussion of our Sixth Principle, this concern about
the degree of government intervention is merely procedural, and
presents no barrier to achieving consensus as long as we adhere
to subsidiarity.
    The Lay Commission does not question the right of the Bish-
ops to venture into the field of economics:

We do not count ourselves among those who think that, in
speaking of economics, the Bishops are overstepping their
proper authority. On the contrary, we take pride in Catholic social teaching. We welcome the Bishops' constructive
contributions to that unfinished tradition, even though lay
Catholics also have a primary calling to contribute to that
tradition. (Ibid., p. 3)

The Novak report also praises the open and democratic manner
in which the pastoral was laboriously drafted, discussed, and
redrafted:

We commend the Bishops for being attentive to their many
critics. (Ibid., p. 2)

We also thank them for the open manner in which they
have proceeded and for inviting public criticism and debate. (Ibid., p. 23)

Indeed, Michael Novak was the only person who was permitted
to appear before the drafting committee three times.

The Novak report makes no comment on the 1986 Pastoral's support for broadened stock ownership, but Mr. Novak's prior writings contain clear endorsements of this principle. For example, in *Freedom with Justice,* he wrote:

> There is one further point about economic development in which Catholic leaders might take the lead. Just as the Homestead Act was designed to prevent the US Middle West from developing in the pattern of Latin America — a few large landed estates, worked by peasants — in favor of a policy promoting as many property owners as possible; so also the time is now ripe to consider methods for broadening the ownership of industry and commerce. It is both sound American practice and an ideal of Catholic social thought that ownership should be diffused as broadly as possible. To a striking extent, this is already true in the ownership of homes, automobiles, and multiple personal resources. It is not so broadly true in participation in the ownership of industry.
>
> (Novak, 1984, pp. 53–54)

Much of the Novak report's criticism of the 1986 Pastoral is based on differences in terminology. For example, the Lay Commission would prefer the Pastoral to use the term "pluralism" instead of "solidarity." Media comments on the Novak report often focus on these semantic and procedural differences, without noting the strong degree of moral consensus between the 1986 Pastoral and its most detailed criticism. As we have seen, this consensus, buttressed by subsidiarity, is broad enough to serve as a foundation upon which we can build a new path to social justice through expansion of work and ownership.

The Protestant Churches

Protestantism has been popularly identified with capitalism ever since the Reformation, notably through the "Protestant ethic," which glorified hard work, thrift, and efficiency, in the name of eternal salvation. As the noted German author Max Weber interpreted Protestantism in his 1904 book, *The Protestant*

Ethic and the Spirit of Capitalism, the ethic was an important factor in the economic success of Protestants during the early stages of European capitalism. But Weber was a sociologist rather than a theologian, and it is doubtful that Protestant theologians such as Luther and Calvin really embraced the capitalist ethic as fully as Weber implies. Professor J. Philip Wogaman of the Wesley Theological Seminary in Washington, D.C., holds:

> Undoubtedly, the Calvinist strain in the cultural development of Switzerland and the Anglo-Saxon countries has had some effect in supporting the ethical claims of laissez faire ideology, although it should immediately be noted that that ideology falls short of the real Protestant ethic at two decisive points. In the first place, the genuine emphasis of Calvinism always had a much deeper commitment to the life of the community. Calvin and the greatest of his followers would have been appalled by the extremes to which laissez-faire capitalism carried individualism. In the second place, the early Protestant would have objected strongly to the implied self-righteousness of the laissez-faire idea of deserving. (Wogaman, 1977, p. 83)

In *The American Ethos,* Professors McClosky and Zaller found that by margins of more than 90 percent, both the general public and political influentials believe that we are made better by the trials and hardships of life, in line with the Protestant ethic. They comment on Weber's writing:

> Weber's thesis is especially appropriate for an understanding of American capitalism. America was, from the beginning, a predominantly Protestant nation, and many of its business leaders have attributed their own economic success to the cluster of beliefs that Weber called the "Protestant ethic." Perhaps the most influential settlements in the New World were those of the New England Calvinists, more commonly known as Puritans. In few parts of the world were the values of Protestantism and early capitalism so mutually reinforcing as in the Puritan colonies....

This radical new religious perspective had important secular implications. Most important, perhaps, was that the deliberate pursuit of wealth and material goods — disdained by the hereditary aristocracy and viewed with suspicion by the Catholic Church — had attained powerful religious sanction....

It is ironic that Protestant theologians valued wealth not for the comforts or pleasures it might afford but for the arduous *process* by which it was acquired. This process, as Protestant ministers repeatedly stressed, tamed the passions, kept one occupied, instilled good habits, and enabled one to avoid the temptations of sin.

(McClosky and Zaller, 1984, pp. 104–106)

All of the surveys reported by McClosky and Zaller indicate an overwhelming approval of the basic principles of the Protestant ethic when the questions are posed in positive form.

The evangelical tradition of mainline American Protestantism included spiritual revivals that paved the way for the Revolutionary War and the abolition of slavery. After the Civil War, this energetic spirit became increasingly directed toward questions of labor and capitalist values. Laissez-faire capitalism as practiced in America gave priority to the rights of capitalists and property owners. This facilitated industrial expansion, but also brought us sweatshops, child labor, monopolies, robber barons, cruel company towns in the coalfields, and Upton Sinclair's "jungle" in the stockyards.

The Social Gospel Movement

Within American Protestantism there arose a group of preachers who recognized that Christianity had to address new social issues created by capitalism's abuses. In an age of pulpiteers, there were powerful preachers of national reputation who had the ear of presidents, captains of industry, and the laboring classes for whom they were advocates. The crusade they formed became known as the Social Gospel Movement. Emanating essentially from the middle-class membership of the evangelical churches — mainly Baptist, Methodist, Congregationalist, and Presbyterian — the Social Gospel Movement developed into a national political force, playing a key role in Theodore Roosevelt's Progressive and Bull Moose campaigns, and helping to win the regulatory changes that forced big business to begin assuming some degree of social responsibility. In fact, some of the social justice issues that have endured to this day were first formulated by the Social Gospel Movement.

In grappling with the abuses of capitalism, the Social Gospel Movement had a formidable adversary — the Gospel of Wealth — which relied on its own brand of religious morality to justify capitalism. Essentially, the Gospel of Wealth claimed divine approval for free enterprise capitalism and the rich men it produced. Andrew Carnegie expressed its philosophy in an essay on wealth published in 1889, in which he maintained that civilization depended on three iron-clad principles: free competition, free accumulation, and the sacredness of private property. Although Carnegie recognized that these principles "may sometimes be hard for individuals," he nonetheless believed "it is best for the race because it insured the survival of the fittest in every department" and produced "a wonderful material development" to the benefit of all.

This sentiment was expressed in the churches as well, although less blatantly, and was also usually accompanied by a reminder that no one needed to go poor or hungry in the vast richness of America. For example, in 1870 a Congregationalist newspaper noted that there were thousands upon thousands of acres of magnificent soil beyond the Mississippi to be secured at a nominal price, ensuring that "no man who is blessed with health and a willingness to work, be his family large or small, need come to the poorhouse." Gradually, however, the frontier began to close, and the safety valve that the historian Frederick Turner popularized in his "frontier thesis" was no longer able to delay the day of moral reckoning. Then did the battle for biblical integrity between the Social Gospel and the Gospel of Wealth begin in earnest.

There are too many diverse voices and movements to detail here, but one of the leading nineteenth-century Social Gospel preachers was the Reverend Washington Gladden, a Congregationalist minister. Gladden opposed both socialism and capitalism, seeking instead to apply "Christian law" to social problems. In a long career that included forty books and hundreds of articles, he denounced American capitalism and its leading lights, including the Harrimans and the Rockefellers. He even tried to get his church to turn down John D. Rockefeller's gift of $100,000 as "tainted money." In his view, the problem with capitalism lay in its basic principles:

> That self-love is the mainspring of human action, and that all rules of conduct must be adjusted to this as the supreme controlling motive, has been the assumption of all our political and practical philosophy.... That this principle has not worked very well through the old days of absolutism and aristocratic feudalism we could see.... What we are witnessing is nothing other than the culmination and collapse of the existing social order which rests on moral individualism. And the Church of Jesus Christ is called to replace this principle of selfishness and strife with the principle of goodwill and service. (Ferm, 1969, pp. 252–253)

Walter Rauschenbusch, perhaps the most influential of the Social Gospel preachers, held a similar view of the essential immorality of pre-welfare capitalism. As a Baptist minister among the poor in New York's "Hell's Kitchen," he saw firsthand the bitter fruits of laissez-faire capitalism and came to these conclusions about the root causes of the poverty he faced daily:

> Our scientific political economy has long been an oracle of a false god. It has taught us to approach economic questions from the point of view of goods and not of man.... Man is Christianized when he puts God before self; political economy will be Christianized when it puts man before wealth. (Hofstadter, ed., 1963, p. 82)

This criticism of capitalism's root and branch did not mean the Social Gospel preachers embraced Marxism or socialism. On the contrary, these foreign ideologies had little appeal in the reformist American churches, and many preachers accurately foresaw the problems inherent in socialism and communism. As Congregationalist minister Charles Reynolds Brown noted in his book, *The Social Message of the Modern Pulpit*:

"Give us government ownership and government control of all the resources and machinery of production," the socialists say, "and these men who are now selfish, narrow and false will be public-spirited, generous and faithful." But will they? What is to reach the springs of action, renew the heart, purify and ennoble the affections, correct and strengthen the will? (Brown, 1912, p. 249)

Most of the Social Gospel preachers, in fact, sought to reconcile capital and labor within a market economy. As Reverend Brown put it:

The right to manage [one's] own business in his own way ... is modified by his obligation to manage it in such a way that his prosperity shall include a fair measure of prosperity for the men whose destinies are bound up with his own in that enterprise. (Ibid., p. 206)

The Social Gospel Movement drew upon the nineteenth-century European Protestant emphasis on the theme of the Kingdom of God. Walter Rauschenbusch and his colleagues organized a Brotherhood of the Kingdom in 1893, to promote the idea of a Kingdom of God on earth as the central thought of Jesus and as the great aim of Christianity, transforming life on earth into the harmony of heaven by Christianizing the social order progressively. Rauschenbusch's final work, *A Theology for the Social Gospel* (1917), contains some concrete policy ideas which parallel those of the Catholic social teaching we have just examined: the dignity of work and the need for full employment, as well as cooperative ownership of the means of production (Yeager, 1986, p. 191).

As Martin E. Marty has pointed out, the Social Gospel stood apart from and denounced socialism:

... Rauschenbusch favored cooperativism but felt that private property did spur morality and participation in the republic. Only in his support of Henry George's single tax did Rauschenbusch come close to the support of a socialist program. Otherwise, socialism stimulated class conflict and violence while for the Christian, he believed, love creates fellowship. (Marty, 1986, pp. 294–295)

There was great optimism in the Social Gospel Movement, with the reformers coming to think that poverty and war would be eradicated. These delusions were shattered by World War I and the Great Depression. But this important strain of Protestantism, adapted to post-Depression conditions, was carried on and led by Reinhold Niebuhr, probably the most influential Protestant theologian of the twentieth century. Born in Missouri in 1892, he was ordained a minister in the Evangelical and Reformed Church (now a part of the United Church of Christ) in 1915.

As a pastor in Detroit from 1915 to 1928, Niebuhr came to embrace Christian socialism, attacking capitalism forcefully in many books, articles, and speeches. But Niebuhr was equally skeptical of socialism as a panacea. After World War II, he became a leading opponent of Soviet expansionism in Eastern Europe, and in his later books he rejected both systems, using the evangelical tradition to denounce their shortcomings. He was one of the earliest advocates of employee stock ownership. In *The Children of Light and the Children of Darkness,* he wrote:

A conservative class which makes "free enterprise" the final good of the community, and a radical class which mistakes some proximate solution of the economic problem for the ultimate solution for every issue of life, are equally perilous to the peace of the community and to the preservation of democracy. (Niebuhr, 1944, pp. 148–149)

In Niebuhr's mature judgment, capitalism and communism both err in failing to view life as the Bible portrays it: a dialectic between freedom and sin. Capitalism errs in misunderstanding human freedom: individuals and societies cannot morally be dedicated solely to their selfish interests, nor is God a mechanistic "invisible hand" regulating these competing self-interests. Marxism, on the other hand, errs in misunderstanding human sin. It presumes to end injustice by rearranging institutional relationships, but it fails to see that those institutional injustices are the *consequences* of human sin, not the cause.

As Martin E. Marty has observed, Niebuhr and Rauschenbusch had a strong influence on Martin Luther King, Jr.:

> At seminary King had read Walter Rauschenbusch and had
> absorbed the Social Gospel. He recalled learning that "the
> gospel deals with the whole man, not only his soul but
> his body." His professors, however, told him that Social
> Gospel progressivism was out of touch with hard reali-
> ties and injected him with a dose of Reinhold Niebuhr's
> "Christian realism." King fused the two motifs, just as he
> blended faith in Jesus with lessons from Gandhi.
>
> (Marty, 1985, p. 441)

The National Council of Churches

The Social Gospel Movement helped to inspire formation of the
Federal Council of Churches in 1908, and the FCC became the
chief agency for uniting movements in support of social Christianity. In 1950, the National Council of Churches of Christ in
the U.S.A. (NCC) was organized to promote and express the ecumenical movement. Today the NCC is composed of thirty-two
church bodies — Protestant, Orthodox, and Anglican — with
combined membership of over 40 million Americans. The NCC
carries on some of the work started by the Social Gospel Movement. However, there is no centralized body to speak for all
the Protestant Churches as the Vatican does for Catholicism.
Neither the NCC nor the World Council of Churches has the
teaching authority or power to set policy for any of its member
churches in this manner. Nevertheless, the NCC over the years
has published economic policy statements that are important
indicators of religious consensus on social justice.

In 1954, the NCC issued a policy statement, *Christian Principles and Assumptions for Economic Life,* which included important declarations on work and ownership:

> Every able-bodied adult has an obligation and the right to
> an opportunity to serve the community through work....
> Large-scale unemployment, or long-continued unemploy-
> ment for any considerable number of persons able and will-
> ing to work is intolerable.... A wide distribution of centers

of power and decision is important to the preservation of democratic freedom.... Since private ownership of many forms of property is a stimulus to increase production of goods and services, and a protection to personal freedom, wider ownership among our people should be encouraged.

The 1958 NCC statement *Christian Concern about Unemployment* concentrated on work. It stated:

> We believe that the federal government should undertake the responsibility of helping those for whom no other public or private aid is available.... We welcome the fact that as a people we are committed to full employment as a national policy. The government should give continued consideration to both short-run and long-term measures to restore and maintain employment levels. The government has a responsibility to use, when needed as stabilizers and other aids, the vast resources available in its fiscal, monetary, public works, and other economic powers....
>
> We call upon churches and church people... to participate actively, as citizens, in community, state, and national programs (including the retraining of workers) which will put workers back to work. The deepest tragedy of unemployment is that work ceases for millions when there is so much work to be done.

The 1966 NCC policy statement was entitled *Christian Concern and Responsibility for Economic Life in a Rapidly Changing Technological Society.* In addition to reaffirming the major points of the previous policy statements, it added:

> Work, understood as creative and responsible participation in useful, meaningful and compensative activity, is both a right and a need of all men.... Man's sense of identity and worth is closely related to his feeling of contributing creatively and responsibly to the meeting of the needs of society. Each human being, within his God-given capabilities, is entitled as a matter of right to opportunity for this form of self-fulfillment.... Against such a catalog of human needs to be met, our immediate task is seen

to be the training and equipment of the present and on-coming generation for kinds of work which society needs and which at least in our time fall outside the scope of automation; and the finding of ways and means which convert work-to-be-done into jobs available at equitable rates of compensation, as well as through special intergovernmental programs such as the Peace Corps.... Voluntary service rendered through a variety of religious and secular community organizations, utilizing time released from the requirements of economic work and livelihood, represents a vast field of opportunity for self-fulfillment and socially valuable self-investment.... Every able-bodied adult has an obligation and the right to an opportunity to serve the community through work.

Beyond these policy statements, the NCC administers many direct action programs designed to fight economic injustice in the United States and throughout the world. For example, the NCC's Division of Church and Society organized distribution of food to the needy at the same time it was alerting the nation to the hardships caused by cutbacks in the federal funding of nutrition programs.

The NCC sponsors the Interfaith Center for Corporate Responsibility (ICCR), a joint venture of many church groups, including major Protestant denominations and various Roman Catholic orders. Organized in 1971, the ICCR's chief purpose has been to force social accountability on major American corporations, mainly through religious-sponsored resolutions at annual shareholder meetings. At first these efforts were ridiculed, and most ICCR resolutions received less than 3 percent of the shareholder vote. But in the 1980s they began to pick up momentum and were joined by a growing number of institutional investors. The ICCR was responsible for many successful anti-apartheid resolutions and played an important role in causing American businesses to withdraw from South Africa.

The ICCR is also interested in broadening ownership, as noted in its 1986 annual report:

...A growing number of institutional investors are affirmatively channeling their investment dollars, making alternative investments in employee and community-owned businesses and cooperatives, enterprises which traditionally are denied access to commercial financing.

The ICCR is active in environmental matters (such as acid rain caused by utilities, the Bhopal disaster, etc.); boycotts of American companies allegedly engaged in unfair labor practices; and the Alternative Investments Clearing House, which promotes community investment through a directory that contains detailed profiles of more than fifty worker-owned businesses, cooperatives, low-income housing projects, and community development credit unions.

The ICCR also sponsors meetings between church investors and innovative community groups seeking funding, and has led opposition to legislation such as the Hatch-Kennedy Bill, which was designed to remove restrictions on the export of pharmaceuticals not approved for sale in the U.S. One of ICCR's long-term projects was fighting the use of baby formula in the Third World.

Most of the major Protestant churches have drafted or have adopted statements on specific economic problems such as poverty and unemployment. For example, the American Baptist Churches published four recent statements, covering *Employment* (1976), *Cutbacks in Employment for Women and Minorities* (1980), *Plant Closings* (1980), and *Feminization of Poverty* (1985).

Several Protestant churches have undertaken comprehensive social justice statements similar in scope to the 1986 Catholic Bishops' Pastoral. While they tend to be less specific about remedies than the Catholic Pastoral, they reflect the strong overall consensus of religious support for broadening of work and ownership. Important examples are two comprehensive statements by the Presbyterian Church (U.S.A.), *Christian Faith and Economic Justice* (1984) and *Toward a Just, Caring, and Dynamic Political Economy* (1986), and a draft tentatively titled *Christian Faith and Economic Life* produced by the United Church of Christ for study and debate, looking to adoption by its General Synod in 1989.

So much for the history of the religious quest for social justice among the major religious groups in the United States. Now let's look at some specific ideas for broadening work (Chapter Four) and ownership (Chapter Five), which can be tested through trial and error, and if successful, can bring us closer to realization of that dream of social justice.

Chapter 4

Expanding Work

ONE OF OUR MOST PERSISTENT PROBLEMS is finding ways to expand employment so that every American can work at a meaningful occupation that provides enough income to avoid poverty. Here we will relate this problem to our Ten Principles to see if they help us toward a solution.

Structural Changes and "Full Employment"

It seems clear that some structural changes in our economic system will be needed to reach the elusive goal of "full employment" (unemployment of 4 percent or less) since we have been trying for more than a decade to bring unemployment down to that figure, without success. In 1986, unemployment remained at an historically high level for a recovery period despite five years of strong economic performance. At the same time, as we have seen, several hundred billion dollars worth of repair to the nation's infrastructure was needed, but there was no effective plan for turning that glaring need into a job-creation mechanism.

While the Reagan administration is proud of the millions of new jobs created during its tenure, the poverty rate remains far above pre-1980 levels. Indeed, wages for many new jobs in both the manufacturing and service sectors provide incomes below the poverty level. Many of those falling into poverty dropped down from the middle class, and for the first time in our history, children of middle-class families face the prospect of a lower standard of living than their parents.

That the nature of work in our society is changing is viewed by most observers as incontrovertible. Many, however, disagree on the extent and nature of these changes. Our search for consensus compels us to examine the ongoing and future changes in the nature of work, as well as the relationship between work and life-supporting income.

The percentage popularly quoted as the unemployment rate provided by the Bureau of Labor Statistics (BLS) describes only a small part of the changing relationship of jobs to income. The rate, by itself, tells us nothing about the length of unemployment of individual jobseekers, the types of jobs lost and the types newly created, or the pay levels afforded by existing jobs. The BLS rate counts everyone as employed if they have worked one hour or more in a week, and it does not count the millions of persons who have stopped looking for jobs but still want to work. And several studies have shown that millions of newly-created jobs are only part-time and pay wages far lower than those being lost (e.g., Dembo and Morehouse, 1987). That there were more than 8 million officially unemployed persons during 1986 (certainly an appalling record for a nation that prides itself on its ability to create jobs) is only one aspect of the more fundamental trend toward a disjunction between the number of traditional wage jobs and the ability of people to support themselves through such employment.

We have drifted toward acceptance of an unemployment rate as high as 7 or 8 percent in *boom* years, even though that rate is twice as high as the rates prevailing from 1950 to 1980, and would probably run well above 10 percent today if all the victims were counted. As Congressman Augustus Hawkins observed, "Full employment has come to mean the highest level of politically tolerable unemployment." If we accept these jobless rates that only yesterday shocked our consciences we will consign millions of people to the scrap heap of society.

The need to redefine our concept of work has been a favorite topic of futurist writers. University of Michigan Professor Frithjof Bergmann notes that until the nineteenth century most people lived on farms and therefore technically did not have jobs, and that "the very notion that everyone could or should have a job came into being only with the Industrial Revolution, and the brief span in which that idea had any viability may now be past." Like other futurists, he questions what will come after the shift from manufacturing to service jobs. He comments:

> The progress of technology has slowly brought about a condition where a conjunction of machines can turn out finished products with a bare minimum of human help. This self-sufficiency of the technological apparatus created the situation where the rich can put their money into a set of machines and can eventually receive much more money in return, but now they no longer need to include anyone else in this small cycle: it is all between them and their machines and themselves....
>
> Throughout — and it is crucial that this is not misunderstood — we are of course not discussing "work." "Work" will naturally always exist in limitless abundance; there is no end of things that any of us can always do. But that is not the issue: we are considering *Jobs;* and that means work which someone else is *willing* but also *able* to pay for. (Bergmann, 1983, pp. 314–315)

Alvin Toffler, author of *Future Shock,* was one of the first popular writers to analyze changes in patterns of work. His 1980 book's title, *The Third Wave,* is the name Toffler gives to the current period, often called de-industrialization. Toffler believes that we have been in a transition phase to the Third Wave since about 1955. This new wave is characterized by "a new way of life based on diversified, renewable energy sources; on methods of production that make most factory assembly lines obsolete; on new, non-nuclear families; on a novel institution that might be called the 'electronic cottage'; and on radically changed schools and corporations of the future" (Toffler, 1980, p. 10).

Toffler's future scenario is for the rising costs of traditional (second wave) energy sources to shift our economy away from industrial-age emphasis on production in large-scale factories to newer forms of production and consumption that acknowledge the new energy economics. The four growth industry "clusters" Toffler identifies for the Third Wave are electronics and computers; the space industry, including space manufacturing; exploitation of the sea for food and energy; and the biotechnology revolution (pp. 140–149).

In a chapter entitled "The Electronic Cottage," Toffler visualizes a shift from mass production to smaller scale runs of partially or completely customized products with many people working at home, aided by advanced electronic communications that would make home work more economical than large staffs working in big buildings (p. 181). Toffler goes on to say:

> We cannot today know if, in fact, the electronic cottage will become the norm of the future. Nevertheless, it is worth recognizing that if as few as 10 to 20 percent of the work force as presently defined were to make this historic transfer over the next 20 to 30 years, our entire economy, our cities, our ecology, our family structure, our values, and even our politics would be altered almost beyond our recognition. (pp. 207–208)

Although Toffler considers the Third Wave an irresistible force, his book does not provide any analysis of its effect on the number of jobs or the level of wages, and so it is not of much use in our quest for structural changes that will expand work opportunities.

Several recent books deal more directly with the expansion of work through redefinition. Two are by English authors: Charles Handy, *The Future of Work: A Guide to a Changing Society* (1984), and James Robertson, *Future Work: Jobs, Self-Employment and Leisure after the Industrial Age* (1985). The third, *The Future of Work and Health* (Bezold, 1986), compiled by the Institute for Alternative Futures, summarizes general analyses such as those of Handy and Robertson, and then focuses on future work patterns in health services.

Handy believes that we must "look beyond employment to a society which is less job-fixated in its values, its structures and its systems" (p. xi). To explore that vision, he poses four basic questions: Who gets the jobs? How do we pay ourselves? What do we use for wealth? And who protects us? (p. 97). Handy's main response is a National Income Scheme, presumably funded from tax collections, that would make it easier for people to choose the type and amount of work they prefer.

James Robertson shares many of Handy's concerns. He pos-
tulates three possible scenarios for the future: business as usual;
HE (Hyper-Expansionist); and SHE (Sane, Humane, Ecologi-
cal). He believes the SHE vision is part of the historical progres-
sion from masters-and-slaves beyond employers-and-employees
toward greater equality:

> As hopes of restoring full employment fade away, the dom-
> inant form of work will no longer be seen as employment
> but "ownwork...." Ownwork means activity which is im-
> portant and which people organize and control for them-
> selves. It may be either paid or unpaid. For the individ-
> ual it may mean self-employment, essential household and
> family activities, and participation in voluntary work. For
> groups of people it may mean working together as partners,
> perhaps in a cooperative enterprise. (pp. 15–16)

Realistically, Robertson sees the immediate future as a combination of all three scenarios, with a blurring of work and leisure;
but he finds ownwork the most desirable. Yet, like Handy, he
suggests no method of paying for ownwork other than a Guaranteed Basic Income, derived from taxes on income and sales.
The Washington newsletter *New Options,* always on the look-
out for SHE-type ideas, found Robertson's ownwork intriguing
but condemned his guaranteed income proposal as "simply a
non-starter" (*New Options,* April 28, 1986, p. 7).

The analysis by the Institute for Alternative Futures reaches
conclusions similar to those of Handy and Robertson. It finds
that many of the new technologies are inherently job-displacing
(Bezold, 1986, p. 69) and that the result will be expansion of
society's underclass (p. 57). Perhaps the most immediate cause
for concern is the fact that such employment opportunities as
exist can no longer be counted on to provide employed people with incomes that will support themselves, let alone their
dependents. Throughout the 1950s and 1960s, income distribution in the U.S. became more equitable. The bottom 40 percent
of the population increased its share of the pie from 16.5 percent in 1950 to 17 percent in 1960 and 17.6 percent in 1970.
The share going to the middle 40 percent also increased from
40.8 percent in 1950 to 41.4 percent in 1970. Beginning in the

mid-1970s and increasingly since 1979, however, the distribution of income has become more uneven, to the point where in 1986 the bottom 40 percent held a lower percentage of total income (15.4 percent) than they did in 1950. And the average inflation-adjusted hourly wage was only $8.75 an hour in 1987, compared to $9.56 an hour in 1978. This growing inequality of income is accompanied by an increase in the number of people living in poverty, which in 1986 was officially defined as income below $11,203 per year for a family of four. The poverty class, which stood at 11.4 percent in 1979, jumped to 15.2 percent in 1983, declining slightly to 13.6 percent in 1986. But even at the "improved" 13.6 percent rate, 32.4 million Americans are living in poverty. And the incidence of poverty is unevenly distributed across society, hitting blacks and Hispanics proportionately harder than others, and affecting women and children most of all. That the incidence of poverty is related to what has been called the "pauperization" of work is evident in the statistics. In 1984, of those with incomes below the poverty level, a full 40.9 percent over fifteen years of age actually were employed during the year. Thus we see that despite the exciting scenarios created by Toffler, Handy, Robertson, and other futurist authors searching for a new philosophy of work, they have not come up with an acceptable means of paying for the new forms of work they envision. A guaranteed basic income would be rejected by most Americans as another form of welfare, and so we must search for other methods of paying for these new forms of work.

Some observers foresee a different problem: a *labor shortage* caused by demographics and lack of work incentives. Whichever view we accept, there is an equal need for creation of more meaningful work and stronger incentives.

Subsidiarity: Private and Governmental Programs

Because the job creation problem has been with us so long and is so intractable, there is a legion of proposals for achieving broader employment through the private sector, the public sector, or combinations thereof. Our subsidiarity principle requires us to achieve as much as we can through the private sector before intervention by government. This would be a good place to begin use of our Subsidiarity Scoreboard, by first evaluating private sector proposals, then moving to local government initiatives, and then to state and federal government programs, if we find that the private sector cannot solve the problem alone.

We can only scratch the surface here by sampling a few proposals of the hundreds available. In this process, we will be using some of our other principles, in addition to subsidiarity: we will be determining feasibility by trial and error, and we will be applying religious teaching to make value judgments on income and wealth distribution questions.

The fact that economic policies are determined by trial and error is made abundantly clear by the number of experiments aimed at solving the problems of unemployment and underemployment. This history of experimentation and futile search for the magic elixir of full employment also demonstrates that it would be a great mistake to leave employment — the major method of income distribution — to the "experts" who have failed to come up with a solution for these many decades. All of us must take a hand in trying to solve this problem, and as members of religious organizations we are at least as qualified to make the necessary value judgments as are economists, business executives, government officials, and others who might be considered experts on broadened employment opportunities.

Private (Non-Governmental) Initiatives

There are at least a dozen promising private initiatives in operation that belong on our Subsidiarity Scoreboard. Many are regional or national programs that work with local organizations in their own form of subsidiarity. The following sampler will serve to illustrate what has been done through trial and error, and how we might be able to expand employment by learning lessons from these valuable experiments.

The Enterprise Foundation

An operating model that is serving as a testbed for many innovative approaches to slum clearance, low-cost housing, and job creation is the Enterprise Foundation, formed in 1982 as a non-profit organization in Baltimore by James W. Rouse, founder and former chairman of the Rouse Company, a successful commercial real estate development company.

The Enterprise Foundation helps to coordinate efforts nationally to build low-cost housing through grants, low-interest loans, and technical assistance. In addition to distributing funds received as contributions, the foundation has organized the Enterprise Development Company as a private, profit-oriented subsidiary, which will attempt to replicate Rouse's success in developing "festival marketplaces" such as Faneuil Hall in Boston. The marketplaces developed by Enterprise are on a smaller scale than the Faneuil project, but already include: The Waterside in Norfolk, Virginia (80,000 square feet, opened June 1, 1983); Portside in Toledo, Ohio (60,000 square feet, opened in May 1984); the Water Street Pavilion in Flint, Michigan (42,000 square feet, opened in June 1985); and 6th Street Marketplace in Richmond, Virginia (67,000 square feet, opened in September 1985). The festival marketplaces include specialty food and clothing shops, with employment preference (both in construction and operation) given to poor residents of the formerly disadvantaged neighborhoods.

Two other subsidiaries organized for profit are the Rehab Work Group, working on lowering the cost of housing renovation, and the Enterprise Social Investment Corporation, which is exploring innovative ways of raising funds for such work. One example is a fund set up by the Baltimore Federal Financial bank and the Enterprise Foundation that pools money from individuals, corporations, and charitable organizations; the money is deposited in a federally insured account at low rates of interest, and the funds are then used to make loans to low-income home buyers. As Rouse puts it, "The appeal of these loans is that people are performing a charitable act, yet they still get their money back."

Rouse is building the Enterprise Foundation into a nationwide network of neighborhood projects. Enterprise has completed studies in Chattanooga, where it is estimated that up to $200 million would be needed for renovation of 13,220 existing units and construction of 500 new units, in order to revitalize all housing occupied by the poor. $2.9 million has been raised from Chattanooga businesses and foundations thus far. In Dallas, Enterprise has a grant to focus attention on that city's housing problems through technical training for local groups and operating model projects to demonstrate what can be done. In

Cleveland, Enterprise helped raise $2.1 million as an initial investment in Cleveland Housing Partnership, which hopes to renovate 333 homes over the next five years.

Rouse describes Enterprise as "a lighthouse to the United States." He says of the foundation's housing efforts:

> More can be done about housing and the life of the poor than our creative, free society has managed to do. All kinds of little problems will respond to little solutions. But nobody's working at it. The government doesn't work at it. Nobody works at trying to build a new system for housing the poor — to take the problem apart; to deal with its pieces, and put it back together with new answers.
>
> ("America's Poor Millions Need Not Live in Squalor," Op Ed piece, *Los Angeles Times,* August 24, 1986)

One vehicle for discovering those new answers is *Cost Cuts,* a monthly newsletter published by the foundation's Rehab Work Group, dealing with the nuts and bolts of renovation and low-cost construction.

The Job Placement Network of the Enterprise Foundation is building a nationwide string of community-based centers to place low-income unemployed people in private sector jobs. In its housing projects, the Foundation attempts to involve the persons directly affected in renovation and rehabilitation. Rouse believes that such community participation is the key to long-term solutions.

While it is too early to determine how successful the Rouse approach will be, it shows enough promising results to warrant careful study as a model program. Here again we need the Subsidiarity Scoreboard to tell us how far we can get without seeking government intervention, and how we can combine private and public initiatives most effectively. Despite his dedication to free enterprise, Rouse himself believes that the problems of housing and jobs for the poor can be solved only by a combination of city, state, and federal government collaboration with private sources. His involvement was inspired by the Church of the Savior, a small parish in a poor section of Washington, D.C., which bought two burned-out buildings and turned them into usable housing despite Rouse's prediction that they would fail.

EXPANDING WORK   111

Meanwhile, Rouse is working harder in his retirement years than
he did while running the Rouse Company, as Enterprise spreads
its network to more than twenty-five cities. Its address is: Enterprise Foundation, 505 American City Building, Columbia,
Maryland 21044.

Its Board of Trustees includes John W. Gardner, Robert S.
McNamara, Charles McCurdy Mathias, Jr., Charles S. Robb,
and Andrew J. Young.

Control Data Corporation

Control Data Corporation, America's fourth largest computer manufacturer, has had a unique history of attempting to
turn social needs into profit-making corporate opportunities —
doing well by doing good. This policy was originated by William
C. Norris, who served as Control Data's chief executive officer
from its founding in 1957 until January of 1986. Norris believes that our society's deterioration will continue unless substantial corporate resources are invested to treat social needs as
profit-making opportunities, in cooperation with government,
religious organizations, and charities.

To carry out this policy, Norris created a number of profit-
seeking programs, both inside and outside of Control Data.
His most ambitious project was PLATO, which stands for Pro-
grammed Logic for Automatic Teaching Operations. It is designed to do nothing less than privatize America's public schools,
providing student education and management of the entire education system through Control Data computers.

Norris also organized Rural Venture in 1980 as a for-profit
consortium capitalized at $3 million. Shareholders included
several corporations, Land O'Lakes (the farm cooperative), and
the Catholic archdiocese of St. Paul and Minneapolis. It was
designed to promote viable small-scale agriculture, again using
Control Data services and resources.

In 1978 he organized City Venture Corporation, another for-
profit consortium. Members included twelve corporations and
two church organizations (the American Lutheran Church and
the United Church of Christ). Control Data bought 35 percent of the stock. City Venture is an urban planning and development operation that contracts with municipal governments
and attempts to create jobs, promote small businesses, and con-

duct remedial education and training. These projects are usually paid for by combinations of city, state, and federal funds. City Venture has caused some resentment and has had some failures because some local government planners and community organizations felt their functions were being usurped by an outside organization, one operated for the profit and glory of Control Data. Therefore, despite some great successes — such as the creation of 1,000 new jobs in a depressed section of Toledo, Ohio — City Venture has had something of a mixed reception.

Unfortunately, Control Data encountered serious financial problems during the mid-1980s, culminating in a 1985 loss of more than $560 million. Norris retired as chief executive officer in January of 1986, and Control Data placed his social needs projects on a back burner in order to concentrate on financial recovery. Norris has vowed to carry on his pioneering work as a private individual.

Polaroid Corporation took a page from Control Data's book in 1968 by creating Inner City, Inc., in Needham, Massachusetts. According to its president, Richard V. Carson, Inner City serves primarily as a youth job training center (with pay) for Boston's unemployed, and has operated since 1968 on a self-sustaining basis with no public-sector funding involved.

Despite the misfortunes of Control Data, we can learn a lot from Norris's pioneering efforts. Norris himself summarized them in a book (Norris, 1983). A recent book by Ralph Nader and William Taylor contains a long chapter on Norris. The authors state:

William Norris, by his concepts and by his practice, is a businessman seeking a future in old rejected markets through the application of new technologies. He looks upon large areas of decay in cities and the countryside not as jettisoned, expendable sectors of the economy but as challenges that should inspire companies to rethink their marketing strategies and product innovations. His industry peers, in contrast, seek new market tiers on top of established markets and ignore low-income consumers.... Constructing plants in the inner city, as Norris has done, is more than just a way to make use of available low-wage

labor. It is a way to help revive a depressed local economy
and produce there a faster velocity of market exchange —
the multiplier effect.

(Nader, 1986, pp. 500–502)

Norris's address is: William C. Norris, Chairman Emeritus,
Control Data Corporation, 8100 34th Avenue South, Minneapolis, MN 55440–4700.

The Local Initiatives Support Corporation (LISC)

LISC is a national nonprofit lending and grant-making institution founded in 1980. Its purpose is to draw private-sector
financial and technical resources into the development of de-
teriorated communities. It invests in rehabilitation and new
construction projects that are being developed by community-
based nonprofit organizations. LISC's emphasis has been on re-
habilitating deteriorating real estate, rather than starting up new
business operations, because such projects offer more security.
LISC packages its support to bring local banks and other private-
sector lenders into each investment, ensuring that its own funds
amount to a small proportion (currently about 10 percent) of
total project costs. As of 1986, LISC had received contributions totalling more than $100 million from over 375 private
corporations and foundations, which it used to make grants or
loans to more than 400 community groups. With that funding,
the local groups in twenty-seven major cities were able to attract
an additional $360 million from public and private sources to
revitalize blighted neighborhoods.

According to a 1985 appraisal of LISC operations by the
John F. Kennedy School of Government at Harvard University (Vidal, 1985), LISC has been quite successful in the role
of a hard-nosed philanthropist conducting a social experiment
"which might provide the basis for a major change in the way
society deals with economically and socially distressed areas" by
facilitating neighborhood revitalization projects and strengthen-
ing community-based organizations.

With continued support from backers such as the Ford and
MacArthur Foundations, LISC is moving to fill a void created
by reduced federal housing aid. It is organizing a national sec-
ondary market for social investments and will purchase loans

originated by social-investment intermediaries to provide them with a continuing source of capital for their community development programs. This idea was first tried on a pilot basis in Boston, through a joint effort by LISC and the Hyams Foundation, with encouraging results. The participating insurance and financial institutions will receive a return of about 7.5 percent while generating funds for community revitalization.

LISC's address is: Local Initiatives Support Corporation, 666 Third Avenue, New York, NY 10017.

The Campaign for Human Development

As we noted in the preceding chapter, the Campaign for Human Development (CHD) was established by the National Conference of Catholic Bishops (NCCB) in 1969 as the U.S. Catholic Church's education-action program to combat domestic poverty and injustice. It is one of the largest national funding programs for low-income worker-owned business ventures.

In its first fifteen years, CHD awarded over 2500 self-help grants in 175 dioceses, with many success stories. For example, $59,000 in CHD grants helped launch Connecticut's Naugatuck Valley Project (NVP) to reverse decay in one of America's oldest industrial areas. Under the leadership of Auxiliary Bishop Peter A. Rosazza of Hartford, NVP mobilized more than fifty area churches, labor unions, and community organizations to rescue existing jobs, bring in new businesses, and organize employee buyouts of local plants. NVP helped the employees of Bridgeport Brass to buy the company from its parent (which was about to shut it down). Now it operates successfully as the Seymour Specialty Wire Company, 100 percent employee-owned. Building on the Seymour success, an NVP delegation helped persuade the Connecticut legislature to establish an $8 million fund for development and financing of worker-owned cooperatives.

In an interview with Arthur Jones for the *National Catholic Reporter* of August 28, 1987, Reverend Alfred P. LoPinto, Executive Director of CHD, said:

> You really have to believe in the parable of the mustard seed (Matthew 13:31). The long process that will see the [Catholic] church in this country as a major supporter of economic development in the lives of low-income com-

munities has begun. [This process] will enable low-income people to take charge of their own economic life.

In reading CHD's 1984 annual report, I was struck by the fact that of the more than $7 million allocated for grants and loans, only $621,000 was disbursed to business ventures cooperatively owned by low-income workers or community groups. The balance of the $7 million in grants and loans went to "social development projects" that organized community groups around issues that affect the lives of its members. Thus, despite CHD's emphasis on self-help business ventures, of the approximately 1,000 applicants for grants or loans, only 17 such ventures warranted funding in 1984. The figures for 1985 followed the same pattern.

The reason for this record is not a policy decision by CHD, but rather a shortage of qualified applicants — i.e., those worker-owned enterprises that seem to have a reasonable chance of survival. People who have the skills and motivation to organize and manage successful businesses are not likely to be found in depressed areas. Something more than money is needed to create successful business enterprises, as our next example will show.

The address of the CHD is: Campaign for Human Development, U.S. Catholic Conference, 1312 Massachusetts Ave., N.W., Washington, DC 20005.

National Minority Supplier Development Council (NMSDC)

The National Minority Supplier Development Council was organized in 1972 as a non-profit corporation to expand business opportunities for minority-owned companies. The Council works with a nationwide network of organizations that direct corporate and government purchasers to minority-owned businesses. The program is similar to government "set-aside" provisions that earmark a certain percentage (usually 5 to 10 percent) of government contracts that must be subcontracted to minority-owned businesses. Government set-asides have been widely abused through "fronting," with the main contractor using a minority figurehead to collect the set-aside percentage and kick back most of it. But the NMSDC seeks to avoid this problem in their private patronage programs by careful screening to verify the ownership and legitimacy of minority businesses.

The Council has been able to certify more than 12,000 minority suppliers for its major corporate buyers. In 1986, under the leadership of Alphonso Whitfield, Jr. (formerly Vice-President for Social Investments at Prudential Insurance Co.) the Council provided some *$9 billion* worth of business to its supplier network, through trade fairs, catalogues, and other promotional efforts.

Patronage of the type generated by NMSDC could make projects like the Campaign for Human Development even more effective by supplying the missing link for many fledgling businesses: a life-sustaining stream of income. If CHD and other religious organizations could mobilize patronage merely from the successful businesses that are managed by their own parishioners, they could take a long stride toward broadening work and ownership.

The address of NMSDC is: National Minority Supplier Development Council, Inc., 1412 Broadway, New York, NY 10018.

The Black Churches

Community-based self-help programs sponsored by black churches are featured in a recent book edited by Robert L. Woodson, *On the Road to Economic Freedom: An Agenda for Black Progress* (Woodson, 1987). Woodson himself is President of the non-profit National Center for Neighborhood Enterprise in Washington, D.C., which has coordinated many successful black church-sponsored programs.

Woodson's book is an outgrowth of meetings sponsored by the National Center for Neighborhood Enterprise (NCNE) devoted to helping blacks to use their own resources to move out of poverty instead of depending on government and welfare. Woodson and his co-authors emphasize ownership and new business development. Woodson documents many self-help programs sponsored by black churches that are actually working. He urges that public housing authorities allow residents to manage housing units through RMCs (Resident Management Corporations), which he says have turned "crime-ridden hell-holes into healthy communities that place a premium on education, family, and self-motivation" (Woodson, 1987, p. 21).

Bill Alexander, a contributor to the Woodson book, covers "The Black Church and Community Empowerment" (Chapter

Three). He states that black entrepreneurship had its beginnings through a church-led process of aggressive self-determination, and that black churches now boast a membership of 20 million and weekly collections of $10 million. He gives many specific examples of successful local development projects led by black churches. Alexander describes the success of the Opportunities Industrialization Centers (OIC) and the Zion Investment Corporation (ZIC), created by a group of Philadelphia ministers headed by the Reverend Leon Sullivan:

> OIC now operates job training centers in more than 200 communities in 42 states, Washington, D.C., and the Virgin Islands.... The Zion Investment Corporation, under Sullivan stewardship, also became successful as a national, yet community-based, economic development project. Through a network of black churches and fraternal organizations, it offered individual shares for $360 each. To attract low-income investors, ZIC devised the 10/36 plan whereby shareholders paid $10 a month for 36 months. (Woodson, 1987, p. 56)

The experience of the black churches supports the validity of our Ten Principles. They are using self-interest, subsidiarity, broadening of work and ownership, varying degrees of government intervention, experimentation, and the galvanizing force of religious organizations to turn the problems of blighted neighborhoods into social justice opportunities.

The address of NCNE is: National Center for Neighborhood Enterprise, 1367 Connecticut Avenue, N.W., Washington, D.C. 20046.

There are hundreds of other private-sector job creation initiatives that are worthy of study and entry on our Subsidiarity Scoreboard. (Many major programs are analyzed in Robison, 1978.) Some involve job creation that would also broaden ownership, but usually it is ownership of weak enterprises whose shares are of questionable value. We have touched on a possible remedy for this shortcoming in our discussion of the National Minority Supplier Development Council's patronage program, and we will return to it later in this chapter under the heading

118 EXPANDINGWORK

of "Combining the Work of Humanity with Ownership: Share-holders In America, Inc. (SIA)."

We move now to governmental job creation, bearing in mind that most of the "private" programs also call for some governmental involvement.

Governmental Job Creation

Our federal, state, and local governments do many things that help private companies to create jobs — everything from giving tax breaks and loan guarantees to building roads and airports. Here we are concerned with direct job creation by government, which did not become American policy until 1933. Again, we have space for only a sampling of the many programs and proposals.

The New Deal Public Works Agencies

The classic American governmental effort to create jobs was launched by President Franklin D. Roosevelt in the depths of the Great Depression. With a third of the work force unemployed, Roosevelt created three major agencies: the Public Works Administration (PWA), the Works Progress Administration (WPA), and the Civilian Conservation Corps (CCC). While designed primarily to provide short-term work relief for the unemployed millions, these agencies made a strong start toward achieving the work of humanity. The PWA in its time (1933–1939) built more than 70 percent of the nation's new educational buildings; 65 percent of its new courthouses, city halls, and sewage disposal plants; 35 percent of its new public health facilities; and 10 percent of its new roads, bridges, and subways. During its eight-year life, the WPA put 8.5 million people to work, building more than 650,000 miles of roads, 125,000 public buildings, 120,000 bridges, 8,000 parks, and 800 airports. Projects in the arts employed thousands of writers, actors, and artists. The CCC employed young men from impoverished families in reforestation and other environmental projects, helping to stem the soil erosion that created the Dust Bowl. At any one time, 25 to 45 percent of a total pool of 16 million unemployed held jobs created by these federal agencies.

Roosevelt himself believed that welfare was "a subtle destroyer of the human spirit" and he was not willing "that the vitality of our people be further sapped by the giving of cash or market baskets" on a long-term basis (Louchheim, 1983, p. 177). He felt that the opportunity to work was as important as the money it brought in, because it helped to rebuild the broken morale of the unemployed. This view has been documented by later appraisals of New Deal agencies. In her study of the WPA program in New York City between 1935 and 1943, Barbara Blumberg describes the heightened self-esteem shown by people moving from welfare to WPA public service jobs:

> On the most elementary level, these government jobs allowed their holders to survive until private enterprise could again absorb their labor.... But creating work that attempted to utilize the individual's skills and training did much more for him than fill his stomach and provide shelter.... Anzia Yesierska, who was on the Writers' Project in New York, recalled the reaction she and her friends had when they first heard about the emergency work program: "people who no longer hoped or believed in anything but the end of the world began to hope and believe again." As she queued up with others to be interviewed for WPA placement, she noticed the changed manner of her companions. "I had seen these people at the relief station, waiting for the investigation machine to legalize them as paupers. Now they had work cards in their hands. Their waiting was no longer the hopeless stupor of applicants for mass relief; they were employees of the government. They had risen from the scrap heap of the unemployed, from the loneliness of the unwanted.... The new job look lighted the most ravaged faces." (Blumberg, 1979, pp. 282–283)

These programs were far more successful than most people thought they would be at the time when the idea was new. Growing up during the Depression, many in my generation looked down on the WPA as a ragged army of lazy men leaning on shovels. Little did we know how much they would accomplish, and how difficult it would be to ever reach their level of effectiveness again despite the hundreds of billions of dollars thrown at the unemployment problem. Professor Russell A. Nixon, who has served as co-chairman of the National Conference on Public Service Employment, summarizes the significance of the New Deal experience:

> From the standpoint of current interests and issues, the experience of the 1930's with job creation suggests four major conclusions:
>
> 1. It is feasible for the government, through direct job-creating intervention, to create large-scale employment and to cut unemployment extensively.
>
> 2. The productive results of direct government job creation are impressive and socially are dramatically useful.
>
> 3. The job programs of the 1930's were primitive by today's standards. They did not include systematic or significant on-the-job or off-the-job training, had no program of employability creating remedial or support services, and included nothing at all in the direction of career development, upgrading, or upward mobility.
>
> 4. Expansion of the job creation programs was successfully opposed by established political powers at all stages so that those programs fell far short of utilizing as fully as possible the idle economic resources at hand. (Nixon, 1981, pp. 131–132)

It is time to take a fresh look at the New Deal programs.

Senator Paul Simon's Proposal

Sen. Paul Simon (Democrat, Illinois) announced his Guaranteed Job Opportunity Program in 1987, both in the form of a book and a platform plank in his campaign for the Democratic presidential nomination. He has drawn heavily upon the New Deal experience to formulate a plan that would guarantee a job to anyone who seeks one. In his political speeches, Simon states his premise very simply: "We shall spend money either to create more jobs or more jails, and I seek an America with more jobs." His book spells out the premise:

Three realities should cause a change in our national employment policy: First, the demand for unskilled labor is
declining.... Second, the pool of unskilled labor is growing... Third, we are not going to let people starve. Faced
with those three realities, we have a choice of paying people
for doing nothing or paying people for doing something. It
makes infinitely more sense to pay people for doing something, to let them be productive, to let them know and
feel that they are needed and contributing toward a better
society. (Simon, 1987, p. 130)

His Guaranteed Job Opportunity Program (GJOP) is designed
to make a job available to every citizen eighteen years of age or
older. It would pay the minimum wage for thirty-two hours a
week, or 10 percent above welfare or unemployment compensation, whichever is highest. Simon's reason for using thirty-two
hours rather than forty hours of work is to have one traditional
working day free to pursue other job opportunities, since the
ultimate goal is to put the unemployed in a position where they
will get full-time jobs in the private sector. The public service
jobs that he enumerates fall within our vision of the work of
humanity:

Teaching others how to read and write, helping with day
care centers, planting trees, assisting in senior citizen's programs, cleaning graffiti off the walls of subways, cleaning
off vacant lots, making bicycle trails, and doing a host of
other things that will improve our society. (Ibid., p. 132)

His plan would be financed by the federal government but would
be administered at the state and local level. It would be limited
to high school graduates or non-graduates eighteen years of age
or older. Those between eighteen and twenty-five who are not
high school graduates would be tested for verbal and mathemat-
ical skills and would have to attend evening or weekend classes
until they earned their high school equivalency diplomas, thus
upgrading the educational level of the unemployed. Each state
would decide whether its people on welfare would be *required*
to sign up for the GJOP.

Simon claims that his GJOP differs from workfare in that it puts more stress on preparing the unemployed for private sector employment; it is not a punitive or mean-spirited program, as some people see workfare; and, in Simon's eyes, his program gives people an incentive to work by paying them more than they would receive under welfare or unemployment compensation.

Personally, I do not believe that wage levels only 10 percent above welfare benefits provide a very strong work incentive. Speaking of such jobs, University of Michigan Professor Frithjof Bergmann said:

> The hurdle that many of these programs must face is that the act of *taking* these kinds of jobs represents defeat and capitulation to these people. It amounts to admitting that one was not sufficiently resourceful, and that one failed at all the other more tempting ways of making a living. Since minimum wage jobs often do not raise the income that many unemployed now make — usually from underground deals combined with money from the public dole — accepting this kind of job means only that for exactly the same pay one had before, one must now jump through the boss's ugly hoops. (Bergmann, 1986)

Simon admits that political support for his program, which would cost a minimum of $8 billion a year, is not there yet. I suggest that if Simon's GJOP was coupled with a stock ownership plan that would enable people entering the program to become owners of stock that paid dividends and had a chance to appreciate in value, the work incentive would be much stronger. I think that many more unemployed people could be motivated to work their way into steady private jobs with the added status of shareholder.

National Youth Service

There are more than forty state and local programs for youth public service, including the New York City Volunteer Corps and the San Francisco Conservation Corps, both patterned loosely after the Civilian Conservation Corps of the 1930s and the Peace Corps and VISTA of the 1960s. Several plans to establish a national program of youth service have been proposed. The main proponents are Representatives Robert G. Torricelli and Leon E. Panetta. Torricelli's legislation would establish a select commission on national service opportunities to study the feasibility and cost of establishing a mandatory national youth service program. The Panetta bill would provide matching federal grants to state and local governments operating voluntary youth service programs.

Representative Morris Udall has proposed an American Conservation Corps, in which young people would maintain public parks and lands. Senator Dale Bumpers would exchange cancellation of federal student loan payments for public service work. Representative Dave McCurdy proposes federal student grants and loans *only* to youths who agree to complete a period of civilian or military service. And Senator Claiborne Pell proposes a five-year test program that would make GI Bill benefits available to students who complete two years of either civilian or military service.

Although President Reagan vetoed a 1984 bill calling for a conservation corps (because of his objections to a large program of public-sector rather than private-sector jobs), a new consensus for a national youth program seems to be building, spurred by the haunting problems of AIDS, drug abuse, and hopelessness among our youth.

Although the number of state and local conservation programs has been increasing, they annually serve less than 10,000 jobless young people. But the Human Environment Center, a Washington clearing house, claims that these programs actually work, pointing to benefits of $1.77 received for every $1.00 spent by the California Conservation Corps, ranging from rebuilt parks to weatherized buildings.

Comprehensive Employment & Training Act (CETA)

Established in 1973, CETA was originally intended to promote locally tailored, federally financed job-training and job-creation programs. The initially modest public service component of CETA (creating 50,000 jobs) was increased following the 1974–75 recession. By 1977, CETA had been further expanded to provide 750,000 public service jobs, and was complemented by the Youth Employment Demonstration Projects Act, which employed 250,000 young Americans annually.

One of the major difficulties facing any such program is providing jobs that are meaningful both to society and to the individual and that will lead to more rewarding positions or will provide the worker with enough skills and self-assurance to find another job in the private sector. CETA jobs were often criticized as "make work" positions not leading to any permanent attachment to the labor force. Some CETA workers were simply assigned to a unit of government and were paid even when there was nothing for them to do. And as Professor Robert Lekachman noted:

> The Act's deliberate decentralization allowed municipalities under budgetary pressure on occasion to divert CETA funds for the payment of policemen, firefighters, sanitation personnel, and other regular employees. Hard-pressed mayors ingeniously converted CETA into a form of federal revenue sharing, effectively subverting the program's objectives. (Lekachman, 1987, p. 65)

Despite these and other drawbacks, Lekachman believes that CETA was reasonably successful in making headway against massive problems (ibid., pp. 66–67).

In 1981, with little opposition from Congress, President Reagan was able to eliminate CETA's public service program, and to replace CETA in 1982 with the Job Training Partnership Act, which has no public job-creation component.

Some recent reviews of CETA have concluded that the program was effective in creating public jobs, targeting disadvantaged groups, and providing training needed to enter the job market. While there were documented abuses, a survey of local officials involved indicated that 95 percent found the work done to be very useful to the community. In 1985, the House of Representatives Committee on Education and Labor published a report which concluded that direct federal job creation could play an important role in assisting people unemployed as a result of adverse economic conditions, disadvantage, or displacement. The report blames conflicting objectives, unrealistic expectations, and poor timing for the unpopularity of CETA, despite its overall promise (C. Johnson, 1985). It makes some positive findings about the value of CETA-type programs:

Despite its negative image, careful analyses of the CETA program have revealed that participants in public service employment programs experienced significant earnings gains. A detailed study of 1976 PSE [public service employment] participants found that their post-program annual earnings were $261 higher than matched controls in 1977 and $326 greater in 1978.... Gross earnings among the most disadvantaged PSE participants from 1974 to 1977 were more than $4,000 over those of comparison groups, indicating that individuals experiencing serious difficulty in labor markets may have profited substantially from CETA. Evidence suggests that public service employment programs under CETA enhanced the ability of participants to secure permanent jobs in the public sector, serving as a "try-out" period and providing on-the-job training for adults with limited prior experience. (pp. 15–16)

As an initial introduction to the labor market, federally supported PSE jobs located in the non-profit as well as public sector, can instill positive work habits and discipline, increase awareness of expected job performance, and provide an employment reference for transition into unsubsidized work. (p. 17)

The scrapping of CETA without making full use of its trial-and-error data is a good example of the need for our Ten Principles, which hold that we must develop equitable policies through experimentation such as the CETA program, and that we must reject a purely ideological approach to the procedural question of government intervention. That CETA was torpedoed by ideology was made clear in the House report:

Currently, this potential for using public employment programs to further economic and social goals has been ignored and rejected on the basis of ideology rather than experience. As a result, the nation is left without a full complement of policy tools, specifically public service employment, to reduce persistent job deficits and boost employment prospects for those in need.... There is no good reason, other than the strength of outmoded beliefs, for the

American people to turn their back on federally financed
direct job creation to assist those groups who cannot make
it on their own. (pp. 39–40)

Job Training Partnership Act (JTPA)

Since the Reagan swing away from direct federal government
involvement with the unemployed and poor, the emphasis has
shifted from job creation to training. JTPA continues the trend
begun under President Carter toward trying to get industry to
be more active in training the unemployed. Private Industry
Councils (PICs), established under CETA in over 400 local communities in 1978, were greatly expanded under JTPA.

The shift from CETA to JTPA is a good example of the need
for a Subsidiarity Scoreboard. CETA went right into federal
job creation without seeking to enlist extensive state, local, and
private participation. Despite its many failures, it developed
a body of trial-and-error data that can be useful for future job
creation programs. Based largely on the Reagan administration's ideological aversion to governmental solutions, CETA was
scrapped in favor of JTPA, which is much more to the liking
of the business community. Under JTPA, employers are reim-
bursed for 50 percent of a new worker's wages if the employee is
receiving on-the-job training. The program is described in glow-
ing terms by James E. Burke, chairman of Johnson & Johnson:

> ...JTPA to date has progressed fairly smoothly and has
> been twice as effective as CETA in placing program par-
> ticipants at half the cost.... In addition to supporting the
> training aspects of JTPA, business is also committed to
> hiring these disadvantaged youths into real jobs and pro-
> viding the support mechanisms to have them remain and
> grow in their work. (Burke, 1987, pp. 222–223)

Burke believes that JTPA is precisely the kind of program that
the 1986 Bishop's Pastoral seeks to achieve. But James Bovard,
who analyzed JTPA for the libertarian Cato Institute, calls it a
corporate welfare program (Bovard, 1986). Bovard questions
the impressive performance figures, pointing out that under
JTPA, workers can quit a current job and enter government-paid
training for another one. Roughly one-fifth of JTPA trainees

have some college or post-high school education. And his big point is that a close study of JTPA in action shows that in most cases, the employers would have had to train the prospective employees anyway, so the only difference is that the government now pays for much of the training.

Despite Bovard's criticism, JTPA carried over from CETA the requirement that 90 percent of the trainees must be *disadvantaged,* meaning that they fall below the poverty line income of $11,000 for a family of four. William A. Kolberg, president of the National Alliance of Business and a strong supporter of JTPA, defends the "creaming" aspect: "Companies ought to find the very best people they can find. This program was never designed for the most difficult to place, like a 45-year-old mother on welfare who can't read or write."

We can learn much about job creation and subsidiarity from the history of CETA-JTPA. Obviously, the trial-and-error experience of both programs shows that some progress can be made, but we still need further experimentation to achieve good results over the broad spectrum of the disadvantaged.

Enterprise Zones

Representative Jack Kemp (Republican, New York) and others have been trying for many years to enact federal legislation to create enterprise zones, which would offer tax and regulatory relief to companies locating or expanding in low-income areas. President Reagan has pushed for enterprise zones since taking office, but the bills have been stymied mainly by House Democrats, who see in these zones the specter of federally protected enclaves of nonunion workers receiving subminimum wages. While this legislation has been stalled in Congress, state and local governments have gone ahead, creating more than 1,300 productive zones in 615 communities (Hayes, 1986).

In 1981, Connecticut became the first state to establish urban enterprise zones, providing special property tax abatements, state corporate tax credits, job creation grants, training assistance, and working capital loans. In 1986, Governor William A. O'Neill pronounced the pilot program of six zones a success, since it helped generate more than $135 million in new investments, created 4,300 new jobs, and helped maintain another 4,200 existing jobs. Connecticut is now expanding the program to create four more zones and to open it to smaller businesses.

Other successful state enterprise zone programs are summarized in Hayes, 1986.

Role of Education

In September of 1987, the Committee for Economic Development (CED) released a report entitled "Children in Need: Investment Strategies for the Educationally Disadvantaged." The report warned that we are creating a permanent underclass of young people who are unemployable because they lack basic literacy skills and work habits. It said that if schools imposed higher standards but failed to provide special help needed to meet those standards, over a million students would drop out and another three-quarters of a million would graduate without the skills necessary for higher education or employment.

The CED is a highly respected non-profit, non-partisan research and education organization, most of whose 225 trustees are top business executives or presidents of major universities. The report was produced by a CED committee chaired by Owen B. Butler, retired chairman of Proctor & Gamble. In addition to citing humanitarian values, the report alerts business people to the threat that poverty and ignorance could cause grave shortages of qualified workers in the future and thereby weaken America's competitiveness in the world economy. Therefore, proposals for radical new interventions in the education process are put forward as a necessary *investment* rather than an expense. The report says that "failure to educate is the true expense."

CED claims that more than a third of our youth grow up severely undereducated. It says that in 1987, more than one million babies will be born who will never complete their schooling and thus will become virtually unemployable. Furthermore, they will soon have children of their own, thus perpetuating the cycle of ignorance, want, and unemployability.

To overcome these deficiencies, the CED recommends three key investment strategies for improving the prospects of children in need: prevention of learning problems through early intervention; restructuring the foundations of education; and retention and re-entry.

The early intervention program would require agencies to work with the targeted parents and their children from prenatal care through age five. It would encourage pregnant teenagers and those with babies to stay in school and it would provide prenatal and postnatal care for pregnant teens and other high-risk mothers; parenting education for both mothers and fathers; quality child care arrangements for teenagers in school and poor working parents; and quality preschool programs for all disadvantaged three- and four-year-old children.

Restructuring the public schools that serve the disadvantaged would include upgrading the quality of teachers; providing smaller schools and smaller classes; support of preschool and child care programs by the school system; updating educational technology; adding support systems within the schools that include health services, nutritional guidance, and psychological family counseling; and increasing emphasis on extra-curricular activities.

Retention and re-entry would involve targeting of students likely to drop out and those who have already left school to provide work experience with education in basic skills.

The report urges the business community to become a driving force on behalf of public education and to be a prime advocate of educational initiatives for disadvantaged youngsters. This includes supporting higher funding levels that would be needed for both the new early prevention programs and for upgrading the public education system.

The report follows the subsidiarity principle, by calling on the federal government only to fund demonstration projects, with the state and local governments to continue paying for the major part of the education bill. But overall, despite its big-business orientation, CED is calling for increased intervention by federal, state, and local government. While the program would involve additional outlays of $11 billion per year, the report claims that every dollar spent on early prevention and intervention can save $4.75 in the cost of remedial education, welfare, and crime further down the road.

The report is available from the Committee for Economic Development, 477 Madison Avenue, New York, NY 10022.

The immediate reaction of Secretary of Education William J. Bennett was affirmative. On the NBC news program "Meet the Press," he stated that "we believe that for disadvantaged children early intervention can help, can make a big difference, provided you bring the family along with them."

From this brief survey of public and private sector job creation efforts, we learn that subsidiarity is actually being practiced. Government officials at all levels are concerned about minimizing expenditures, and they focus on creation of private sector jobs as the ultimate solution. To a large extent, public and private programs already follow the suggestions in the 1986 Bishops' Pastoral:

> We believe that an effective way to attack poverty is through programs that are small in scale, locally based and oriented toward empowering the poor to become self-sufficient. (No. 200 C)

Broadening Work Opportunities

As we saw in Chapter Two, there is a strong consensus favoring work opportunities for all who want them. Most of us also favor substitution of work for welfare and the creation of public service work (the work of humanity) if it can be funded economically.

Welfare and Workfare

The primary problems of the present welfare system are these: it discourages welfare recipients from finding jobs; the safety net does not extend broadly enough, nor does it provide assistance at adequate levels; and it fosters the break-up of the traditional family by providing greater benefits to single-headed families than those with two parents.

Workfare, in its various versions, attempts to get people off welfare through training, education, or job placement. Lately, there has been much discussion of a federal workfare program, but as of late 1987 the most likely outcome was further experimentation at the state level.

Thirty-nine states have experimented recently with workfare. One of the best known experiments is the ET (Employment and Training) program in Massachusetts, which offers training to

welfare recipients and contracts with private and local government agencies to find jobs for the trainees. Because agencies are
paid to find higher-paying jobs ($5/hour or more) which last at
least 30 days, the program's supporters claim that it will keep
people off welfare on a voluntary basis, thus reducing overall
welfare costs.

The ET program points up some of the weaknesses in workfare programs generally. Massachusetts has one of the lowest
unemployment rates in the country, with actual labor shortages
in many job categories. Its ability to find jobs paying above
the minimum wage (and high enough to avoid poverty) is very
specific to that state. ET's initial success is not necessarily main-
tainable on a continuing basis. Often in such programs, those
most likely to hold down jobs are put through the program first
and their rate of success in securing longer-term employment is
not attainable by the larger population at which the program is
aimed.

Many of the new workfare proposals call for mandatory work
near the minimum wage level. It is hard to see how such programs would bolster a recipient's desire to work, as the wages
would be far below the poverty level.

In 1987, the Conference of State Governors proposed workfare with these provisions:

A flexible state-designed work program which accommo-
dates remedial education, training and job placement and
experience for participants in Aid to Families with Dependent Children (the largest welfare program).

A requirement that all recipients of cash assistance with
children aged 3 or more participate in a work program.

A binding contractual agreement between the recipient
and the government which lays out mutual obligations —
the client to strive for self-sufficiency and the government
to provide adequate support services for a designated period of time as the client moves toward economic independence. (*New York Times,* February 24, 1987)

Workfare appears to be a consensus idea whose time has come.
This is the conclusion reached by a comprehensive British study,
Would Workfare Work? written by John Burton, Research Di-

rector of the Institute of Economic Affairs (Burton, 1987). He surveys the workfare experience in Sweden, Switzerland, and the United States, and concludes that it "has slowly evolved from a somewhat cranky conservative notion to one with broad support" (p. 47). Particularly valuable is his analysis of the acceptability of workfare to the actual participants in Arkansas, West Virginia, Sweden, and Switzerland, which he finds to be very positive. In Arkansas, "participants interviewed claimed they liked their jobs, believed they had learned something, and stated that they felt better about getting welfare when working for it" (p. 45). In West Virginia, surveys showed that the workfare program "gave high levels of job satisfaction and acceptance of the fairness of the workfare principle" (p. 45). As a caution, Burton notes that "workfare generates a net increase in employment by exerting downward pressure on wages, and will only generate such a net increase to the extent that it does this" (p. 35). His report concludes:

> It is demonstrably the case that workfare can work even though precise quantification of the costs and benefits remain elusive. Success depends on many factors including administrative streamlining, commitment, the establishment of performance standards and more controversially, a degree of coercion. (p. 59)

A detailed survey of experimental state welfare reform programs was made by the Manpower Demonstration Research Corporation (Gueron, 1987). Assessing the results of on-going programs in eight states, the MDRC report reached mixed conclusions. Most of the programs stressed job search. A few included education and training, while true workfare (requiring unpaid public service work in exchange for welfare benefits) usually lasted only thirteen weeks when it was used. The major findings were:

> It is feasible, under certain conditions and on the scale at which the demonstration programs were implemented, to tie the receipt of welfare to participation obligations. . . .

In cases in which states chose to operate mandatory
workfare, the interim results do not support the strongest
claims of critics or advocates....

The programs led to relatively modest increases in employment, which in some cases translated into even smaller
welfare savings. Nonetheless, the changes were usually
large enough to justify the programs' costs, although this
finding varied by state and target group.

(Gueron, 1987, pp. 26–28)

Despite the strong consensus for workfare, we should not build
up extravagant hopes for its potential. Senator Daniel Patrick
Moynihan (Democrat, New York), one of our most knowledge-
able welfare experts, introduced a bill in July 1987 that included
all the reform for which he felt he could muster legislative support. Even with the Democrats in control of both houses, Senator Moynihan's bill, by his own count, would permit no more
than 75,000 of the 3.8 million adult welfare recipients to receive
job-training and placement.

Thus, further experiments with workfare are in order, but
we must continue to search elsewhere for the key to full employment.

The Work of Humanity

We now examine one of the major paradoxes of our time: the
fact that our society is desperately in need of work to be done
while more than 7 million people are unemployed.

As we saw in Chapter Two, the nation's infrastructure is rot-
ting because we have not found a way of organizing and paying
for the needed repairs, and our society is ravaged by the lack of
low-income housing and repair, services for the elderly and the
handicapped, child care, and environmental protection. Senator Paul Simon compares these needs and opportunities with
the WPA days:

...we could teach many more than the 1.5 million adult
Americans that the WPA taught to read and write; we could
help day care centers; we could develop parks and play-
grounds,; we could assist in recreational programs for the

handicapped; we could help develop industrial parks; we could plant 200 million trees a year. The list can go on and on. There is no shortage of needs; there is no shortage of personnel. What we have a shortage of is creative and courageous political leadership.

(Simon, 1987, p. 155)

Religious organizations can prop up the politicians' creativity and courage by marshaling grassroots support for the work of humanity.

More often than not, unemployment and the need for the work of humanity are viewed as separate issues with separate — if any — solutions. Yet the work of humanity is as much a possible solution to unemployment as it is a challenge in itself. In addition to infrastructure and public service work, there is the "informal economy," defined as economic activity that does not show up in the Gross National Product. We are not interested here in the negative or criminal side of the informal economy, but rather in the legitimate activities for which people are not paid in a formal sense. The largest category is work done around the house, including childrearing, cooking, and cleaning.

As with the work of humanity, much of this work is vital to people and their communities, especially in maintaining integrity of the family structure. If it were monetized, it would account for a significant portion of the GNP. Along with the growth in what James Robertson calls "ownwork" (i.e., activity which is purposeful and important, and which people organize and control for themselves), the activities of the informal economy present significant opportunities for redefining work and creating new methods of financial support. We shall return to this concept when we discuss universal share ownership in Chapter Five.

It is clear that there is a crying need for the work of humanity, and that overall we have the resources to accomplish it. What is lacking is the packaging of those resources in a way that is salable to the majority of voters. The lack of such a package brings us to the need to work from a base in our Ten Principles.

Combining the Work of Humanity with Ownership: Shareholders In America, Inc. (SIA)

Because we cannot achieve full employment without government job-creation programs that appear to involve unacceptable costs, and because the work of humanity would create millions of new jobs and greatly improve our society, it is clear that we need to experiment with methods of paying for the work of humanity without massive public funding.

First, as we have noted, despite our high unemployment rate, many jobs are going begging. For the most part, these are low-paying dead-end jobs that do not appear to be any more attractive than welfare except to the most ambitious of the unemployed. Let us first consider the need for incentives beyond the below-poverty-level wages that most of these jobs offer.

Richard B. Freeman is Director of Labor Research at the National Bureau of Economic Research and Professor of Economics at Harvard University. Writing about the monumental problem of black youth unemployment, Freeman says:

> While they [black youth] are willing to work at jobs and wages comparable to those of white youths, they are generally unwilling to take worse or lower paying jobs despite higher unemployment.... The problem is not one of creating jobs, but of creating jobs that offer career opportunities that dominate alternative opportunities, such as crime.... While the research indicates that black youths, like others, respond rapidly to market incentives, changing the incentives will require much more than traditional job training programs and anti-discrimination activity.
>
> (Freeman, 1986)

We have all seen "help wanted" signs in supermarkets offering checkout jobs at $5 to $6 an hour, but they are difficult to fill even though they pay far above the minimum wage of $3.35 per hour. During the summer of 1987, there were 2,000 jobs unfilled at the Cape Cod resorts, even though resort owners were offering transportation, housing, and wages as high as $9.00 per hour. Both the supermarket and the resort jobs were offering little in the way of career incentives.

Even idyllic places of employment such as Disneyland have trouble recruiting students for summer jobs. In the summer of 1987, they offered wages of $4.25 an hour plus many other benefits, but still had more than 200 vacancies. One reason for this shortfall, in addition to the lack of incentives, is the fact that the low birth rates of the late 1960s and early 1970s have caused a comparative shortage of younger people in the job market. And many of the jobless youngsters are stuck in center city ghettos, having no way of getting to suburban areas where service jobs go begging.

This demographic labor shortage is the subject of *The Birth Dearth* by Ben J. Wattenberg. Pointing out the declining birth rates of western nations, Wattenberg predicts that there will be a growing labor shortage in the service sector, and then in housing. He questions the viability of Social Security, with a growing herd of oldsters supported by a shrinking number of younger workers. His solution is to offer bounties for a higher birth rate in the form of higher tax exemptions and lower Social Security taxes for those having more children (Wattenberg, 1987).

Since it does not appear feasible to solve this problem entirely through higher wages, other incentives are needed, both to induce young people to take on low-paying jobs, and to get them to complete the education needed for higher skilled jobs, which to some young people (especially those living in ghettos) seem like illusions. The first step is to create a fairer society in which it is apparent that everyone has an opportunity to participate, through both work and ownership. This would require us to actually offer ownership opportunities to those who normally would never receive them: those struggling at low paying or dead-end jobs.

We will treat in detail some proposals for universal share ownership in the next chapter. Here it is convenient to consider one form of expanded ownership that ties in particularly well with our discussion of the Campaign for Human Development, the work of humanity, and Senator Paul Simon's Guaranteed Job Opportunity proposal, because it might provide a missing link needed to make those programs successful. I call it "Shareholders In America."

I organized Shareholders In America, Inc., as a for-profit Delaware stock corporation, for two purposes: to lend a touch of realism to the essay contests on broader share ownership that I have been sponsoring, and also to provide a vehicle by which American business could attempt to solve some of our serious economic and social problems without government intervention. In the following discussion, I use SIA merely as a symbol for an unfinished idea. Anyone is free to appropriate all or part of the idea.

SIA would offer share ownership and dividends, in addition to paid employment, as incentives for the unemployed and disadvantaged to work their way out of welfare. All shares of SIA would be owned and voted by its worker-owners; no shares would be held by investors. Shares in SIA would be available only to those who are willing to work at relatively low salaries, doing whatever is needed to improve their own communities and ultimately, society and the economy. No new government funds would be needed to launch or sustain SIA, although it could draw upon whatever government resources are currently available to all private businesses.

Successful business companies would play a major role by establishing a stream of profits upon which SIA could be built, through set-asides, subcontracts, and patronage. For example, IBM could volunteer to engage SIA for some janitorial and trucking services, and Philip Morris could award SIA a contract for a small percentage of its printing and painting requirements, without increasing their costs beyond the amounts presently paid for such necessary services. This concept is already working, as evidenced by the *$9 billion* annual patronage organized by the National Minority Supplier Development Council (NMSDC). Business could also lend the services of top management at the outset, giving way to worker-owners of SIA as soon as they are ready to take over.

SIA affords the business community a chance to prove that there is a lot more to capitalism than greed and exploitation. By providing the poorest segment of our society with the opportunity to become working capitalists, business can advance capitalism to a much higher stage of development as a moral, humane, and effective system that does not need to be sustained by the huge doses of welfare transfers that we have been feeding it for the last fifty years. Instead of welfare capitalism, which Harvard economist Joseph Schumpeter described as "capitalism in an oxygen tent," we can move up to universally shared capitalism, without government funding.

Set-asides, subcontracts, and patronage by the granting of business opportunities could start SIA's lifeblood flowing. Eventually, SIA could develop its own captive market to serve the needs of its worker-shareholders and the communities in which they live. This could be done along lines similar to the producer-cooperative and consumer-cooperative movements, with the additional bonus of stock ownership for employees. The strong stream of profits flowing from the set-aside and subcontracting programs would furnish a sound basis for successful cooperatives, which often flounder if started without such a foundation.

Government User Charges

If SIA succeeded in taking people off the welfare rolls and making them worker-capitalists, it would relieve federal, state, and local government agencies of costly unemployment and welfare benefit payments. These benefits, along with losses of tax revenues due to depressed economic activity, are now estimated by the Congressional Budget Office to cost government about $35,000 per unemployed person per year.

SIA should be entitled to receive as a bounty or user charge a reasonable percentage of the $35,000 saved by government for each person it takes off the unemployment and welfare rolls. Many government programs have paid such user charges to private companies in the form of tax credits for creating employment, for which SIA would be eligible as a taxpaying private corporation. In addition to present tax legislation, perhaps future legislation could grant a special ongoing user charge to SIA and companies similarly organized, if they demonstrate the ability to give many people the opportunity to work their way out of welfare into the higher status of worker-capitalist. With or without such user charges, the $35,000-per-person cost to government of welfare and unemployment should provide government agencies with a strong incentive to favor SIA with contracts and other revenue-producing opportunities.

User fees have played an important role in development of turnpikes, bridges, canals, and highways, reaching back to seventeenth-century England (Albert, 1972). Today, user charges are being revived by beleaguered government budget officials. President Reagan's budget message for fiscal year 1988 seeks to impose increased user charges totalling $3.2 billion:

> *User Fees.* Some of the services the Federal Government provides are utilized by narrowly defined groups or individuals. Agencies should recover a portion of their costs for providing these services through "user fees," in which recipients of the service are charged directly. Direct charges to users are appropriate because those who benefit from the service pay the cost; taxpayers do not. User fees increase efficiency of service delivery by reaching those willing to pay. Cost-based user fees may also provide an incentive for the private sector to provide comparable service at lower cost.
>
> The administration proposes to: Increase fees in the mortgage finance programs of the Federal Housing Administration and the Government National Mortgage Association; increase fees for Veterans Administration home loans; charge for Coast Guard services; increase recreation user fees; charge user fees for the Food Safety and Inspection Service; reform pension benefit guaranties; revise user fees for guaranteed student loans; establish user fees for the United States Travel and Tourism Administration; and increase user fees for Commerce products and services.

Private User Charges for Community Improvement, Crime Control, and the Work of Humanity

If SIA cleans up a slum neighborhood, reduces crime, and turns the community into a more valuable resource for companies having business operations there, it would seem reasonable for the companies to pay a user charge for these services. Businesses are paying the equivalent of such user charges indirectly now, through their own security forces (with more than 600,000 security guards on private business payrolls in 1983) and through their substantial expenditures for public relations and community relations activities. They are also paying dearly for the lack of favorable community conditions, through lowered morale, oppressive working conditions, and losses to crime.

According to *Business Week,* business expects to pay more of
the bill for "The Crumbling of America" through both tax hikes
and user fees (December 1, 1986, p. 62). It should be possible
to design appropriate user charges that would be a continuing
source of income for SIA.

Such special user charges are imposed by governmental units
now. For example, local businesses in Miami, Florida, have been
struggling with the problems of crime, decaying neighborhoods,
and poor public transportation. A new "Metromover" transportation system has been installed, and the downtown businesses served by the new system are paying a special assessment
fee to help retire a $20 million bond issue. Though the fees
are decreed by the government, businesses are paying them in
the expectation that the new transportation system will increase
property values and ease access to a crowded area. Crime and
the decay of neighborhoods are even more threatening to local
businesses than the inadequacy of local transportation which the
Metromover system is designed to alleviate. A similar plan to
create a Business Improvement District in the Grand Central
area of New York City would assess property owners 10 cents
per square foot a year for improvement of the neighborhood's
ambience, including security patrols, garbage pickup, and aid
for the homeless. Fees from the landlords would be collected by
the city with property taxes and then turned over to the Grand
Central Partnership, a consortium of businesses that is developing the plan.

It remains for SIA to develop a method of quantifying the
value of such services so that reasonable user charges can be
collected. SIA could arrange user charges by contract with businesses in the area before revitalizing a neighborhood. Major
companies in the area could agree in advance on reasonable
user charges, thus giving SIA a concrete challenge and a sound
business basis for organizing the project. A minimum charge
could be agreed upon, payable monthly, subject to cancellation
if SIA does not produce results.

The "value-added" concept is used in many government and
business functions today. It should be possible for SIA to apply the same principles in order to establish reasonable user
charges. Although it calls for development of a new management skill, this could be accomplished with the help of business,

religious organizations, universities, and community improvement groups.

SIA and Its Worker-Shareholders

SIA could change some losers into winners simply by treating the disadvantaged as owners. The heightened self-esteem that flows from treating workers as partners is an important part of successful business strategy, as documented by *In Search of Excellence* (Peters, 1982, pp. 238, 247).

Obviously, the compensation package would have to be more attractive than welfare benefits in order to motivate potential SIA employees. In this connection, I received a valuable insight from Theodore M. Hesburgh, President Emeritus of the University of Notre Dame and one of America's leading social reformers. Father Hesburgh has a special interest in ghetto youth, and has often been frustrated by the refusal of thousands of them to learn to read and write well enough to hold down a steady job. He told me he thought there would be a greater prospect of motivating these young people to acquire the basic skills required for employment if we offered them a block of stock. "If we could put something on the table — $5,000 or $10,000 worth of stock, let's say — and say to these people, here — this is for you — all you have to do is to learn to read and write. If we could do that, I think we would have a much better chance of motivating these people." Similarly, conservative Congressman Newt Gingrich (Republican, Georgia) has suggested that government give financial rewards to those who overcome illiteracy (Gingrich, 1984, p. 167).

No matter which future scenario we accept — that automation will reduce job openings, or that many people will not be working because of lack of skills or insufficient incentive — SIA could help to solve the problem. If SIA could supply the missing incentive through shareholder dividends and enhanced status as a capitalist, many of those who are avoiding the job market might take the trouble to train and discipline themselves to become useful members of the work force.

There seems to be no doubt that small business activity of the type envisioned for SIA will continue to be the main source of new employment. Large corporations have reduced their overall

payrolls at every opportunity, especially during down cycles, and
they rarely return to their previous high staff levels during up
cycles. They prefer to expand through automation and increased
capital investment, leaving it to the small business sector to pick
up the slack in job creation.

This business policy creates another opportunity for SIA:
development of a temporary-help service. Nearly a quarter
of all private sector jobs are temporary, contingent, or part-
time. Many people were surprised when the largest American temporary-help service provider, Manpower Inc., drew a
takeover bid of over $1.2 billion in 1987. Manpower Inc.
built a highly profitable business through fees of 5 to 7 percent
of the wages paid to "temps," of which they have more than
700,000 available. SIA could provide a similar service and earn
healthy profits while providing employment to its shareholder-
workers.

SIA and Religious Organizations

The Reverend Erskine White, a minister of the United Church
of Christ, worked with the Campaign for Human Development
at its headquarters in Washington and also on field projects designed to empower the poor by helping to finance their attempts
to organize profit-making business enterprises. Reverend White
believes that churches have the raw materials needed for a new
inner-city economy: poor people who want to work and would
like to own a share of a successful business; access to capital
through church pension funds, along with the ability of churches
to raise money for social programs; and access to business expertise through more successful members of the church congregation. But these raw materials have yet to be mobilized into
a program that reduces unemployment significantly or creates
substantial ownership opportunities. Reverend White and other
religious leaders to whom I have spoken believe that SIA is certainly worth a try and that it should attempt to use the good
will and resources of religious organizations in its quest for profitable operations. Indeed, the organized business patronage of
churches alone would go a long way toward making SIA successful.

To summarize, SIA would provide worker-owners with two

types of business opportunities. First, patronage and subcontracts from large successful companies would get SIA off the
ground and enable it to build management and performance
skills, while distributing profits to the worker-owners. Second,
SIA would gradually develop its own stream of profits by organizing and performing the work of humanity in its own community, while continuing to profit from the patronage and subcontracting program.

The Council on International and Public Affairs has published a booklet describing SIA in more detail (Speiser, 1986b).

Religious Expertise and Input

From the foregoing panorama of frantic efforts to create employment, it is clear that the experience and energy of religious
organizations are sorely needed in the quest to redefine work,
open work opportunities to all, and devise ways of paying for
that work within the American consensus that balks at handouts
of tax funds.

Religious organizations are particularly well suited to lead
the way in the work of humanity. It is, in a large sense, a moral
concept, and can be shaped from the original clay, unlike the
paid employment system that we have to take largely as we find
it.

We have seen the great strides taken by the Reverend Leon
Sullivan and other black church leaders. The experience of the
Church of Jesus Christ of Latter-day Saints (the Mormons) may
also contain some useful ideas. While the rigors of Mormon
lifestyle are not for everyone, they have developed a very comprehensive program that they call "welfare service" but that is
actually based on a highly developed work ethic and a cooperative method of helping people to help themselves. Their objective is to completely eliminate poverty in Mormon communities, and this they have accomplished to a surprising degree
in their practical programs of welfare assistance and self-help
promotion.

For example, section five of the *Mormon Welfare Services
Resource Handbook* describes the "storehouse resource system"
through which temporary assistance is given to the poor. As the
handbook notes, "This is to be done not as a dole, but in recog-

nition of their willingness to labor to the extent of their ability."
While temporary help is given in the form of cash, social services, and rehabilitation, the primary object is to find regular
jobs for those able to work.

Deseret Industries is a part of the Mormons' storehouse resource system. As the handbook states,

> Deseret Industries is a non-profit enterprise built on the
> principles of thrift, giving, work, and sharing. The pur-
> pose of Deseret Industries is to help people help themselves
> by encouraging independence rather than dependence, and
> work rather than idleness.

Its specific objectives are to provide meaningful employment
and work training in an environment that will enable the needy
to become self-sustaining. Deseret Industries, is, in a way, a
working model of Shareholders In America, based on religious
principles. The initial operating funds for a Deseret Industries
unit are provided from Mormon Church collections. Thereafter,
units are expected to be self-sustaining. There is a strong element of patronage, since Mormon Church leaders are instructed
to encourage members to shop at Deseret Industries retail stores,
to contribute useable items for refurbishing and sale, and to
share their talents by training workers. The Deseret Industries
home craft program provides work opportunities for the needy,
the homebound, and others who are able to learn and contribute.
This is a promising way of accomplishing some of the work of
humanity.

From our brief survey in this chapter, it is apparent that
there is a lot of raw material to which the galvanizing force of
religious institutions can be applied. There is a huge reservoir
of energy, good will, and determination to overcome the unemployment and poverty problems. Many experimental programs
have been taken a long way over the road of trial and error. And
there is the genuine concern and commitment of many business
executives, as we have seen in the work of the Committee for
Economic Development and in the $9 billion worth of support
given by business to the National Minority Supplier Development Council.

Future Shortages:
Jobs, Skills, Workers, or Incentives?

If you are a little confused about the future of work and employment, you are not alone. The views of twenty-three leading
employment and welfare specialists were compiled by University of Wisconsin Professor Sheldon H. Danziger and USHHS
economist Daniel H. Weinberg in *Fighting Poverty: What Works
and What Doesn't* (Danziger and Weinberg, 1987). They concluded that by 1984, twenty years after Lyndon Johnson's declaration of war on poverty and the start of the Great Society,
social spending had been greatly expanded but poverty had declined little (p. 2). Not surprisingly, they found that increasing
employment was the best way to fight poverty, but the specialists could not agree on how to actually increase employment
(p. 10). After noting that "as is so often the case in the social
sciences, convincing evidence is hard to come by" (p. 343), the
book closes with a prescription for much more research.

As we have seen, economists and other forecasters are divided on the effects of automation. Some believe that it is already destroying many jobs (as it is designed to do) and that
the number of new jobs it creates will not nearly make up for
the loss of existing jobs. Others believe it will create whole new
industries and open up more jobs than we can fill. One thing
seems clear: the new jobs, which are mostly in the service sector, are not paying as well as the jobs being destroyed, and so
automation seems destined to contribute to the pauperization
of work, with the landing of a job no longer a guaranteed ticket
out of poverty, and middle-class children facing a tough struggle
to equal their parents' living standards.

Another fairly safe prediction is that automation will up the
ante on skill requirements. Millions of workers will need computer skills in order to fit in to the economy of the future. As the
1987 report of the Committee for Economic Development concluded, we are breeding an underclass of unemployable people
who will not have the skills to participate in the economy unless
we make some drastic changes in our education priorities.

We have already seen that in the late 1980s, at a time of
high unemployment for a recovery period, unskilled jobs that

pay wages close to the poverty level are going begging. This situation will be much worsened when the 1987 immigration law reforms take full effect. As this is written, many employers of menial workers who were being paid wages at or below the minimum wage are desperately seeking an alternative to the illegal aliens who filled those jobs. It seems doubtful that this problem can be solved completely by raising wages for unskilled people, since our economy could not remain competitive with other nations if we did not either keep wages down or increase skills and productivity.

All of these conflicting forces lead to some reasonable conclusions we can draw. While there is no gross shortage of "jobs," there is already a shortage of jobs that pay above-poverty-level wages and that provide strong incentives through the prospect of substantial future wage increases. So the problem is not really job creation, but job *enhancement*. Therefore, creation of new incentives is the great challenge of the future. This leads us to Chapter Five, where we will face the task of formulating specific plans for increasing incentives through the broadening of capital ownership.

In its article marking the twentieth anniversary of the 1967 ghetto riots, *Time* magazine observed:

No one seriously thought the inner city could be transformed overnight. But few were cynical enough to envision what actually happened: an entire generation would pass as life in the black ghettos of a rich nation went from bad to almost unimaginably worse.

The article, entitled "The Ghetto: From Bad to Worse" (August 24, 1987), concluded that the success of the civil rights movement, which broke down segregated housing, caused middle-class blacks to take the new opportunity to move beyond the ghetto walls, leaving behind those who "care less." The article ended on this note:

Twenty years of failed programs, from community development to public housing, point to a depressing conclusion: little will be done to make the ghetto an acceptable place to live and raise children. This by no means suggests abandoning those trapped in the inner city. Rather, the emphasis of both government and private philanthropy must be on helping the black underclass escape the social isolation of these inner-city wastelands. What successes there have been come not through cosmetically improving the ghettos but by providing residents with opportunities through jobs and education to rise out of them. Saving people, not inner-city neighborhoods, may be the only way America can redeem the promises that were made against the charred urban landscape of that terrible summer of 1967.

I do not think we need to accept this pessimistic appraisal. While the ghetto picture is very disturbing, we don't have to abandon whole communities in order to save people one by one. Indeed, as we have seen in the work of LISC and James Rouse's Enterprise Foundation, one of the best opportunities for saving the people in the ghettos is to mobilize them to take advantage of the need for rebuilding their burned-out wastelands, through new methods of expanding work and ownership. Every decaying ghetto is an opportunity as well as a blight.

The Israeli Kibbutz as an Educational Model

The Israeli kibbutz (Hebrew *Qibbutz,* meaning "gathering" or "collective") has captured the imagination of the world as an efficient application of socialist principles. The first one was founded at Deganya in 1910. In their early years they concentrated on agriculture, but have now become industrialized as well. Each kibbutz member owns one share and has one vote at the weekly general meetings that provide the community government. Today's kibbutzim have from 60 to 2,000 members, each of whom performs an assigned task but receives no salary because all needs are provided by the kibbutz. After provision of members' needs, including social and medical services, profits are reinvested in the community. Adults have private quarters, but children are housed and cared for as a group, with frequent visitation by the parents.

The Israeli kibbutzim evolved from the Marxist orientation of their founders. In their early days they were so opposed to the institution of private property that a man who sent his shirt to the kibbutz laundry would be likely to get back somebody else's shirt in return.

Here we are not concerned with the ownership or governance aspects of the kibbutz, since (as we shall see in the next chapter) there are many other models for cooperative and universal ownership that do not depend upon Marxist origins. Let us focus on the unique system of childrearing pioneered by the kibbutzim. Can it serve as a model for experiments with the rearing and education of disadvantaged American children?

The early kibbutzim, organized in Palestine during the first decade of the twentieth century, needed to free mothers from childrearing duties so that their labor could help establish a foothold for the precarious Jewish settlement. So began the practice of providing separate collective homes for the children. The system has evolved so that in the 1980s, all children of a kibbutz spend the first year of their life in an infant house cared for by a *metapelet* (upbringer) who takes care of four or five babies. During the nursing stage, mothers feed their babies in the infant house. The next stage is the toddler house, containing eight children aged from one to four. These children visit their parents for a few hours each day. In the next stage, kindergarten, children from three to seven are under the care of a teacher and three assistants.

In the words of Israel's leading guidebook:

> Of all the characteristics of a kibbutz, none is more prominent than the care and education of the children. From the moment babies return from the maternity home they are placed in Baby Houses under the care of nurses who invariably are not their mothers. This communal responsibility for raising children continues through a succession of children's homes from kindergarten through high school, where they live, eat, study and play in groups of children of their own age. It is a highly successful system that frees the mother for other tasks on the kibbutz. It also introduced women's lib before it became fashionable in the outside world. Inevitably the children come to regard the entire kibbutz as "home." Studies show that this group education and fostering of team spirit from childhood gives them a re-

sourcefulness and self-reliance that is responsible for their
leadership qualities. Delinquency is rare indeed.

(Bazak, 1985, p. 92)

It is this kibbutz function of the substitute home for children,
and their rearing during the critical years by experts rather than
by harried working mothers, that holds promise for dealing with
the problem of the American underclass.

As we have seen, the Committee for Economic Development
deplores the development of a permanent underclass of young
people who are unemployable because they lack basic literary
skills and work habits. In addition to the CED's warning, the
National Assessment of Educational Progress, a federal project
to monitor student knowledge of basic subjects, concluded that
we need a stronger academic core for the basic high school curriculum. Secretary of Education William J. Bennett released
a proposed future curriculum in December of 1987, which included three years of mathematics, three years of science, and
two years of foreign language study, among required courses.
And the Hudson Institute, a think tank commissioned by the
Labor Department to do research on employment, income, and
occupational trends, concluded in its report, *Workforce 2000*,
that even though the average American's standard of living will
be rising for the rest of this century, income distribution will be
more widely skewed because jobs for the least skilled members
of the labor force will shrink while those for the most skilled
will grow more rapidly (Johnston and Packer, 1987).

All of this underscores the need for education of the underclass. It also appears that no matter how much we spend on
present programs, the children of the underclass are not likely
to be inspired in large numbers to educate themselves to the required levels while they are living in the kind of home environment that contributes heavily to their disadvantaged status. If
we are to solve our domestic problems and start to catch up with
the Japanese, we must change the home environment that now
spawns the undereducated underclass. I can think of no more
promising experiment than the establishment of Israeli-type kibbutzim, which would relieve American mothers of many home-
making tasks, leaving them free to work while being assured that
their children are getting a good education. The children in turn

would be partially raised and counselled by expert professionals dedicated to their education and welfare. They would be indoctrinated in the work ethic and the importance of education for future job success. This experiment could begin with fatherless families in a few large cities, and the results could be evaluated relatively quickly by comparing post-kibbutz academic and work performance with the children's earlier records.

Bear in mind that even if we made such radical changes as revival of the WPA or the type of public works projects proposed by Senator Simon, there is little evidence that the work habits needed to make use of such programs are present in the contemporary underclass. In the WPA days, the problem was not lack of the work ethic — rather, it was the absence of available work. Millions of unemployed people were lined up waiting for any kind of job and could be counted on to work diligently once they were given even the meanest opportunity. Today, many jobs paying more than public service wages are going begging, while the skills and work habits needed to fill these jobs are fast eroding.

We have postponed discussion of share ownership plans, apart from their role in SIA. Now it is time to see whether we can open share ownership to everyone. Is capitalism strong enough to do this? Some capitalist thinkers who have had the foresight to explore the relationship between work and ownership are optimistic. One of them is David Howell, Member of Parliament and formerly a minister in the Thatcher cabinet. In his latest book, he concludes:

> Yet it could well be that the miserable and baffling phenomenon of high unemployment constitutes not a rejection of the ideal of a property-owning democracy but a direct challenge which it is more capable of meeting than other great philosophies. (Howell, 1986, p. 138)

Chapter 5

Expanding Ownership

AS WE SAW IN CHAPTER TWO, the idea of sharing ownership broadly is as old as John Adams and Thomas Jefferson and as fresh as Ronald Reagan and the Catholic Bishops' 1986 Pastoral. Yet the question persists: How do we achieve this? How can we open capital ownership to everyone and thereby make our economic system as democratic as our political system? We should note that while socialism *politicizes* the economy by putting ownership and control in the hands of bureaucrats, universal capitalism would *democratize* the economy by putting ownership in the hands of individual citizens.

To democratize our economy, we would have to spread ownership of the means of production (MOP) more widely and more equitably. Many people are under the impression that we already have widespread ownership, but this is not the case. The subject of MOP ownership has been neglected because most economists see it as value question that is beyond their responsibility. Therefore, there are few statistical studies, but from those available it is clear that the distribution of MOP ownership (evidenced mainly by shares of corporate stock) is dominated by a tiny pinnacle class. Indeed, Ronald Reagan, when he was a privately employed radio commentator, estimated in a 1975 broadcast that "only 6 percent [of Americans] are true capitalists in the sense of deriving their income from ownership of the means of production."

Dr. Robert Hamrin spent four years studying future economic growth as a staff economist for the Joint Economic Com-

151

mittee of Congress (JEC). In a 1976 staff study for the JEC based on the latest statistics then available, Hamrin found that half the individually owned corporate stock was owned by the richest 1.04 million Americans (one-half of 1 percent of the population). In his 1980 book, *Managing Growth in the 1980s: Toward a New Economics,* Hamrin analyzed the privately held wealth of the nation and concluded that only about 5 percent of Americans really share in the benefits of capital ownership (pp. 261–262). In this respect, the great egalitarian economy of the United States is on about the same level as the economy of India.

In 1981, the New York Stock Exchange proudly reported that some 32 million Americans (14.4 percent of the population) were individual owners of corporate stock and mutual fund shares. But closer examination reveals that only one-sixth of these shareholders (5.9 million Americans) owned shares worth $25,000 or more; and only 3.1 million owned shares worth $50,000 or more. Given the present state of dividends, the average annual return on portfolios worth $25,000 to $50,000 would be less than $5,000. Therefore, no more than 3 to 5 million Americans receive more than $5,000 of their annual income from stock ownership. Of course, there are other important sources of capitalist income, such as income-producing real estate, saving accounts, and bonds — but the studies indicate that the same pinnacle class owns most of those assets as well.

It is ironic that this figure of 6 percent (or less) of the population controlling the means of production is duplicated in the Soviet Union where membership of the Communist Party (which controls the MOP) is just about 6 percent of the total population. Thus, at the very moment in history when capitalism and communism are engaged in a death struggle arising (at least partially) from their differing ownership ideologies, it is plain that neither system provides equitable sharing of the income derived from MOP ownership.

A study by the Survey Research Center of the University of Michigan, commissioned by the Federal Reserve Board in 1983, found that the wealthiest 10 percent of American families (7.5 million households) own 84 percent of the nation's assets, with the richest 1 percent (840,000 households) owning fully half of the nation's wealth. The same study found that 90 percent of the American people have little or no net worth (Avery, 1986). MIT

Professor Lester Thurow dramatized this disparity by pointing out that those on the *Forbes* magazine roster of the 400 wealthiest American families could control 40 percent of U.S. business capital, if they simply borrowed an amount equal to their wealth (Thurow, 1984).

Note that we are talking here about individual ownership. Shares owned by pension funds and other institutional investors do not make their beneficiaries capitalists, since the beneficiaries do not own any shares individually and do not receive income from MOP ownership before retirement. Even then, they receive the fruits of labor rather than capital.

This overconcentration of capital ownership is a major stumbling block for those claiming that American capitalism is a morally just system. In addition, it may be the source of other weaknesses. For example, in his best-selling book, *The Great Depression of 1990* (written long before the October 1987 stock market crash), Southern Methodist University Professor Ravi Batra bases his prediction of impending economic disaster on the extreme overconcentration of wealth that occurs about every 60 years, which leads to speculative excesses, collapse of the stock market, and weakening of the banking system (Batra, 1987, pp. 116–124). In his foreword to the Batra book, M.I.T. Professor Lester Thurow explains:

> Depression is seen as a product of systematic tendencies for the distribution of wealth to become concentrated among a few. When this happens, demand eventually sags relative to supply and long cyclical downturns commence.
> (Batra, 1987, pp. 14–15)

Batra's cyclical theories of "historical determinism" are not accepted by most mainstream economists, but he has been highly accurate in past forecasts of major events, and his book presents much concrete evidence that depressions (as distinguished from recessions) are caused by the extreme inequality of ownership that builds up every two generations, which in turn damages the securities and banking systems so badly that recessions turn into long-running depressions. One of major remedies suggested by Batra is much broader and more egalitarian stock ownership to minimize the wealth disparities that cause depressions (Batra, 1987, pp. 182–184). Batra's remedies draw upon capitalist sources such as Adam Smith, and he rejects socialism and communism because they restrict the freedoms he regards as essential for a prosperous and just economy (pp. 181–182).

Plans for broadening share ownership have taken three basic forms. Plans in the first group, which we shall call *Type A*, are based on the employment relationship. *Type B* plans are based upon savings enhanced by tax relief, and *Type C* covers the broadest plans, opening ownership to all citizens regardless of their employment status and their savings or lack thereof.

Type A Ownership: Employment-Based

Ownership of a piece of the action by a firm's employees is the simplest and most attractive method of broadening ownership, but as we saw in Chapter One, it is not possible to spread capital ownership broadly among the people through employee ownership. It brings no benefit to the unemployed, the very poor, and those who are not fortunate enough to be long-term employees of continuously successful private companies. Therefore, the great majority of Americans who need the help that ownership can bring are simply not in a position to achieve it through employment. Nevertheless, it is important to study the great progress that has been made through employee share ownership recently, because it has started the process of broadening ownership, and it can serve as a foundation for the Type C plans needed to achieve real diffusion.

Employee Stock Ownership Plans (ESOPs)

ESOPs, the most widely used of employee ownership plans, are financed by employer contributions, which are used to buy stock of the employer company. The stock is then held in trust for employees. Generally, shares are allocated on the basis of each employee's relative wage, but some companies make equal contributions for all employees, regardless of their compensation. Employees receive this stock only after their employment has been terminated. As with other employee benefit plans that qualify for tax benefits under the Internal Revenue Code, ESOPs must be established and operated for the benefit of the employee participants.

ESOPs are sometimes used when the federal government steps in to bail out a troubled corporation. For example, under the Chrysler Corporation Loan Guarantee Act of 1979, Chrysler was required to set up an ESOP and contribute approximately $40 million a year until the trust's assets totaled $162.5 million of Chrysler stock, to be divided among the company's 94,000 American and Canadian employees. This stipulation was the work of Senator Russell Long, who believes that whenever the government is called upon to rescue a business, the benefit should not go exclusively to its creditors and stockholders but should also make the workers part owners, even though their ownership does not take effect until they retire or otherwise leave the company.

We have space for only a brief overview of the ESOP. Since Louis Kelso and Senator Long went to work on the project in 1973, ESOPs have grown from practically zero to the point where the General Accounting Office reported in December 1986 that there were at least 7,000 active ESOPs with more than 7 million participants and over $19 billion in assets (General Accounting Office, 1986). The GAO report concluded:

> GAO's analysis indicates that ESOPs do provide a broader distribution of stock ownership among covered employees than generally prevails in the U.S. population. But ESOPs cover only a small percentage of employees and hold only a small percentage of outstanding stock. These facts place an upper limit on the likely effects of ESOPs on the overall distribution of stock ownership to date.... GAO estimates that the cost of ESOP tax incentives averaged between $1.7 billion and $1.9 billion per year during the period 1977-1983, for a total of $12.1 billion to $13.3 billion over that period. (p. 5)

The GAO felt that this total cost of about $13 billion in tax breaks to create about $19 billion in stock held by workers was a very high price to pay (p. 6). The GAO declined to make any recommendations based on their study, indicating that we are at a very early point in the history of ESOPs.

A more optimistic view of the impact of ESOPs is given
in the comprehensive book compiled by the National Center
for Employee Ownership (Rosen, 1986). It documents many
individual ESOP programs, showing how they have benefited
employees and improved company performance. Such unsuccessful ESOPs as the Hyatt-Clark program do not necessarily
invalidate the ESOP principle, since Hyatt-Clark was a roller
bearing manufacturer whose 1987 bankruptcy (after converting
to employee ownership in 1981) may reflect nothing more than
the obsolescence of smokestack America, which has caused termination of many businesses that are not employee-owned.

It is not necessary for us to get into the debate about the
overall usefulness and equity of ESOPs. As we have seen, they
are microeconomic tools that may be beneficial to a particular
company and its employees. They can also be useful in rescuing
jobs by enabling workers to take over ownership when a parent
company wants to shut down a plant or get rid of an unprof-
itable division. Sometimes this is facilitated by the employees
cutting back their own salaries and pension benefits in order to
make the company profitable, looking toward future dividends
and stock price appreciation to make up the difference. This is
a strategic matter to be considered on a company-by-company
basis. In general, it is in tune with the religious quest for social
justice. Indeed, when ownership is mentioned in religious documents (such as *Laborem Exercens*), employee ownership usually
is stressed because it is the best-known variety. But we must
face the fact that employee ownership and profit sharing have
been around for more than a hundred years, without apprecia-
bly changing the social justice picture — nor are they capable of
doing so, because of the inherent limitations of moving through
the employment channel to broaden capital ownership.

In 1976, Peter F. Drucker announced the coming of "pension
fund socialism," based upon the fact that pension funds had become the biggest player in the stock market, predicted to own a
majority of the shares of all American publicly-held companies
by the year 2000 (Drucker, 1976). However, the workers involved in the pension funds have nothing to do with the investment of the funds, this being handled by trustees whose duty it is
to get maximum mileage out of the investments to provide cash
payments to retired employees. Therefore, instead of pension

fund ownership leading to worker ownership or control, pension fund domination of the financial markets has done just the opposite. Like other financial guardians, pension fund trustees have focused on the bottom line, managing their portfolios to produce maximum income through dividends and stock appreciation, which in many instances has resulted in the loss of jobs by the very workers who supposedly are owners under Drucker's vision of pension funds.

Note that the foregoing discussion relates to tax-advantaged share ownership plans. There is nothing to prevent an employer from paying bonuses or sharing profits with any of its employees, either in cash payments or in stock. In either case, the employer will receive a tax deduction for paying that extra compensation, just as the employer receives a tax deduction for the regular payroll. But the employees would have to pay income tax immediately on cash or shares received in that way, unless the payment was made under a "qualified" tax-deductible plan. In order to qualify, such plans (whether pension, profit-sharing, stock bonus, or ESOP) must include all employees, and the benefits cannot be received by the employees until they retire or terminate the employment. As a practical matter, ESOPs have emerged as the dominant method of making employees owners, because of the tax advantages to both employers and employees that Senator Long and his colleagues engineered.

Other Forms of Employee Ownership and Profit Sharing

The idea of workers owning shares in the enterprise that employs them is older even than Marxism. In 1826, German economist Johann Heinrich von Thunen wrote a book on this subject called *The Isolated State.* Von Thunen, however, did not confine himself to theoretical speculation. He owned large agricultural estates, and he applied his theories to his own farm workers, paying them the prevailing wages, and in addition, agreeing to share his profits with them. But instead of paying these profit-sharing bonuses in cash, he reinvested this money in equipment that would improve his farms' productivity. Each employee had an individual account to which his share of the profit was credited each year. The interest on this share was paid out annually in cash to the worker, and when the worker retired or left von

Thunen's employment, he received his share of ownership in cash.

During the nineteenth and twentieth centuries, von Thunen's idea was carried on through many types of profit-sharing and ownership-sharing plans within individual companies throughout Europe and the United States. There are many individual success stories, notably the Sears Roebuck and Eastman Kodak profit-sharing plans, which invested their funds mainly in stock of the employer company. This made the employees, at least indirectly, owners of substantial shares in the company for which they worked.

Modern American profit-sharing plans, as IRS-qualified retirement plans, usually invest in a diversified portfolio of shares of many companies, and proceeds are accumulated by trustees and paid to workers on retirement or leaving the company. However, it is perfectly feasible for a company to pay out shares of their profits in cash annually. The worker receives the cash immediately and must pay income taxes at the ordinary rate. Such cash incentive plans have worked very well in many companies. Many workers prefer to get cash in their hands before retirement so they can use it when they are younger.

The Weitzman Share Economy

In his 1984 book, *The Share Economy — Conquering Stagflation,* M.I.T. economics professor Martin Weitzman suggests that American business should abandon the practice of paying fixed wages and instead compensate workers in relation to their employers' revenues or profits. He attributes stagflation to the universal practice of paying employees fixed wages. When sales decrease during recessions, companies have difficulty reducing prices because they often cannot reduce wages and indeed sometimes even must increase them. Therefore, business managers choose instead to cut production and lay off employees. Thus, even as wages go up, unemployment rises and inflation persists. Weitzman suggests that if workers agreed to accept a fixed share of the company's revenues or profits, then when revenues dipped during a slump, workers' income would drop accordingly and the firm could then reduce prices in order to revive sales. Because all workers would take a temporary cut, no one would have to be laid off, and the burden of the recession would be spread throughout the whole work force.

Weitzman also claims that in such a share system, the company would have more incentive to hire new employees during better times. The new workers would help increase production when sales were climbing, but they would not reduce earnings when business was bad because the employee's average pay would fall along with decreasing sales. He feels that workers might be willing to take a pay cut in exchange for job security. From this premise, Weitzman reasons that if many or all companies installed the share system, the pool of qualified people looking for work would be quickly depleted, and we would have full employment. The increased purchasing power to take up all of this new productive capacity would come from the sizeable increase in employment, which would create more demand for goods and services.

While labor unions have expressed opposition to the Weitzman scheme because in the first instance it would reduce wages and increase the number of workers sharing the pie, Weitzman believes that this opposition could be overcome by having the government give income-tax breaks to those workers who accept the plan, in the form of lower tax rates on the portion of their income that is contingent on profits.

Weitzman cites Japan as a successful example of the share system, for in many Japanese companies, as much as half of a worker's pay comes in the form of a bonus that is tied to the company's performance. Weitzman's suggestion, although not adopted by business or labor groups immediately, has attracted widespread media and political interest, especially in the United Kingdom, where in 1987 the Thatcher government enacted "Profit Related Pay" legislation giving tax relief to employees who agree to make part of their wages contingent on profits.

Obviously, Professor Weitzman's challenging ideas deserve careful consideration and further development. But even if all his assumptions are correct, it seems to me that his profit-sharing scheme would require an additional source of income in order to be palatable to labor. In the first instance, it requires wage reductions and increases in the work force that would be very frightening to those who already hold well-paying jobs. Beyond that, the scheme would create or heighten formidable new conflicts of interest that workers might well see as a threat. One of the most troublesome of those conflicts that might be heightened by the changes is that between management, which would have a new incentive to forego capital investment in favor of a more profitable labor intensive policy (see Davidson, 1985), and the present jobholders, who would resist cutting their own take-home pay in order to make jobs for outsiders. Without some substantial counterweight to these negative forces, the Weitzman scheme would appear to be politically risky, since its implementation requires massive wage reductions that could easily be characterized as anti-labor.

To make the Weitzman plan viable, I believe that workers choosing to accept profit-related wages would need to have access to a second income from ownership of shares of enterprises other than the one they work for. Therefore, universal (Type C) share ownership, which we shall discuss shortly, may be the missing link in the Weitzman plan.

Employee Convertible Debentures

The idea of Employee Convertible Debentures occurred to me after reading the winning essay in the 1985 contest, submitted by Professor Jon Wisman of American University. He suggested that we can accomplish for employee share ownership what the FHA mortgage loan guarantee program accomplished for home ownership, if we use long-term credit guaranteed by the federal government.

Debentures, like bonds, are issued by businesses in exchange for loans that pay fixed interest rates over a fixed period (e.g., a $1,000 debenture paying 7 percent interest over thirty years). *Convertible* debentures give the purchaser the option of holding the debenture to maturity (in our example, collecting $70 interest each year and then receiving the $1,000 principal back at the end of the thirty-year period) or converting the debenture into the company's common stock. The conversion price is fixed at the time the debenture is issued. Usually it is only slightly above the then market price of the common stock, so that the debenture holder can profit from any substantial future rise in the company's stock price. In our example, if the stock of the company issuing the $1,000 7 percent thirty-year debenture was then selling at $20 per share, the conversion price would probably be fixed at about $25 per share. This means that at any time during the next thirty years, the debenture holder could exchange the debenture for forty shares of the company's common stock (forty time $25 equals the $1,000 face amount of the debenture). Thus, if the company's stock rose to $50, the debenture holder could exchange the $1,000 debenture for $2,000 worth of common stock (forty shares times $50 per share).

Normally, an employee borrowing $1,000 from a bank to buy a $1,000 7 percent debenture would have to pay more than 7 percent interest on the loan. But if the government guaranteed repayment, participating banks would be able to grant loans to employees at about the same interest rate as the employees would receive on the debentures (e.g., a 7 percent loan to buy a 7 percent debenture). As shown in Table 1, if the employee receives 7 percent interest ($70) on a $1,000 thirty-year debenture each year, and pays 7 percent interest on the government-guaranteed $1,000 loan that enabled the employee to buy the debenture, the employee receives $1,014.93 more in interest than he or she pays out over thirty years, which difference is enough to defray the $1,000 principal cost of the debenture.

Column A of the table on p. 162 shows the thirty years of the debenture's life, with the middle years grouped in five-year increments for brevity of presentation.

Column B shows the principal payments of $33.33 that would be made by the employee each year to repay the $1,000 loan the employee received to buy the debenture.

Column C shows how the $33.33 principal payments reduce the unpaid balance each year. This explains why the interest payments in Column D get smaller each year.

Column D shows the interest the employee must pay each year on the unpaid balance of the original $1,000 loan, moving from $70 in the first year all the way down to $2.34, and totalling $1,085.07 over the thirty-year life of the debenture.

Column E shows the interest received by the employee each year ($70) as the holder of a $1,000 thirty-year 7 percent debenture, totalling $2,100 over the thirty years, which is slightly more than the $2,085.07 that the employee pays out ($1,000 for principal, Column B, and $1,085.07 for interest, Column D).

EMPLOYEE CONVERTIBLE DEBENTURES

Payments made and interest received on a $1,000 thirty-year 7 per-cent debenture financed through a thirty-year 7 percent government guaranteed loan.

A. Year	B. Principal Payments on $1,000 Loan	C. Unpaid Balance of $1,000 Loan Principal	D. Interest Paid on $1,000 Loan	E. Interest Received on $1,000 Debenture
1	$33.33	$1,000.00	$70.00	$70.00
2	33.33	966.67	67.67	70.00
3	33.33	933.34	65.33	70.00
4	33.33	900.01	63.00	70.00
5	33.33	866.68	60.67	70.00
6–10	166.65	700.00	268.33	350.00
11–15	166.65	533.38	210.02	350.00
16–20	166.65	366.73	151.68	350.00
21–25	166.65	200.08	93.35	350.00
26	33.33	166.75	11.67	70.00
27	33.33	133.42	9.34	70.00
28	33.33	100.09	7.00	70.00
29	33.33	66.76	4.67	70.00
30	33.43	33.43	2.43	70.00
Totals:	$1,000.00	—	$1,085.07	$2,100.00

Total received by employee (Column E) $2,100.00
Less: Total paid by employee (Columns B and D)   −2,085.07

Net to employee after payment of principal and interest: $14.93

Table 1

Use of the leverage created by such a government-guaranteed loan program could enable corporations to offer a very favorable capital acquisition program to their employees. Since these Employee Convertible Debentures (ECDs) could be convertible into the common stock of the corporation during the entire debenture term of thirty years, each employee could profit by converting if the common stock price rose above the original conversion price at any time during the thirty-year period. Each employee who bought debentures in this relatively painless way would have a continuous day-to-day interest in the company's stock price and the performance that underlies that price. Therefore, ECDs should have all of the motivating factors present in ESOPs with the added incentive that the employee is actually buying the securities with his or her own principal payments and becomes a debenture holder (and potentially a common stockholder) while active on the job, instead of having to wait for retirement as is the case in ESOP and other post-employment benefit programs.

Details such as redeemability and limits on total accumulation of ECDs would have to be worked out. The government loan guarantee need not indemnify the employees against losses, so that if a corporation that issued ECDs went into bankruptcy, the employees would still owe the unpaid balance on the debentures. Some cushioning might be desirable in such cases, since the employees would be left without the debenture interest and would be liable to the lender for both principal and interest. This risk can be minimized by limiting the ECD program to companies that register the ECDs with the SEC and deliver an appropriate prospectus to all employees. If complete revenue neutrality is required, then an insurance factor can probably be built into the loan charges at reasonable cost.

I see many potential advantages for ECDs. *The employer companies* gain access to a cheap method of financing made possible by long-term government loan guarantees, and at the same time can increase employee motivation and create a new community of interest with the workforce. The companies also eliminate the sales commissions (usually 2 to 3 percent) charged by underwriters who sell debentures to the public. For these reasons, I do not believe that any tax relief for the companies issuing ECDs would be necessary or appropriate. *For employees,* ECDs represent a low-risk method of getting a piece of the action. Over a forty-year work expectancy, each employee could buy as much as $40,000 worth of ECDs on very attractive terms. Many of them would have the opportunity to make substantial capital gains by converting at times of peak common stock prices. *For the nation,* ECDs would be an improvement over ESOPs because there would be no tax subsidies involved. ECDs would provide a method of increasing savings, spurring productivity, and moving toward a community of interest among capital, labor, and government. This is the basic formula for economic renaissance advocated by Jack Kemp, Henry Kissinger, Kevin Philips, Mario Cuomo, and Lester Thurow, among many others.

If common stock were used in such a government-guaranteed loan program, I do not believe that the results would be as favorable as in the use of ECDs. The stock would rarely pay for itself out of its own dividends, leaving the employee with the burden of paying both the purchase price of the stock and the interest on the thirty-year loan. Also, the employee would be locked in to the stock price at the time of issue each year, whereas ECDs give the employee the benefit of becoming a common stockholder at the most favorable time: when the stock price is higher than the conversion price fixed in the debenture.

While legislation would be needed to establish the government loan guarantee, ECDs comply with subsidiarity because they are voluntary for both employer and employee, and they operate at the level of the individual private-sector company. One or more states could experiment with ECDs by providing loan guarantees for local businesses, producing the trial-and-error experience that could prove the case for federal loan guarantees.

Building a Bridge from ESOP to USOP

Seven million Americans are already owners of employee shares, and ESOPs receive across-the-board political support. How, then, can we build on this foundation to achieve our goal of universal share ownership? There are no definitive answers as yet, but this is one of the topics being addressed in the USOP essay contests.

One possibility arises out of the principal shortcoming of employee ownership. ESOPs and similar plans have been criticized because they tend to put all the workers' eggs in one basket. It is not uncommon for an ESOP to be substituted for a pension plan, thus making the retirement nest egg of the employees, as well as their living standards during their working lives, dependent on the financial performance of the employing company. Commentators from the political left, right, and center have pointed out this shortcoming.

But USOPs could overcome this problem by providing that, under certain conditions, ESOP shares could be converted to USOP shares. This would give employees the lifetime security that is missing in the ESOP-type scheme. It would also make employee ownership much more saleable to employees, for then employers could bargain for the replacement of pension plans by ESOPs without endangering the workers' future security.

The convertibility feature has two important facets. First, it serves as a safety net for those employees who are depending upon ESOP shares in their retirement years; and second, it is a potential means of getting the best out of ESOPs by limiting convertibility to those plans that contain the features most likely to enhance worker productivity and security.

Mondragon: 100 Percent Worker Ownership

Firms that are entirely owned by employees also have a long history. The most successful current examples are the Mondragon worker-owned producer cooperatives in the Basque region of Spain, which have built an impressive record of successful operations since 1960, both in the growth and recession phases of the Spanish economy. The Mondragon cooperatives are the creation of a Catholic priest, Reverend José María Arizmendi, who was assigned to Mondragon in 1941 to assist the young and the poor. During the 1940s and 1950s, he taught the young of Mondragon a social doctrine that emphasized cooperation and the primacy of people over things. In 1956, several of his students who had gone on to college left their jobs to form a new company (Ulgor) to implement his teachings. Raising initial funds from the Mondragon townspeople, Ulgor opened a small paraffin stove factory employing twenty-four. Soon they converted to butane stoves and within a year they had 117 worker-owners and had bought two other foundries.

The Ulgor pioneers incorporated the enterprise as an agricultural cooperative since that was the only legal structure available. This remained true until the laws were amended in the 1970s. From this small beginning has grown a mighty industrial complex. By 1987, the Mondragon group encompassed 172 industrial, service, and consumer cooperatives, employing over 20,000 worker-owners. Most of them are small enterprises, since Mondragon learned from the Ulgor experience that 500 workers is about the optimum size for successful cooperative management. Some of the manufacturing cooperatives failed during the oil crisis (1981–1986) and some new ventures such as medical and fishing cooperatives were unsuccessful, but nobody was fired. Because Mondragon is dedicated to job creation and security, jobs for the employees of the failed ventures were found in other Mondragon cooperatives.

The Mondragon cooperatives have some unique features. Each worker-owner has one share of voting stock, regardless of the size of financial interest. The entire association of cooperatives is private, and there is no government involvement. Seventy percent of annual profits are distributed among the worker-owners in proportion to salary scale and number of years of service. Profits are not distributed in cash, but in the form of additions to capital account, on which 6 percent interest is paid annually. Ten percent of profits go to charity, and the remaining 20 percent is reinvested to create more worker-owned jobs.

A crucially important step for Mondragon was the development of its own bank, the Caja Laboral Popular, which now has 120 branches. Since its founding in a church basement in 1958, it has helped the Mondragon community to create nearly 20,000 worker-owned jobs in 100 cooperatives, while operating a successful loan business. This tradition of doing well while doing good is one of the great legacies of Father Arizmendi, who died in 1976. He did not believe that there had to be a tradeoff between equity and efficiency. In his words:

A company cannot and must not lose any of its efficiency just because human values are considered more important than purely economic or material resources within that company. On the contrary, such a consideration should help increase efficiency and quality.

Many religious organizations that have studied the Mondragon experiment find in its principles of unity, common good, and love of neighbor the seeds of a moral breakthrough in economics. Arthur Jones, Editor-at-Large of the *National Catholic Reporter,* visited Mondragon and wrote in the August 28, 1987, issue:

> For the past 31 years, Mondragon has been a crucible of experiments that have applied Catholic social teachings to everyday economic life to interweave job security with the family's needs, career training with a Gospel-based value system, a Christian-based education system with today's industrial, hi-tech needs.

While Mondragon has served as an inspiration to others seeking to promote worker-owned business, some observers believe that Mondragon will be hard to replicate in other places, pointing out the singular solidarity of the Basque people, deepened by Franco's outlawing of their language and the virtual occupation of their territory by the Spanish police. Two English authorities on worker ownership concluded:

> The Mondragon model may therefore flourish in isolated areas where strong community ties prevail and limit mobility; it is unlikely to be easily transplanted elsewhere.
>   (Bradley and Gelb, 1986, p. 70)

I do not think that the last word on Mondragon's replicability has been written, given its newness and the lack of concerted experimentation elsewhere. Surely Mondragon is worthy of intensive study by American religious organizations, especially in light of its genesis and flowering under religious auspices.

There is already an extensive bibliography on Mondragon. Some of the leading works are: Campbell, 1977; Johnson and Whyte, 1977; Oakeshott, 1978; Eaton, 1979; Thomas and Logan, 1982; Bradley and Gelb, 1983; Mollner, 1984; Whyte and Whyte, 1988.

American Producer Cooperatives

American worker-owned cooperatives have had a checkered history. Many have failed because they were not based on valid business ideas in the first place, often being the result of a desperate attempt to keep a failing enterprise alive to save the jobs involved, without regard to the foredoomed nature of the business itself. However, there are many successful worker-owned producer cooperatives, of which fifteen made *Fortune* magazine's 1986 list of the top 500 industrial companies in America. Some examples are Farmland Industries, Agway, Land O'Lakes, Ocean Spray Cranberries, and Sunkist. (For further data on American cooperatives, see Jackall and Levin, 1984; Jones and Svejnar, 1982.)

The worker-owned cooperative is strongly favored by those taking a religious approach to social justice, as evidenced by its support in the 1986 Bishops' Pastoral (Nos. 300, 301). The Bishops particularly recommend cooperative ownership in "new entrepreneurial enterprises," since it is easier to go co-op when starting a small business from scratch than trying to convert a successful going business owned by nonworkers.

While the scope of worker-owned cooperatives is limited by the relatively meager savings of the workers, there are leverage factors that may be applied to overcome this. The Mondragon bank is one example. Other ways can be found to capitalize the worker-owner's willingness to work for a little lower salary and minimize fringe benefits. Positive lessons can be learned from the experience of the Naugatuck Valley Project, which obtained great leverage from a $59,000 Campaign for Human Development grant, and the subsequent appropriation of $8 million by the Connecticut legislature to finance employee buyouts. Another model to be studied is Weirton Steel Company, which was bought by its employees through an ESOP in 1983, after its parent company threatened mass firings. The workers took 20 percent pay cuts to save their jobs and make the buyout possible. Since 1983, the workers' share of profits has largely offset their wage cuts, as Weirton became the most profitable American steel producer. Employment, reduced to below 7,000 at the time of the buyout, rose to over 8,500 in 1986.

Shareholders In America (SIA), which we discussed in Chapter Four, is an attempt to implement full cooperative ownership from the beginning of a new entrepreneurial enterprise with the help of a stream of income in the form of patronage from major successful companies, without government intervention.

Type B Ownership: Savings-Based

One of the earliest savings-based plans to broaden stock ownership was the Capital Formation Plan developed by the Sabre Foundation (McClaughry, 1972). It was designed to stimulate greater use of equity financing and to encourage people with low or middle incomes to purchase shares through tax incentives. Specifically, the plan proposed that all people with annual incomes below $20,000 could take a tax deduction for the amount they invested in corporate stock up to $3,000. To encourage firms to engage in greater equity financing, a split rate corporate income tax schedule would be adopted, through which retained earnings would be taxed much more heavily than those that are distributed. To encourage companies to sell their new equity issues to the capital formation funds (CFF) from which the individuals would buy their diversified stock portfolio, dividends paid on shares sold to a CFF would be tax-deductible. The revenue loss to the Treasury, though substantial in the early years, would be gradually offset by the increased income taxes on dividends received and also by the reduction in the amount of interest deductions taken by companies.

In some respects, the Capital Formation Plan resembles the French Loi Monory, or Monory Laws, named after the scheme established by French Finance Minister Rene Monory in 1978. Basically, the Loi Monory is a form of tax incentive to encourage individuals to invest in equities either directly or through specifically designed funds. The objectives were to improve the equity base of the corporate sector, especially in the face of rising interest rates that inhibited capital expenditures; to strengthen the role of the stock market; to lure the private investor away from traditional investments such as savings banks and building society accounts — which are basically short-term investments — toward a long-term commitment to trade and industry; and to reverse the ever-increasing percentage of share ownership gobbled up by institutions as opposed to individuals.

Under the original 1978 scheme, each French household was allowed to deduct from taxable income up to 5,000 francs per year of new net investment in shares of French companies. Individuals could buy shares directly through the Bourse (the French stock exchange), or units in specially designated funds called Monory Sicavs, provided the funds maintained at least 60 percent of their portfolio in French equities. In 1983, this scheme was succeeded by one known as the Loi Delors, under which the tax credit was reduced to 25 percent of purchase price, but its limits were increased from 5,000 to 10,000 French francs, with an allowance of 14,000 francs for a married couple. In order to qualify, the investment must be a fresh one rather than based on proceeds of sale of shares in an existing portfolio. The investment must be held for at least four years.

The Loi Monory and similar plans in Belgium, Sweden, and Norway have been fairly successful in adding new shareholders, increasing equity investment in business, and causing share prices to rise. In Great Britain, the Thatcher government introduced the Personal Equity Plan (PEP) in 1987. It allows everyone aged eighteen and over to invest up to $2400 a year in a PEP. If the shares are held for two years, capital gains and reinvested dividends will be free of tax for so long as the investor retains his or her PEP investment.

The Capital Formation Plan was the basis for legislation proposed by President Gerald Ford in 1976; the new plan was known as BSOP (Broadened Stock Ownership Plan). The general idea of BSOP was to allow every person a tax deduction of up to 15 percent of earned income, with a maximum deduction of $1,500, for buying shares that would be held for a minimum of seven years. The maximum deduction of $1,500 would be available only to those with earned income below $20,000. For those with income from $20,000 to $40,000, the benefits would gradually reduce, reaching zero at $40,000. If the shares were held for seven years and then sold, the proceeds would be taxed as capital gains; but if any were sold before seven years, gains would be taxed as ordinary income.

Some critics dubbed BSOP "the Stockbrokers' Relief Act of 1976," since it would increase sales of shares and probably drive up the market price because more people would bid against each other for the existing public supply of shares, and then they would be holding on to these shares for seven years to get the tax advantages of BSOP. Other critics of BSOP said that it probably would not result in new savings but would merely shift savings from bank accounts into the stock market. BSOP, in any event, did not capture the imagination of Congress. It was voted down by the Senate in 1976.

The Individual Retirement Account (IRA), enacted by Congress in 1982, has some of the attributes of the Capital Formation Plan. Tax-deductible contributions were limited to the lesser of 15 percent of earnings or $2,000 per year. However, unlike the Capital Formation Plan, no distribution can be made from an IRA until the person establishing the account dies, is disabled, or reaches age 59 1/2. Under the Tax Reform Act of 1986, the tax-deductibility of IRA contributions was limited to those individuals who are not covered by any other qualified plan established by an employer. The earnings of all IRAs are still tax-free until paid over to the beneficiary.

We also have the Keogh Plan, a form of qualified retirement plan covering self-employed individuals, who may contribute up to 15 percent of net earnings to a maximum of $7,500 per year on a tax-deductible basis.

Plans to stimulate the purchase of shares through tax relief have some merit, but obviously they benefit only those who have savings and so they really represent tax benefits for the sector of our society that is well-off compared to those in poverty. Nevertheless, such plans contain some elements that could be worked into the ideal plan for universal capital ownership, and so we must study them for that purpose.

Type C Ownership:
Universal Share Ownership Plans (USOPs)

We now come to the type of expanded ownership that is at once the most difficult to work out and potentially the most rewarding: Universal Share Ownership Plans (or Citizen Share Ownership Plans, as they are known in Great Britain). No such plans are in operation, with the exception of a tiny model in the Canadian province of British Columbia (discussed below under "Privatization").

The first form of USOP we will examine is one designed by me, derived from the writings of Louis Kelso and the ideas of others, including the Joint Economic Committee of Congress. Originally I called this plan SuperStock. More modestly, I have also called it the Kitty Hawk Plan of universal share ownership, in recognition of its primitive nature and in the hope that it will eventually soar like the invention of the Wright brothers. I propose it as one possible starting point in the search for an ideal USOP, rather than as *the* ideal plan itself.

The SuperStock (or Kitty Hawk) Model

Is there anything inherent in capitalism that would prevent us from spreading ownership of the means of production to all of our people? You will search in vain for any such restriction in the Constitution or laws of the United States. Yet most economists, even liberals, have not opened their minds to such a concept. There is no reason why capitalism cannot function when the means of production are owned by the majority rather than a minority. In fact, if we could find a way to open ownership of the means of production to all Americans, we could make our economic system consistent with our political democracy and our concept of fairness.

One possible way to make capitalism work for everyone is the plan I call SuperStock. Its purpose is to spread ownership of newly formed capital through society, enabling the noncapitalist 94 percent to derive income from direct participation in capitalism. Because its purpose is to spread *newly formed capital,* there would be no confiscation of wealth and no need for new taxes.

The Hidden Reservoir

There is a vast hidden reservoir of unowned wealth in this country, in the form of the *new capital* created each year by American business. This hidden reservoir of wealth could be the source of a substantial amount of income for those Americans who presently own little or no capital. (Capital, in this context, does not refer to money, but rather to the plants and equipment that companies build or buy every year.)

Financial people call this new capital "self-liquidating." It is designed to *pay for itself* out of the increased profits flowing from expanded production. So, for example, the cost of constructing a new automobile factory will be covered by the sale of new cars rolling off the factory's assembly line.

This new capital is designed to pay for itself *regardless of who owns it*: a wealthy investor, a struggling janitor, even a Teddy Bear (see Figure 1). In theory, then, anyone could become an owner of this new capital — *if* he or she were extended the necessary credit with which to purchase shares of stock in the companies creating the capital. In practice, however, credit for the purchase of stock or other income-producing capital is available only to those who already have savings or other holdings — those who can provide good collateral for loans.

In 1986, American business invested over $300 billion in the construction and purchase of new plants and equipment. Under our present system, 95 percent of these new capital expenditures are paid for by a combination of debt (loans or bonds) and internal funds; 5 percent is financed through the issuance of new common stock. The main vice of this system is that it perpetuates the overconcentration of capital ownership. Billions of dollars are kept bottled up in the corporations for capital expenditures. Wealthy stockholders believe this practice serves their interests, for they would otherwise have to pay income taxes on substantial dividend income. They prefer to have this money remain in corporate coffers where the value of their holdings can increase untaxed.

Even the 5 percent of capital expenditures that is paid for by the issuance of new stock can be owned only by those who have cash savings or credit. As long as this system remains intact, so too will the process of concentrating ownership of the means of production in the hands of a mere 6 percent of the population. Expanding employee ownership (Type A) will not reduce this concentration significantly. There is, however, nothing sacred or immutable about this system. It is simply one method — and not necessarily the best method — of financing a modern economy.

Outline of the SuperStock Plan

SuperStock is one possible way of reversing this overconcentration. It is designed to make stock ownership in America's

Figure 1: *The Teddy Bear Principle: Access to long-term credit determines who will own income-producing capital. This principle is used in Super-Stock, and may also be used in other ownership plans, such as Employee Convertible Debentures and the National Mutual Fund.*

2,000 leading corporations available to everyone through a system that would funnel ownership of new capital directly to the 50 million families or households that now own little or no capital. To understand how it would work, let's take as a case in point the fictitious Peerless Pizza Parlors Corporation, which we shall imagine as one of the nation's 2,000 leading corporations. Let us assume that Peerless is building a new $10 million plant to meet increased demand for its new pizza oven. Thus Peerless is creating $10 million worth of new capital *that is not presently owned by anyone* and that will *pay for itself* over time through the increased production and sale of pizza pies.

Under our present corporate system, Peerless would finance such an expansion primarily through internal funds and debt, which automatically funnels ownership of 95 percent of the new capital into the hands of the current Peerless shareholders. At the heart of the present system, then, is a mechanism for producing capital ownership that has been employed for centuries by wealthy individuals and businesses: *long-term credit.* At the heart of SuperStock is the same mechanism, but with one key difference: now long-term credit will be extended to the noncapitalists, under our Teddy Bear principle (Figure 1).

Let's assume you are one of the noncapitalists. Here is how SuperStock would make you a capitalist:

Financing new capital. Under the new federal legislation adopting SuperStock, Peerless will not pay for its new plant through internal funds or debt. Rather, it will be induced or required to finance its capital growth by issuing $10 million worth of a special type of stock, to be known as SuperStock shares. This stock will not be available to the 6 percent of Americans who already own a substantial number of shares. Instead, you and the rest of the noncapitalist 94 percent will be able to acquire a given number of SuperStock shares.

How do you pay for the SuperStock shares? You don't. A loan will be arranged to provide the money needed to pay Peerless for the stock — and eventually the stock will pay for itself, out of its own earnings (Figure 1).

The loan. SuperStock legislation will establish a government-guaranteed long-term loan program. In effect, *you* will be using the credit power of Peerless to acquire shares of its stock — just as Peerless now uses its credit power to acquire further capital ownership for its present shareholders.

A bank loan of $10 million will be arranged to provide Peerless with the entire cost of the new plant; Peerless will then issue $10 million worth of stock. But the loan will not be owed by you or by Peerless. It will be owed by the SuperStock fund. Until the loan has been repaid, the Peerless shares earmarked for your account will be held in escrow by the bank that made the $10 million loan.

Repayment. The SuperStock legislation requires Peerless and the rest of the 2,000 participating companies to pay out all their earnings as dividends (except those reserves actually needed to run the company). It also exempts Peerless from the federal corporate income taxes on those earnings. Thus, as Peerless begins to realize higher profits from the output of the pizza machines made in the new factory, these profits will be turned into higher dividends which are used to pay for the SuperStock shares issued to you. For a number of years, these dividends will be paid directly to the bank, until such time as it has recouped its $10 million loan plus interest. Then you become the outright owner of your SuperStock shares, and you will receive all future dividends directly. Thus, the new SuperStock system ensures that Peerless's $10 million worth of new capital is owned by those who previously had no real access to capital ownership.

The 2,000 Participating Companies

I have oversimplified SuperStock to give you a bird's-eye view from the standpoint of a single company, Peerless Pizza. Actually, it is designed as a group plan, involving at the start America's 2,000 leading companies, such as General Motors, IBM, ATT, Xerox, and Exxon. These are the companies that every year create most of America's $384 billion of new capital (which I rounded off to $300 billion above to represent the expenditures of these major companies).

To pay for this capital, each company would issue shares of its stock at market value. Each year these shares would be pooled in a sort of mutual fund, with each company contributing to the pool the number of shares needed to pay for its new capital expenditures. Shares would be parcelled out to those families and households eligible for the SuperStock program. Every SuperStockholder would receive a piece of every participating company; there would be no big losers if one of the 2,000 companies did poorly.

Eventually, we should be able to include smaller companies in the SuperStock system. But we begin with our 2,000 largest successful companies because we are trying to plug our neediest people into the strongest sector of our economy.

Role of Government

Apart from administrative functions, the government's primary role in the SuperStock program would be (1) to induce or order our 2,000 leading companies to issue stock in payment for their new capital additions, and (2) to guarantee the loans the banks would make to pay for SuperStock shares.

Obviously, it would be preferable to provide inducements for voluntary participation by the 2,000 leading companies. But if you're wondering whether Congress has the power to order them to issue stock in payment for their new capital additions, the answer is yes. Back in 1937, the U.S. Supreme Court decided that Congress, by virtue of its power to provide for the general welfare, could require companies to make Social Security contributions for their employees. Thus, if Congress decided that a national policy of capital ownership would promote the general welfare of the American people, it would have the constitutional power to enact the necessary legislation.

There are also precedents for government guarantees of long-term credit. Following in the footsteps of the FHA mortgage program, World War II veterans were able to secure government-guaranteed low-interest home mortgages under the G.I. Bill of Rights. Certainly, if the government can guarantee loans for nonproductive items like homes, it should be able to guarantee loans for capital outlays that are both productive and self-liquidating.

Who Would Receive SuperStock Shares?

There would be a lot of tough decisions for Congress to make in establishing the priorities for access to SuperStock. We might start by excluding all households whose current net worth equals $100,000 or more. Or we could establish a point system for eligibility. Points could be awarded for low wages, lack of savings or capital ownership, physical disability, and many other criteria. As we have seen, handing out valuable shares is not politically feasible, so those eligible would have to *earn* their shares. This opens the way for accomplishing the work of humanity, paying for it by issuance of SuperStock. Other experimental programs, such as the Weitzman plan, could be paid for partially by Super-Stock, and ESOP shares might be made convertible into Super-stock. We could also test the concept of including "ownwork," child rearing, and household chores in the work of humanity, thus providing new support for family integrity.

Once eligibility has been determined, how much could Super-Stock shareholders actually expect to receive in stock and income? According to consensus projections, American business will create at least $5 trillion worth of new capital over the next twenty years. If that figure is divided among the 50 million households (out of 86 million) that presently own little or no capital, each household would receive $100,000 worth of Super-Stock shares. So at the current pretax return rate of 15 to 20 percent on invested capital, each household could expect to receive about $15,000 to $20,000 in dividends per year (after their SuperStock shares have paid for themselves).

Would a guaranteed yearly income of $15,000 to $20,000 impair the incentive to work? Perhaps. To prevent this, we might make participation contingent on continuing to work, including performance of society's unwanted tasks by those who do not have regular jobs.

Restrictions on Shareholders

SuperStock is designed to provide income that eventually would perform the functions of Social Security, welfare, and other transfer payments. Since SuperStock shares would be issued to a lot of people who have no experience in ownership of capital, we would have to put restrictions on the right to borrow against it or sell it, so that the recipients could neither squander it nor be cheated out of it. Here we can learn a lesson from the Homestead Act, under which the federal government gave out ownership of over 250 million acres of public land — only to see most of it bought up by commercial interests after the five-year residence requirement had been met.

The question of voting rights is more difficult. SuperStock would be structured like a mutual fund, and the holders of such fund certificates do not have any voting rights in the companies whose shares the mutual fund purchased. Furthermore, the immediate purpose of SuperStock is to heal our economically divided society by using stock ownership to make income distribution more equitable. Thus, it would seem that voting rights are not required to achieve that purpose. Obviously, voting rights would make SuperStock legislation more difficult to enact, since the plan would be seen as a threat to corporate management. Nevertheless, many people who otherwise approve of Super-Stock would question its suitability without voting rights. This problem could be solved in the manner of the established mutual funds, by creating a national SuperStock Board of Trustees which would be elected by the SuperStock shareholders. This Board in turn could be empowered to elect one or more directors of the 2,000 companies constituting the SuperStock fund.

Other Problems of SuperStock

While the steps in the SuperStock plan are fairly simple to visualize, the ramifications are complex because it has the power to make many deep changes in our society. Apart from the knotty problems relating to earning the shares, maintaining the work ethic, eligibility, transferability, and voting rights, there is the key question of whether the 2,000 leading companies should be *required* to participate. Under our subsidiarity principle and the laws of practical politics, it would be much preferable if they could be induced to participate voluntarily, in exchange for elimination of the corporate income tax (which would not be needed by the Treasury if all earnings were paid out as dividends and were taxable to the shareholder-recipients) and gradual reduction of the employers' Social Security contributions, to the extent that Social Security is replaced by SuperStock dividends. The participating companies could advertise their participation and promote consumer preference for "equal ownership" organizations. They would also benefit from a larger market for their products and services through the increased purchasing power of the USOP shareholders, and the overall advantages of changing an army of welfare recipients to corporate shareholders. They would also reduce debt and thus have lower interest obligations.

All these questions, together with possible effects of Super-Stock on the economy and various interest groups, are discussed in detail in *The USOP Handbook,* the guidebook for the American and British essay contexts of 1986 (Speiser, 1986, Chapters 3, 4, 6, and 7). The economic feasibility of SuperStock is also discussed (Chapter 5), and the findings of the 1977 seminar at the Brookings Institution, as well as the articles by Professors Paul Davidson and Robert Lekachman, are reprinted in the appendix.

SuperStock as a Starting Point

After more than a decade of immersion in this subject, I remain convinced that SuperStock, while not a complete or ideal plan, is worthy of consideration as a starting point in the design of the ideal USOP. I believe this because I think SuperStock is consistent with America's greatest traditions, both liberal and conservative; it can achieve the vital goal of increasing productivity by facilitating savings and investment in new plants and equipment; it provides a more logical and humane substitute for our outmoded welfare system; it opens the way for the work of humanity; it increases the incentives and support for family integrity; and it can be integrated with other plans to achieve much wider employment and a more equitable society, bringing us closer to the economic counterpart of political democracy.

Nevertheless, I believe that we can design and implement a Universal Share Ownership Plan without using SuperStock. There are other ways to do it, some of which are discussed below. Whatever approach is taken, I think that the Teddy Bear principle of democratizing access to self-liquidating long-term credit, even if totally divorced from SuperStock, is a very useful tool that can make achievement of USOP much easier. At the moment, it is being used widely by some of the most successful Wall Street entrepreneurs, under the label of "Leveraged Buyout" (LBO). Formerly known by the more descriptive title of "bootstrap financing," the typical LBO will involve a few top executives of a large corporation (or even outsiders) who want to take over ownership for themselves, using the income-producing assets of the company as collateral for huge loans with which to buy out the present shareholders. LBOs do not create jobs, raise profits, increase production, or improve management. Yet our lenders have made billions of dollars available for LBOs, and few questions have been raised about the legitimacy of using assets of major companies to create huge profits out of mere paper transactions.

The Teddy Bear principle, if used in a USOP, would put the credit power of our major companies to work for the 50 million noncapitalist households instead of the handful of wealthy people who benefit from LBOs. Indeed, LBOs themselves could be used to create stock ownership for the poor instead of aggravating overconcentration of wealth. Proponents of LBOs justify them by claiming that they challenge or remove complacent managers who are not maximizing share values. This objective could be accomplished without limiting the benefits to a few rich people who seize control of the companies' credit power. LBOs could just as well be organized so that the credit power is used to spread ownership to disadvantaged families, since in either case the leveraging loans will be repaid from the companies' assets and profits rather than by those who become shareholders.

Work Sharing Combined with SuperStock

A fully implemented SuperStock plan would capture the entire reservoir of the $300 billion annual capital expenditure and spread its ownership among the 50 million disadvantaged families. But, as we have seen, there are political obstacles to such a sweeping change, and implementation would probably have to start much more modestly. For example, we could focus initially on only 20 percent of the $300 billion annual capital expenditure and combine it with a work-sharing scheme. Suppose that we went to a four-day work week in certain appropriate occupations, such as those paying less than $25,000 per year. This four-day work week would produce only four days' pay, and so we would have to make up the missing 20 percent of the paycheck. This could be accomplished by the dividends on the USOP shares created by our mini-SuperStock plan. To earn these shares, USOP stockholders would perform the work of humanity for one day each week. If all of this worked out, we could increase employment by as much as 20 percent without decreasing anyone's wages; we could accomplish some of the work of humanity; and we could make a start on the road to universal share ownership.

Universal Share Ownership Plans
Suggested in the Essay Contests

In the 1985 and 1986 essay contests, the entrants were free to discuss SuperStock, modify it, or discard it and suggest their own form of Universal Share Ownership Plans. Therefore, we shall now shift from "SuperStock" to "USOPs" since the Superstock label applies only to the plan that I have just described.

The winning 1985 essay, written by American University Professor Jon D. Wisman, made the major innovation of relating broadened stock ownership to the type of credit guarantee afforded by the federal government under the Federal Housing Administration loan-guarantee programs. It was the Wisman essay that led to the idea of using FHA-type financing for Employee Convertible Debentures, discussed above. The Wisman essay is reprinted in full in K. Taylor, 1987.

The 1986 contests in the United States and Great Britain yielded more new ideas for USOPs, reprinted in Speiser, 1988. The American first prize winner, University of Kansas Professor David Burress, embraced the democratic consensus and the idea of the common good, which he found to be the basis of the SuperStock plan, but he found some technical deficiencies, which he proceeded to correct in his paper (Burress, 1988). He criticized details of the plan's execution, and suggested modifications that would control inflation, limit inefficient investment choices, and avoid reduction of government revenues. He also addressed the political strategy of providing adequate incentives for enlisting the support of business managers; the importance of voluntary participation by corporations; the need for monetary policy to control inflationary pressures; and the desirability of competitive allocation of USOP investments. His scholarly paper has advanced the prospects for a feasible USOP. In his own words, he sought to move USOPs forward from Kitty Hawk to the Spirit of St. Louis.

The second-prize winner in 1986, Villanova University Professor Kenneth B. Taylor, based his paper on a form of USOP that he calls "The Common Fund." His goal was to design a new social policy incorporating equity, efficiency, and elimination of the present social welfare apparatus. As part of his research for the paper, he assumed the existence of a SuperStock-type plan and made a computerized simulation of its five-year effects on two major companies, General Electric and DuPont. He found that the general idea of SuperStock would be feasible, with important modifications that are detailed in his essay. He designed the Common Fund plan to enhance management decision-making flexibility, retaining the traditional corporate objectives and leaving the stock market position unaffected. Taylor also made use of the Shareholders In America (SIA) concept, and he carried the program through an eleven-year computer simulation to reach the point where the Common Fund would replace Social Security and welfare (Taylor, 1988).

Third prize was won by the Reverend John A. Sedlak, a Roman Catholic priest in Greensburg, Pennsylvania, where he serves on the Diocesan Peace and Justice Commission. Father Sedlak's paper concentrated on the importance of relating USOP to work, for religious as well as economic reasons. His plan would replace Social Security and other retirement programs with individual stock ownership and would supplant most of welfare with guaranteed work opportunity. Guaranteed minimum wage jobs — one per household where no one is otherwise able to find full-time employment — would be funded largely from monies no longer needed for welfare and from revenues formerly applied to Social Security and other compulsorily-funded retirement programs. Using a modified version of Super-Stock to establish a revolving national stock fund, he proposes that this stock be awarded to U.S. citizens to supplement their wages and to build their individual retirement portfolios. Additionally, his plan would annually award stock to disabled citizens; to full-time students in college or technical schools; and, reflecting Father Sedlak's concern for nurturing stable families, to either nonemployed parent with the full-time job of raising children under eighteen years of age within the home.

In addition to the three prize winners, there were dozens of other useful papers submitted. More than twenty 1986 U.S. essays are reprinted or summarized in the CIPA book (Speiser, 1988). For example, Shann Turnbull, a management consultant in Sydney, Australia, submitted an essay based on his long-

standing work on a cooperative land bank and other innovations for broadening ownership, which are detailed in his book,
Democratising the Wealth of Nations (Turnbull, 1975). And Oscar B. Johannsen, Executive Director of the Robert Schelken-
bach Foundation in New York City, contributed one entitled
"Land Based Shares," in which he proposed that title to more
than 600 million acres of federally-owned lands in thirteen western states be given to thirteen separate "public" corporations.
Shares of these corporations would be given to every living
American, to revert to the corporations after the death of each
shareholder. The corporations would lease the lands to the highest bidder and would receive income from the leases and from
the natural resources on the lands. This income would be paid
to all Americans as dividends on their Land Based Shares.

Robert A. Carlton of Rochester, New York, did not submit
a formal essay, but he made a valuable contribution after reading the contest material. He suggested that the federal government should elicit a *quid pro quo* for various forms of assistance
to business, by requiring the beneficiary businesses to issue an
appropriate number of their shares to a USOP that would be
owned by all Americans. For example, government funding of
research and development projects should stipulate that profits
derived from such research should be "shared by the people of
the United States as part of the USOP pool." And when the government bails out a failing company (e.g., Chrysler, Lockheed,
Continental Illinois) or an entire industry (e.g., semiconductors)
the USOP pool should receive shares of the companies involved
to compensate for that government assistance.

Likewise, there were many excellent papers in the 1986 British essay competition, administered by the Wider Share Ownership Council. An essay submitted by Susan Potterton proposed
a National Social Work Scheme that would contain many of the
features of Senator Simon's Guaranteed Job Opportunity Program, as well as the Shareholders In America (SIA) approach
to community development. Her plan would assign to the unemployed, the handicapped, the housewife, and the pensioner
social work that is not presently carried out, creating a pool
of shares to pay for such work and allowing these shares to be
traded in the normal way (Potterton, 1988). Her essay antici-
pated the object of the 1988 essay competition: "How can we

use share ownership to alleviate the problems of unemployment, under-employment, and below-poverty-level wages?"

Another British entry, by Jack B. Grant of Glasgow, proposed a USOP-type experiment in the depressed Easterhouse district of Glasgow (Grant, 1988). Grant is trying to activate his Easterhouse USOP as a real-life experiment.

The results of the 1985 and 1986 essay contests were very gratifying. The outpouring of support for the concept of universal share ownership was combined with a very high standard of scholarship, three of the first four American prizes being taken by university professors of economics. Then came the kind offer of Professor Kenneth B. Taylor to edit a volume based on the 1985 entries, and his agreement to assist me in compiling a similar volume based on the 1986 essays. We have decided to continue the essay competition every two years (beginning in 1988) under the sponsorship of the Council on International and Public Affairs in the United States and the Wider Share Ownership Council in Great Britain, giving us time to digest the entries and publish a book based on the leading essays. This will give future essayists access to the past scholarship, thus multiplying our cumulative knowledge.

Progress in the difficult area of Type C Ownership must be measured now in intellectual terms. We cannot expect real political progress until we have done the intellectual spadework required to move ahead from the Kitty Hawk-Spirit of St. Louis era. Religious organizations can expedite this progress by sponsoring similar essay contests, especially through affiliated universities and publications.

The National Mutual Fund

The National Mutual Fund (NMF) was introduced by James S. Albus in *Peoples' Capitalism* (Albus, 1976). Dr. Albus, an internationally recognized authority on industrial robotics with the National Bureau of Standards, proposes creation of NMF as a semiprivate investment company. NMF would use money borrowed from the Federal Reserve to make stock and bond purchases from private industry. This increased availability of investment funds would stimulate the economy and increase productivity. Profits from these investments would be paid to the general public in the form of dividends, making every adult citizen a capitalist to that extent.

Albus estimates that per capita income from the NMF could reach $6,000 to $10,000 a year within sixteen years, assuming reasonably successful investment of sufficient capital. At a dividend rate of 15 percent per year on invested capital, a total investment of around $9 trillion would be needed. In order to accumulate this amount within sixteen years, the NMF would have to invest enough to raise the United States investment rate to a level comparable with that of Japan, i.e., from the current U.S. rate of about 10 percent of GNP (about $300 billion per year) to almost 30 percent of GNP (about $900 billion per year). Albus suggests that the NMF ramp up its investment rate to $600 billion per year over a period of seven years, and then continue to invest at about 20 percent of GNP thereafter. He predicts that the resulting investment rate would produce productivity growth, and hence real growth in GNP, of about 9 percent per year. The cumulative effect would produce the required total investment of $9 trillion within sixteen years.

Of course, if the NMF were to raise investment by $600 billion per year through borrowing alone, it would create strong inflationary pressures due to growth in the money supply. To counteract this, Albus designed a "demand regulation policy" through which savings from consumers would be temporarily withheld in order to prevent disposable income from rising before productivity gains from NMF investments were actually realized. This mandatory savings plan would be designed so that low-income people would be less affected, and they would earn interest in excess of current inflation. Savings withheld from consumer income would go into industrial development bonds to be used by the National Mutual Fund for investment. This would reduce the requirement for NMF funding by direct loans from the Federal Reserve Bank, and counteract the inflationary impact of NMF investments.

Albus's concept has been supported by the Social Credit movement in Great Britain and New Zealand. His book, *Peoples' Capitalism,* is well worth reading and his National Mutual Fund deserves careful consideration. It is another form of USOP that uses the Teddy Bear principle (Figure 1), and it has some advantages over SuperStock. It would not change the way that large companies finance future growth, because each company would have the choice of selling or not selling its shares to the NMF. Therefore, it would attract more support from the business community than would SuperStock. There are elements of the NMF that could be combined with some features of SuperStock, especially as SuperStock has been modified in the 1985 and 1986 essay contests.

The NMF reflects the strong religious commitment of Dr. Albus. He designed a painting for the cover of his book, *Peoples' Capitalism,* which portrays social justice elements of the Old and New Testaments. He also states in the preface:

> Peoples' Capitalism is a political program which attempts to anticipate the scope of the coming robot revolution and to subject its enormous productive power to the influence of the ancient Judeo-Christian precepts.
>
> (Albus, 1976, p. ii)

The Albus NMF proposal is discussed in more detail in Speiser, 1988. For further information, write to: Dr. James S. Albus, 9520 W. Stanhope Road, Kensington, MD 20895.

The National Dividend Plan

The National Dividend Plan was first proposed by Florida industrialist John H. Perry, Jr., in his book, *The National Dividend* (Perry, 1964). Perry has refined the plan during the last twenty years and has spent over $7 million promoting it. The thrust of the plan is to take the collections from the corporate income tax and place them in a National Dividend Trust Fund. From this fund, a yearly check would be issued to every registered voter, once the federal budget is balanced. These dividends would be tax-free. Every year that the budget fell out of balance and into deficit, the money in the National Dividend Trust Fund would be used to reduce the deficit instead of being distributed to the registered voters. This would give every voter a vested interest in resisting federal deficits — no balanced budget, no national dividend check.

For our purposes, the plan need not be tied to the separate issue of the balanced budget. We could consider the possibility

of collecting the corporate income tax and paying it out to the
registered voters in equal shares. This would give each voter
approximately $400 to $500 per year, since there are about 110
million registered American voters, and the corporate income
tax raises about $50 billion per year. In my opinion, this would
not accomplish any of the major purposes of USOP, other than a
token step toward allowing disadvantaged people to share in the
profits earned by corporate giants. But it has the advantage of
simplicity, and it might be a way of opening the door to USOP.
Certainly John Perry is to be commended for his dedication to
the difficult task of promoting economic change.

For further information, write to: John H. Perry, Jr., Americans for the National Dividend Act, Inc., 1901 N. Ft. Myer
Drive, 12th Floor, Rosslyn, VA 22209.

Privatization

Privatization — the sale of government-owned assets and services that could be owned and operated privately — has come
into vogue throughout the world during the 1980s. This movement was led by the Conservative British government of Margaret Thatcher, which in its first six years returned twelve major
state-owned companies to the private sector, including British
Aerospace, Brit Oil, Jaguar cars, and British Telecom. After
France turned out the socialist Mitterand government it too privatized many formerly nationalized companies. Other nations
in Europe and Africa have followed suit. Unfortunately, this has
been done by selling shares in the public market, instead of using
these nationalized companies as reservoirs for spreading ownership by distributing shares to all citizens. The latter course —
using privatization as a means of creating universal share ownership — is favored by Samuel Brittan, chief economic commentator for London's *Financial Times* (Brittan, 1983, 1984a,
1984b, 1985), on the grounds that these companies are actually
owned by all the people, and distributing shares in them is much
more equitable than reducing taxes of the wealthy by selling the
shares for the account of the national treasury. Under Thatcher's
version, privatization serves only the cause of efficiency; under
Brittan's, it could serve equity as well.

While the United States has no exact counterpart of the

British nationalized companies, it does have "national assets" that some American conservatives believe would be better operated by the private sector. This is the theme of *Privatizing Federal Spending: A Strategy to Eliminate the Deficit* by Stuart M. Butler, director of domestic policy studies at the Heritage Foundation in Washington, D.C. (Butler, 1985). Some of Butler's leading candidates for privatization are the postal service, public housing, the Amtrak railroad system, and the air traffic control system. Butler's views were largely endorsed by President Reagan's Commission on Privatization in its final report, issued in March of 1988 (Linowes, 1988). The commission, chaired by University of Illinois Professor David F. Linowes, also recommended sale of the Naval Petroleum Reserves at Elk Hills, California, and Teapot Dome, Wyoming. While the Linowes report suggests that Employee Stock Ownership Plans be used extensively in privatization (especially as a means of gaining the support of the present government employees) it does not mention the privatization method that we are discussing here: distribution of shares in privatized companies to the public at large.

Canada's third largest province, British Columbia, furnishes a model for the use of USOPs in privatization. The New Democratic Party held office in British Columbia from 1972 to 1975, during which it bought substantial shares of several leading local natural resource companies. But British Columbia voters, disenchanted with the socialist bent of the New Democrats, voted them out in 1975 and elected as prime minister William R. Bennett, leader of the Social Credit Party and the millionaire son of a previous British Columbia prime minister. Bennett, known as a champion of free enterprise, decided to privatize the natural resource companies owned by the province, but instead of selling off the shares to the lucky few who had the savings to pay for them, he came up with a new idea. He organized British Columbia Resources Investment Corporation (BCRIC) to hold the shares of the natural resource companies, and he pushed through legislation that provided for distribution of 80 percent of its shares on an equal basis to every adult citizen of British Columbia. Each citizen received five shares. In addition, BCRIC offered shares for sale to the public, which scooped them up enthusiastically.

BCRIC took over government-owned assets worth several hundred million dollars and raised nearly $500 million through sales of additional shares. Of special significance is the fact that Premier Bennett is known as a pro-business conservative. He seized the opportunity to make every citizen of his province a capitalist. Historically, British Columbia has experienced bitter class divisions going back to the early years of the century when radical labor leaders such as Joe Hill and Big Bill Haywood were organizing workers. Even today, British Columbia has a higher proportion of unionized workers than any other Canadian province.

The gift of five shares each went to some 2.4 million Canadian citizens who resided in British Columbia for at least the immediately preceding twelve months. Application forms were handled by credit unions, banks, investment dealers, trust companies, and other financial institutions. All those eligible for free common shares were also permitted to buy up to 5,000 shares at $6 per share, the public offering price fixed in June 1979. The initial Board of Directors included the chairman of Okanagan Helicopters, Ltd., the chairmen respectively of a bank, a development company, a department store chain, and a tractor manufacturing company, and a barrister-solicitor. There are no government representatives on the board or in management.

In announcing the distribution of free shares on January 11, 1979, Premier Bennett said:

> It is a unique, once-in-a-lifetime opportunity for the greatest number of people to become owners, not tenants in our land.... We want people to be able to see and feel their ownership in the form of tangible share certificates. This share ownership will bring home to everyone, and particularly those who have never owned shares before, the value of ownership which can pay rich personal dividends.... Too often we hear that only the wealthy and privileged have a chance to enjoy such an opportunity. Now every resident of our province has a chance to get a piece of the action.

The prospectus states, "In order to significantly reduce registration costs, voting and registration rights are restricted to share holdings of 100 shares or more." This means that the free shares, while common shares, do not have voting power, since each recipient got only five shares. However, all shares are freely transferable. The shares that were distributed free to all citizens are called "bearer" shares and can be transferred like bearer bonds.

In 1984, BCRIC established a Shareholder Liaison Committee, chosen from a list of more than 1,700 names nominated by BCRIC shareholders. The Committee visits company operations and meets with company management at least twice a year, at which time the Committee members report the concerns and questions of shareholders. For further information on BCRIC, write to: British Columbia Resources Investment Corp., 1176 West Georgia St., Vancouver, B.C. V6E 4B9, Canada.

Kelso's New Ownership Plans

In 1986, Louis Kelso and his wife, Patricia Hetter Kelso, published *Democracy and Economic Power: Extending the ESOP Revolution* to chronicle the success of ESOPs and to outline some new plans that could lead to much broader distribution of capital ownership than ESOPs (Kelso, 1986). In all, the Kelsos identify eight financing tools designed to "redemocratize the U.S. economy," of which only the ESOP "has gained some visibility in the business world. Its growing acceptance should make it easier to introduce the others" (p. 59). They present a broader concept of ESOPs, with the federal reserve system being called upon to monetize the ESOP program by discounting notes that would be used to buy stock. Then the Kelsos go on to suggest the following new plans:

The Mutual Stock Ownership Plan (MUSOP) would be used to pool the shares of several corporations, each of which is too small to afford the professional and administrative costs of a properly prepared ESOP. MUSOPs could be local, regional, or even national, thus furthering the development of ESOPs in smaller companies.

The Consumer Stock Ownership Plan (CSOP) is "the capitalist equivalent of the socialist-derived producer cooperative," modeled after Louis Kelso's success with Valley Nitrogen Producers Inc., a chemical fertilizer manufacturer headquartered in Fresno, California (Speiser, 1977, pp. 165–67). The CSOP technique is intended to build consumers' ownership of the capital of public utilities and other businesses having monopolistic consumer relationships. Proposed CSOP legislation would permit these companies to require each of its individual consumers to subscribe to a proportionate number of shares. The subscriptions could be paid from dividends resembling the patronage dividends paid by consumer cooperatives.

The General Stock Ownership Plan (GSOP) could be used "to build ownership of major gas, oil, or coal transmission lines into all economically underpowered citizens in the states through which they might pass, or into Social Security recipients in those states, under transition formulas that would reduce Social Security payments as their GSOP dividends rise. It could also be used to privatize publicly-owned productive facilities, like the postal service, by putting ownership into specified classes of economically underpowered consumers" (Kelso, 1986, p. 75). GSOP is similar to the Financed Capitalist Plan first advocated in *The New Capitalists* (Kelso and Adler, 1961).

The Individual Capital Ownership Plan (ICOP) would provide loans to poor people to buy venture capital stock. Eligible people would include those who do not have a "viable capital estate," with other considerations being personal merit, individual need, and residence in a depressed area.

The Commercial Capital Ownership Plan (COMCOP). Pointing out that the largest repository of capital wealth in the United States is commercial structures, the Kelsos seek to democratize its ownership by increasing taxes on the present "morbid" ownership, to encourage sales of such properties to the democratically owned COMCOP.

The Public Capital Ownership Plan (PUBCOP) is a device for financing the privatization of the public sector and spreading its ownership broadly through society. It would also finance stock ownership for employees of the government entities that are being privatized, thus saving enormous sums in public employee pension costs.

The Residential Capital Ownership Plan (RECOP) would give the home buyer access to low-cost loans, provide the home buyer a deduction from personal income taxes for depreciation, and exempt the income used to acquire a home from personal income taxes within certain brackets.

All of these plans would be undergirded by *commercially insured capital credit,* a new concept advocated by the Kelsos.

The Kelsos' new book (their first since 1968) insists on continuing the war between one-factor and two-factor economics, and so it is not likely to receive a warm welcome among consensus economists. But this should not stop us from considering its many insights into the broadening of capital ownership, especially since it emanates from the team that started the ESOP revolution.

Summary of Potential Reservoirs for USOPs

As we have seen, there are numerous potential reservoirs that could be tapped to provide universal share ownership:

1. Capital additions of major companies, as featured in the SuperStock model of USOPs. This is probably the deepest ownership reservoir of an industrial economy.

2. New stocks and bonds to be issued by American business (as in Albus's National Mutual Fund), which would go into the modernization of business to increase productivity.

3. Corporate profits, which are the smallest and most difficult reservoir to tap because there are already many claims on them. Perry's National Dividend Plan is an example.

4. Privatization, that is, government-owned assets (including over 600 million acres of federal land in the western states) and government services that could be owned and operated privately.

5. The credit power of major companies, as illustrated by the Teddy Bear principle (Figure 1) and as used now in leveraged buyouts.

6. Consumer payments to public utilities, as in Kelso's Consumer Stock Ownership Plan.

7. *Quid pro quo* provisions for government assistance to business (such as research grants and loan guarantees),

which would require the businesses receiving such assistance to issue shares to the USOP fund.

8. Extension of the USOP principle beyond shares of corporate stock to other privately owned assets such as real estate and art objects. This is an undeveloped idea that has been suggested by British Nobel Laureate James E. Meade (Meade, 1984).

9. A requirement for companies to issue new shares without any payment, the shares to be allocated to the new USOP shareholders. This has been suggested in Great Britain, but would not be supported by the American consensus because it requires dilution of present ownership (Speiser, 1986, pp. 116–118).

Synthesis of USOPs with Social Security and Pension Plans

The ideal plan of universal capital ownership should include a synthesis of several forms of ownership, income, and security. Our subsidiarity principle requires us to work with existing government and private sector programs before more government intervention is considered. The whole area of pensions, for example, is related to capital ownership, even though the workers' rights in pension plans do not actually make them owners of corporate stock. Then there are the existing capital ownership plans based on employment, such as profit-sharing plans and ESOPs. In addition, Social Security and government transfer payments should be synthesized with USOPs so that benefits do not overlap and recipients are given an incentive to progress from the welfare system to active participation in capitalism. And the insurance industry should be encouraged to synthesize present and future forms of life insurance with USOPs.

The precarious future financial position of Social Security is well documented. An effective USOP program that provided millions of households with substantial income from capital ownership would, of course, ease the strain on Social Security and eventually make it possible for the government to phase it out. In this connection, Stuart M. Butler suggests that the Social Security system could be privatized, at least partially (Butler, 1985). He believes that Social Security should be split into two distinct parts: a welfare element and a social insurance element. The welfare element would be financed from general taxation, as in the case of other welfare programs. The social insurance element would be financed according to normal actuarial principles, with payroll-related contributions and benefits strictly related to those contributions. This latter portion — the social insurance element — need not be operated by the federal government; it is a pure insurance system that could be transferred to the private sector. A detailed plan for such a privatized Social Security system was presented by Peter Ferrara in his book, *Social Security Reform* (Ferrara, 1982). He likens the pure insurance function of Social Security to an expanded version of the Individual Retirement Account (IRA). Some of the privatizing concepts of Butler and Ferrara may help open the way for synthesis of the Social Security system with USOPs.

Great Britain is ahead of the United States in that it has partly privatized Social Security. In 1978, Britain embarked on a comprehensive opting-out plan with the support of both the Conservative and Labour parties, and now has a two-tiered Social Security system. The first tier is mandatory and provides a basic minimum pension. The second tier provides a pension based on earnings and is voluntary. Private companies, not individuals, can opt out of this tier if they establish a plan for their workers at least as good as the state system. Since 1978, more than 45 percent of all workers have been privatized out of the second tier. The opting-out program has strong union support, and has substantially reduced the British government's Social Security expense.

Pensions are an even more promising area of synthesis since they are already privatized and voluntary on the part of nongovernmental employers. Pension funds in the United States today absorb over $100 billion in new contributions each year, and the estimated total of fund assets is $1.25 trillion. This is just slightly less than the national debt, and by the year 2000 the total is expected to increase to more than four trillion dollars in pension funds. By that time, pension funds overall will own a majority of all the common stock in America. But as we have seen, this does not democratize capital ownership, since pensions are strictly a retirement benefit and they do not confer ownership status on the beneficiaries. They represent funds that workers have earned and in some cases have actually contributed to.

Universal Share Ownership and Our Ten Principles

Our study of USOPs shows that they can be designed to be consistent with each of our Ten Principles. USOP would bring structural changes that can make American capitalism more moral and just, while appealing to the self-interest of most Americans — *if* the USOP shareholders are required to earn their shares and thus avoid dilution of present holdings (First and Second Principles). In the process of earning their shares, the USOP shareholders would be performing useful tasks, especially the work of humanity, in accordance with our Third and Fourth Principles.

Government intervention can be kept to a minimum through use of the subsidiarity principle. Indeed, achievement of universal share ownership (Fifth Principle) does not require any government intervention that is inherently offensive to the majority, provided that the shares are earned and the USOP benefits the overall economy, especially by increasing production and consuming power. While most of the problems of our economy can and should be dealt with at the local level, we also can benefit from a macro-economic remedy like a USOP — a massive injection of equity that can make local programs more effective and give everyone the feeling that the overall system is a fair one. Our Sixth Principle (subsidiarity) does not preclude use of macro remedies where private and local measures have been tried and found unequal to the enormous task of achieving social justice.

Development of an ideal USOP will require much trial and error, but there are no theoretical barriers (Seventh Principle). USOP is the essence of our Eighth Principle, which calls for experiments combining public service employment with stock ownership. We have seen that most existing employment programs (reviewed in Chapter Four) do not provide sufficient work incentive to cure major social justice problems. It is not certain that share ownership will solve these problems, but it is the most attractive incentive that has not been tried in the existing programs.

USOP involves questions of income and wealth distribution, in which religious organizations are fully capable of participating (Ninth Principle). Because USOP involves the work of humanity as a means of paying for shares, the expertise of religious organizations in achieving that work, as in our Tenth Principle, comes into play. And although we have all the component parts needed for a USOP, we seem unable to put them together without a massive galvanizing force such as the energy inherent in our religious organizations.

In this analysis of the interplay between USOP and our Ten Principles, it is instructive to consider why the seemingly successful experiment of the WPA and the other New Deal public works programs disappeared when America entered World War II. The programs were terminated then because we needed all our human resources for the war effort, but why did we not reactivate them after the war ended? Because we had faith in the ability of the private sector economy to reach full employment; because there is a liberal bias against forced work; and because the conservatives among us believe that it is cheaper simply to give the poor a welfare check than for the taxpayers to maintain workfare bureaucracies and to shoulder the nonlabor costs (materials, design, supervision, etc.) of the work they do.

The addition of USOPs to this equation opens exciting vistas. Granted that public service work is more expensive than welfare handouts, if wages must be paid. But suppose that instead of paying for public service work entirely by wages, we also paid the participants the wages of capital, in the form of dividends from USOP shares, or SIA shares, or both — would this change in the source of payment enable us to recreate the achievements of the WPA and the CCC in a way that is economically and politically feasible?

Such jobs would still carry some of the makework stigma of the WPA, but working as an owner of corporate shares rather than as a recipient of public handouts should make a big difference, in my opinion. Wealthy men and women do lots of dirty chores in *their own* gardens and stables. And there are many stories about the CCC boys of the Depression days who had proprietary feelings about the trees they had planted, and went back years later to see them grown tall.

Here, then, is the embryo of a monumental idea. We could

give welfare recipients two choices: they could remain on welfare, with payments cut to the lowest level consistent with responsible government; or, they could work their way out of welfare by moving into the USOP or SIA program, earning their shares by avoiding criminal activity and doing assigned tasks in the work of humanity. And we could accomplish the work of humanity economically because we would not have to pay the wages of welfare to the USOP shareholders.

From Kitty Hawk to the Concorde

The Wright Brothers' 12-horsepower Flyer made its historic fledgling flight from the sand dunes of Kitty Hawk, North Carolina, in 1903. Millions of people who were alive then lived to see the Concorde fly the oceans at supersonic speed. Why can't we do the same in our quest for social justice? We can begin by putting together some of the primitive elements discussed in this chapter, galvanizing them into a nationwide movement through religious organizations, and then letting the trial-and-error process do its work.

Here are some of the component parts we could start with:

- A limited experimental SuperStock plan, starting with about 5 percent of the annual $300 billion in business capital additions, on a voluntary basis, with incentives such as credits against the corporate income tax for those companies that volunteer. The goal would be to move up from 5 percent to 20 percent of business capital additions within a year or two, and then work toward a four-day work week for millions of employees with the fifth day to be devoted to the work of humanity.

- Testing Shareholders In America (SIA) units for the jobless in five or six cities, and experimental integration of SIA shares with USOP shares.

- A 5 percent experimental version of the National Mutual Fund, with controls to test for productivity increases.

- Leveraged buyouts of five or six companies, utilizing the companies' own credit power as collateral for self-liquidating loans, with share ownership to be distributed to disadvantaged citizens who are given the opportunity to earn these shares, preferably by performing the work of humanity. Community organizations could become the conduits for leveraged buyouts that would pass ownership of local business operations to disadvantaged neighborhood families, thus following subsidiarity.

- A voluntary experimental program of Employee Convertible Debentures (ECDs) for 1,000 companies, to expand worker ownership, to apply the FHA financing principle of long-term credit guarantees to worker ownership, and to increase savings.

- Privatization of government-owned assets (e.g., postal facilities) on a small test scale, with shares in the privatized companies to be issued to all citizens or to all disadvantaged citizens.

- Testing of Oscar B. Johannsen's Land Based Shares, by conveying title to several tracts of federal land in two western states to two new corporations whose shares would be placed in a pool, to be issued later to all citizens if the program proved workable.

- Testing of Kelso's Consumer Stock Ownership Plan with the customers of twenty-five public utilities.

- Testing of Robert A. Carlton's Quid Pro Quo plan, by establishing a pilot program to offer government loan guarantees or research grants to qualified companies that agree to issue USOP shares in return.

- Testing of the Weitzman Profit-sharing Plan on a voluntary basis, with USOP shares made available to those workers who agree to limit cash wages.

- Making ESOP shares convertible into USOP shares, on a small test scale.

- Testing the Mondragon cooperative concept with small startup businesses in several states, both with and without use of SIA shares.

Chapter 6

Business Ethics

IN THE 1980s, concern about the ethical deterioration of American business began to build. Can our Ten Principles improve the morals of the marketplace?

The Problem

David Sarnoff, who built RCA into one of America's leading companies, said that "competition brings out the best in products but the worst in people." And an enterprising author named Jay L. Walker published *The Complete Book of Wall Street Ethics* in 1987, consisting of 158 blank pages.

All around us there is evidence of severe crisis in business ethics. The cover story of *Time* magazine for May 25, 1987, was "Whatever Happened to Ethics?" It reported on a January 1987 poll conducted for *Time* by the Yankelovich Clancy Shulman organization, in which 90 percent of the respondents agreed that morals had fallen because of lack of proper training by parents; 76 percent believed that lack of ethics in business contributed to tumbling moral standards; and 74 percent said that political leaders failed to set a good example. The article went beyond business ethics, touching upon the 1987 scandals in religious television ministries, Iran-Contra, the Ivan Boesky insider trading debacle, Gary Hart, and a rogues gallery of more than 100 Reagan administration officials who have faced allegations of questionable activities. The article stated:

If greed is the main motivator in the surge of white-collar crime, pressure to perform also plays a part. Many individuals and companies feel much more competitive stress these days. The flood of baby boomers into the job market has created a crowding effect as they squeeze together toward the top.

Time decried the absence of "conscientious naysayers," but pointed out that "whistle blowing is usually a high-risk business. People who have tried to ask the embarrassing question have a very, very dismal record in succeeding in their later careers." The conclusion of the *Time* article calls for nothing less than a change in our entire value system:

> If Americans wish to strike a truer ethical balance, they may need to reexamine the values that society so seductively parades before them: a top job, political power, sexual allure, a penthouse or lakefront spread, a killing on the market. The real change would then become a redefinition of wants so that they serve society as well as self, defining a single ethic that guides means while it also achieves rightful ends.

The New York Times is even more pessimistic. In its Sunday Business Section for January 25, 1987, the lead article, "Remaking the American C.E.O.," was based on interviews with chief executive officers of many leading companies. Its conclusions were:

> The new order scorns loyalty, in favor of market leadership, profits and a high stock price. Many [CEOs] are adopting a new creed that puts corporate survival above all else. The result: a generation of ruthless management.

I believe it is unfair to put the blame so heavily on our business leaders, who are trapped by the same system that most of us support and seek to benefit from. Many business leaders are among the best people our country produces. They support our churches and synagogues, lead our charity drives, serve in our armed forces, and give liberally of their time and money for social and civic causes. But when they perform in our business system, they feel — probably correctly — that they would not survive if they practiced the golden rule. If they used the same moral standards in their home and social life as they did in business, we would have a thoroughly miserable society. But it is tacitly understood that the requirements of the business world are such that morals and ethics must take a back seat. Now that we are beginning to study the problem, we realize that individuals and even companies and universities cannot buck the tide. There is no tolerance in the system for lack of aggressiveness that leads to loss of business or failure to cash in on a business opportunity, even if ethical corners must be cut to succeed.

While we pay lip service to traditional moral and ethical values, these are very easily lost in the competitive business struggle. Consider the leveraged buyout (LBO), which we examined in the preceding chapter as a use of the Teddy Bear principle to narrow — rather than widen — stock ownership. In the LBO that was engineered for Safeway supermarkets, the company was forced to borrow more than $4 billion. To pay the interest on this mountain of debt, Safeway had to lay off hundreds of workers at their headquarters in Los Angeles. They also closed several supermarkets located in ghetto areas, where most of the customers do not have cars, are not mobile, and were relegated to high-priced delicatessens for food shopping because of these closings. Yet this LBO was not seriously questioned because it was considered an efficient use of capital and a clever business move, which is within the code of business ethics. Indeed, some of those who profit from LBOs are institutional investors representing organizations that are supposed to be guardians of our highest moral values.

There is terrific pressure on portfolio managers of pension funds and other institutional investment pools to bring in the maximum return for every dollar invested. These investment advisors have no choice, as they are selected by the institutional investors on the basis of their performance. Often the institutional investor will parcel out portions of the investment funds to a dozen or more advisors, and closely measure their track records by the total income from dividends and stock appreciation. Thus, the portfolio managers are subjected to the tyranny of the bottom line, and they in turn impose a short-term mentality ("quarteritis") on our economic system by focusing entirely on immediate return.

The *U.S. News and World Report* featured as its cover story on February 23, 1987, "Lying in America." On business ethics, it concluded:

> Is there more dishonesty in the business community today? Many observers think so. One often cited culprit is the current business climate, with many big companies retrenching and streamlining their staffs and others playing the big-bucks corporate takeover game. Another factor is a pervasive ethic of pragmatism: Do whatever is necessary to succeed and beat the competition. "People come to feel like suckers if they're honest, if the companies they are competing against are not," says Gary Edwards, executive director of the Washington-based Ethics Resource Center. . . .
>
> "The yuppie generation are very good game players, but morally, ethically, they have no idea what they're about," says Art Wolfe, professor of business law at Michigan State University. "To them, justice is efficiency, not fairness."

Again, I believe it is unfair to single out the yuppie generation, because they find themselves in a system that is not of their own making and does not offer any clear standard other than pragmatism. They are charged with the duty of producing immediate profit, and those above them are driven by the same force.

One bright spot in this dark picture is that we are beginning to examine the problem honestly. Unethical business practices have always been with us and were much worse in the time of the robber barons, when few dared to even raise a question about methods of making money. Now that we are a mature economic society, we have taken the first step toward solving the problem: asking the right questions. We have an increased awareness of business practices through television and massive media coverage. Competition among business journalists for the latest breaking scandal story is helping to create pressure for reform.

Solutions Now Being Tried

Teaching Ethics in Business Schools

On March 30, 1987, John S. R. Shad, outgoing chairman of the Securities and Exchange Commission, announced a $30 million gift package that will support a Harvard Business School program on ethics. Mr. Shad himself is donating most of this money. He believes that business schools can improve business ethics by selecting candidates for admission who have high ethical standards, and then training them by incorporating into *all* courses — finance, marketing, and production — a high standard of ethical behavior, rather than merely teaching a single course in ethics (Shad, 1987). Shad says that "companies like Johnson & Johnson and IBM demonstrate that the marketplace does reward quality, integrity, and ethical conduct. Ethics pays." What he did not mention is that Johnson & Johnson and IBM for many decades enjoyed semi-monopolistic positions that lifted them above the valley of economic Darwinism where most of our business people are competing head to head to keep their companies from losing market share, knowing that such losses could cost them their jobs.

Certainly, Shad's concern about the ethics of business school students is justified. It was heightened when as chairman of the SEC he saw that his agency was bringing criminal charges against Baker Scholars, Rhodes Scholars, and Phi Beta Kappas. He said, "It's the cream of the crop, and that's what is so shocking and causes my concern." As *Business Week* reported on April 13, 1987, the Harvard Business School students refused to vote on an ethics code for the school in 1985. The article quoted one Harvard teacher: "MBAs aren't interested in ethics. They're obsessed with getting jobs and competing with each other." And in *Time* magazine's ethics cover story of May 25, 1987, moral philosopher Kenneth Goodpaster was quoted on his experience when he came to the Harvard Business School from Notre Dame in 1980:

There was a certain cynicism that said, what good will philosophy do when everyone knows the bottom line is profit?

Why bother putting a veneer over that when in fact the driving impulse is going to be amoral if not immoral?

Obviously Shad's generous gift is a step in the right direction and can help to focus attention on the problem, if not move it toward a solution. However, other noted observers were not so optimistic about teaching ethics in business schools or any other schools. Lester C. Thurow, Dean of the Sloan School of Management at M.I.T., defends the record of business schools by pointing out that business students come to them from society:

> If they haven't been taught ethics by their families, their clergymen, their elementary and secondary schools, their liberal arts colleges or engineering schools or the business firms where most of them have already worked prior to getting a business degree, there is very little we can do.
> (Thurow, 1987)

Thurow goes on to say that he does not know of any way in which business schools can determine from their applicant pools which candidates are most likely to adhere to high ethical standards. Obviously, having reached the level of applying for admission to a business school, the candidate has learned to mask evidence of low ethical standards. Thurow concludes:

> Sacrificing self-interest for the common good is not going to be advocated by business schools or accepted by our students unless a majority of Americans also support the premise. In the end, business ethics is merely a reflection of American ethics. (Thurow, 1987)

Felix G. Rohatyn, senior partner at Lazard Freres, is pessimistic about the role of business schools in general. He comments on the apparent breakdown of morals and ethics in business, blaming it on the evolution of the so-called service society:

> Whereas making things, and the activities related to products, were the main preoccupation of prior generations,

making money, and the activities related to money, are the driving forces of our society today. (Rohatyn, 1987)

Rohatyn echoes Lester Thurow's conclusion that ethics must be taught at home and in society, and that it is too late to try to instill ethics at the level of the graduate business school.

These views support my contention that we must raise moral and ethical standards by making structural changes in the economic system. Only then will we be able to improve business ethics — unless we want to wait around for a change in human nature.

Company Ethics Programs

Many companies are spending time and money on ethical training for executives and other employees. On September 9, 1986, the *Wall Street Journal* reported in its front-page column, "Labor Letter," that "ethics training gets a boost at many companies." It quotes Kirk Hanson, a Stanford University teacher who has run ethics workshops for fifteen companies. Hanson suggests that companies must overcome an assumption by many employees that top management wants profits no matter how they have to be achieved. The article mentions programs at Union Carbide Corporation, Boeing Company, Sun Company, and Hercules Inc., where managers must sign forms saying they have abided by corporate ethics policies. But isn't this merely paying lip service to ethics? As reported by *U.S. News & World Report,* February 23, 1987, in its cover story on "Lying in America," whether corporate ethics programs actually work is a matter of considerable dispute. The screening tests for honesty, for instance, are highly controversial. Do they really test what they purport to? And many critics charge that the in-house codes and programs are often just window dressing. Writes Sissela Bok: "They function all too often as shields; their abstraction allows many to adhere to them while continuing their ordinary practices."

The Bureau of Business Practice, a division of Prentice-Hall, is offering a complete course entitled "Business Ethics: Guidelines and Commitment Video Seminar Program" for $129; it includes video tapes and accompanying manuals. All of this activity is constructive because it focuses attention on the problem and no doubt it will result in some improved ethical behavior. But again, this medicine is hardly up to the virulence of the disease.

Professor Irving Kristol, in an Op-Ed piece for the *Wall Street Journal* of September 15, 1987, noted:

> Apparently, most corporate executives know, without prior instruction, the fundamentals of what is right and what is wrong in the conduct of their affairs. Getting people to do what is right, and to refrain from doing what is wrong, is another matter, of course. But, then, it always is.

Kristol concluded that ethics are formed "by the structure of incentives one encounters in real-life situations." That is why structural changes are needed in the economic system itself.

Tougher Laws and Stricter Enforcement of Existing Laws

Some observers feel that stricter enforcement of present laws and the enactment of tougher new laws may improve business ethics. No doubt some improvement can be made through massive effort, but again, without structural changes that make the system fairer by bringing everybody into participation, law enforcement can hardly be expected to make much of a dent.

This problem was dramatized in August of 1987, when the FBI announced the results of a sting operation in the northeast, from Long Island to the Canadian border. A single FBI agent, posing as a crooked salesman of steel products, offered bribes to 58 public officials, promising to pay them cash kickbacks in exchange for government orders. In a two-year period, 106 bribes were offered, and 105 of them were accepted. Sadly, the one rejection was not based on ethical principles but rather on the fact that the bribe was considered too low.

In fairness, these crooked officials were not selected at random but were targeted because of suspicion of prior illegal acts. Nevertheless, the pervasiveness of low moral standards demonstrated by this sting operation shows that public officials and people in business *expect* this sort of thing to happen under the present system. Everything that they did was clearly illegal under present law, and they will be prosecuted. But will this actually improve business ethics, without a structural change that, for example, allows public officials to become shareholders of major companies and thus feel that they are a part of the money-making business system? This could be done under USOP, and one of the strongest incentives for bribery and corruption could thereby be reduced.

Nevertheless, vigorous enforcement of the present law and innovations such as the very useful federal RICO statute, under which business cheats can be prosecuted and sued for treble damages as racketeers, are helping to weed out some of the worst offenders.

Social Investment Funds

Another hopeful sign has been the development of "socially responsible investing." This new phenomenon is summarized in a recent article by Yvonne DeAngelo and Jean Heck:

> The philosophy of such groups is based on a "morally right approach" to investing, which will ultimately improve the bottom line. They believe that the company that does well while doing good will be successful over the long run. This philosophy is based on the view that socially responsible companies will not be bogged down in environmental disputes, court suits and strikes that cost them money.... If this sentiment grows, business will experience more pressure to be responsive to ethical issues. While companies may experience less pressure from government, there may well be increasing and important pressures from investors.
> (DeAngelo and Heck, 1987, p. 23)

The good news is that the major mutual funds that have been established to carry out the socially responsible investment agenda have been quite successful, in that most of them have outperformed Standard & Poor's 500 Index. Some of the leading socially responsible funds are the Dreyfus Third Century Fund, Garden City, New York, with $2.8 billion dollars under management; the Pioneer Funds of Boston, with over $4 billion; the Calvert Social Investment Funds of Washington, D.C., with over $200 million; and the Working Assets Money Fund of San Francisco, with over $100 million. The *Directory of Socially Responsible Investments,* which includes data on community development loan funds, banks, and advisors, is published by the Funding Exchange, 666 Broadway, New York, NY 10012.

The criteria used for social screening varies from fund to fund. For example, Dreyfus Third Century avoids firms that pollute the environment and seeks investments in companies that manufacture quality products and have good records on equal opportunity, occupational health, and safety. Other funds avoid companies doing business in South Africa or that produce weapons. It is not always easy to maintain a socially pure investment record, because of merger activity, business operations that are kept quiet, and other obstacles to full disclosure. Not every company publicizes dealings with South African sources of supply, for example. But for the increasing number of investors who are seeking to "invest their conscience," socially responsible funds provide an important service.

As of 1987, the total size of these mutual funds was approximately $3.2 billion, compared with an estimated pool of $5 trillion invested in securities in the United States. But this is a relatively new field and it is growing, propelled by the successful investment records produced by double screening: socially responsible *and profitable* companies are sought. Some religious organizations are participating in social investing.

The Council on Economic Priorities (CEP) has published a ground-breaking book, *Rating America's Corporate Conscience: A Provocative Guide to the Companies Behind the Products You Buy Every Day* (Lydenberg, 1986). CEP sent detailed questionnaires to major companies, seeking information on the following "conscience" issues: charitable contributions; representation of women and minorities on board of directors and in top management; extent of disclosure of "social information"; involvement in South Africa; involvement in manufacturing conventional and nuclear weapons; nature and extent of participation in political action committees; and extent to which products and supplies are purchased from minority vendors. Since the major objective of CEP was to provide information that might influence consumer support of particular companies and products, the study was limited to 130 major companies that dominate the food, health, appliance, home products, airline, oil, hotel, and automobile industries.

The result is a handy guide to socially responsible companies. The front section is arranged by products, and so you can choose to buy pasta or peanut butter from a company that is not involved in South Africa or with nuclear weapons, if you so desire. The back section has profiles of the 130 companies, with more detailed information than will be found in the product checklists. The emphasis is on factual data rather than subjective ratings and on positive examples rather than horror stories. The CEP project furnishes an important incentive for major companies to act responsibly. It is too much to ask every homemaker to check these charts before buying a can of baked beans, but I believe that the mere act of sending out questionnaires and publishing the results will help to make major companies more socially responsible.

Rating America's Corporate Conscience is the result of over fifteen years of compiling social responsibility records of major companies by CEP. Their address is: Council on Economic Priorities, 30 Irving Place, New York, NY 10003.

The Jesuit Mission to Wall Street

In 1980, the New York Province of the Society of Jesus opened the Jesuit Office for Faith and Justice at 50 Broad Street in the heart of the Wall Street area. Its mission was twofold:

1. Ministry to individuals in their need to be nurtured in their lives of faith, including prayer, pastoral counseling, and theological education.

2. The promotion of justice within the Wall Street community in fostering a greater awareness, especially among policy makers, of the opportunities and challenges facing the financial community in matters of economic justice.

The Jesuit Office has put on many useful seminars and has published studies and newsletters that are given wide circulation in the Wall Street community. Included in the newsletters are reports on creative ways in which some Catholic business people are approaching work, economic justice, and charitable activities. Great emphasis has been put upon the 1986 Bishops' Pastoral as a teaching document, and the Jesuit Office has held seminars and roundtable discussions on specific applications of the Pastoral to life on Wall Street.

Reverend Joseph S. Dirr, S.J., Director of the Jesuit Office, says that during its early years the emphasis was on pastoral counselling of individuals troubled by problems related to their work. Since 1983, more resources have been devoted to the structures that confront those working in the financial community. Father Dirr and his associate, Father Andrew C. Dittrich, S.J., believe that the Jesuit Office can and should deal with specific gray areas in business ethics, but in ways that facilitate rather than dictate corrective action.

From the personal and institutional standpoints, the establishment of a Jesuit outpost in Wall Street is an important step toward fruitful religious involvement in structural reform of the economic system.

The Need for Structural Changes in the Economic System

The sorry picture of business ethics that we have just examined is but a reflection of the pervasive feeling throughout our society that the economic system, as productive as it is, was not designed for fairness or equity. This automatically puts pressure on people to act selfishly by trying to beat the system, since their incentive to participate within the existing structures is dampened by the apparent unfairness of some of those structures. While the efforts to raise ethical standards at the company and university levels are commendable and important, I do not believe that universities or business executives can change the practice substantially within firms or within the business world as a whole. Business people know that what is really required of them is bottom-line performance, with no searching ethical questions asked. Good men and women are forced to do bad things under the excuse, "That's business."

Consider how the picture would change if we started with a

fairer system, one that allowed all Americans to participate in work and ownership in a meaningful way. This would reduce exploitation and remove some of the supposed justification for unethical behavior. The incidence of unethical behavior should drop substantially, and of equal importance, our tolerance for unethical behavior would be far lower than it is now.

I do not suggest that broadening work and ownership are complete solutions to the ethical problem. We would still be left with a system that apparently requires aggressive opportunism to sustain productivity and prosperity. But at least all of us would be sharing its benefits more equitably, and we would dampen the economic Darwinism that is at the root of our ethical dilemma.

Chapter 7

International Issues

EXPANDING WORK AND OWNERSHIP to achieve greater social justice within the United States is a huge project that could easily take the rest of the century to complete. Therefore, it may seem unrealistic to delve into the economies of other nations. I did not include any international or Third World aspects in the Ten Principles because I do not believe there is a 75 percent consensus in the United States on what actions we should take with respect to the economies of Third World and other foreign countries, due to preoccupation with our own domestic social and economic problems. However, discussion of a religious path to American social justice would not be complete without at least considering its implications for the Third World, since so many religious people have strong feelings about the injustices existing there. For example, an entire section of the 1986 Catholic Bishops' Pastoral was devoted to "The U.S. Economy and the Developing Nations: Complexity, Challenge, and Choices" (Nos. 251–294). Hence, we will discuss briefly the implications of our Ten Consensus Principles for the Third World.

We have space to touch on just two other international aspects. First, it is worthwhile to take a look at the British economy because in many ways it is a precursor of our own. Just as the sun moves from east to west, so has the metamorphosis of industrial capitalism. Adam Smith's theories, the Industrial Revolution, and Keynesian economics took root first in Great Britain and then found their way across the Atlantic. While there are many differences between the British and American economies, there are also important similarities from which we may be able to learn valuable lessons. Also, in Great Britain, the search for ways to expand work and capital ownership has, in some areas, progressed further than in the United States.

The last international aspect that we will touch on briefly is the potential impact on world peace (particularly on Soviet-American relations) of our quest for full participation in the economic system by all Americans.

The Third World

Here we consider two basic questions. First, what effect would the expansion of work and ownership (particularly the adoption of USOP) in the United States have on Third World nations? Second, what can the United States do to help Third World nations to expand work and ownership, particularly through a program like USOP?

As to the first question, it seems clear that successful implementation of expanded work and ownership in the United States would at least raise curiosity in Third World nations, which might find in the American example features that they would want to experiment with locally. Therefore, we move on to answering the second question, and our discussion will relate mainly to expanded ownership, since we can assume that Third World nations will try all the traditional remedies for unemployment on their own.

USOP, of course, is designed for industrialized nations whose large business enterprises furnish a ready foundation for broadening ownership through such reservoirs as corporate credit power and the ability to make self-liquidating capital additions. But what about the developing nations, a category that includes most countries and most of the earth's population? (These nations are also called nonindustrialized, underdeveloped, Third World, or just plain poor.) What they are trying to develop is a higher standard of living, and almost invariably they see industrialization as the quickest way to that end.

Even now, the industrial countries are deeply involved in helping developing nations to industrialize. These efforts involve three forms of financing: foreign capital in the form of loans or equity investments, foreign-aid handouts, and capital investments made in conjunction with wealthy local financiers or businesses. In all three cases, little or no new capital ownership is created among the local residents, most of whom were poor before such aid and remain poor afterwards. Therefore, this financing, even in the form of handouts, is generally not much appreciated by most local residents. In fact, their resentment often results in the expropriation of foreign investments. Moreover, the few jobs created by these efforts usually do not significantly increase the purchasing power of developing nations. To reach that goal, industrialization combined with the diffusion of capital ownership would appear the best approach. This opens the way for the United States to improve relations with developing nations by helping them to install their own USOP systems.

Obviously, Third World implementation of USOP would not be easy, but there is at least one potentially viable scenario. Suppose that American multinational corporations were able to secure the necessary guarantees of credit through the World Bank. This would enable them to establish industrial enterprises that would eventually be owned by the local citizens once the USOP shares paid for themselves out of earnings. The multinationals could supply the management and the technology. At the same time, they would be taking advantage of lower costs of raw material and labor, which might result in higher profits and quicker repayment of capital investments. That has, in fact, always been one of the big attractions of the Third World for the multinationals.

This use of USOP, if viable, would improve our relations with many foreign countries and make us much more popular in the United Nations General Assembly. It would also create new customers for American business. Local industries would be able to pay the multinationals for their goods and services, and the local residents, with more cash in their pockets from capital ownership, might become customers for imported goods and services. How such a plan could be implemented in specific Third World countries would require detailed study, of course, but it appears to have a much better chance for success than any of the strategies currently employed by the State Department and our multinationals. And it could enable Third World nations to build enterprises that would ultimately be owned directly and individually by needy citizens, rather than corrupt government officials or a few wealthy locals who bank the profits abroad.

Franklin R. Stewart, director of the Center for Study of Expanded Capital Ownership in Washington, D.C., is a former U.S. State Department official who has spent much of his life assisting developing nations. He believes that the USOP concept has a broad application to the Third World. In association with Professor Edward E. Azar, director of the Center for International Development at the University of Maryland, he has been exploring the possibilities of converting some portion of the external debt of Third World nations to equity, with that equity to be widely owned by the people of those countries. Their acquisition of the equity could be financed through some form of democratization of credit, such as USOP. The debt situation and the potential privatization of government-owned assets in the Third World provide a golden opportunity to make a start toward universal capital ownership there, to the long-term benefit of all concerned.

In 1987, there was a surge of activity in debt-equity swaps, with American banks and other lenders seeking to sell shaky Third World loans to investment bankers at a discount. The investment bankers in turn would arrange for issuance of equity securities, preferably backed by specific assets such as Mexico's oil reserves. There was even an attempt to make a new securities market out of this, led by Michael Milken, the architect of junk bonds for Drexel Burnham Lambert. As of late 1987, none of these efforts had come to fruition, but all of them seem to me to be misplaced. At best, they would get American banks off the hook on loans that were doubtful in the first place, at the expense of Third World nations and with no real benefits to the impoverished people of those nations. Such debt-for-equity swaps result in foreign ownership, which would throw us back to the old days of Yankee imperialism and probably lead to expropriation. This is not a politically feasible long-term program, nor is it likely to motivate the employees of privatized enterprises. Only individual ownership will do that.

In "Development Diplomacy," Professor Edward E. Azar demonstrates the importance of adding a new moral dimension to our relations with Third World nations:

I suggest that the core goal of any meaningful development plan must be to reduce inequality. Not only does growth of the economic sector without reduction of inequality seem morally lacking, but I would argue that it will also be doomed to failure as the economic system becomes hyperdeveloped and is no longer organically related to the rest of the social organization.... Because no sustained economic growth can occur unless it is accompanied by reorganization of the rest of the social system with which the economy is interdependent, development policies focusing solely on economic development are doomed to fail. (Azar, 1983, pp. 138–143)

Professor Azar sees universal local ownership as a means of reducing inequality within Third World nations. Therefore, he recommends intensive study of USOP as a potentially valuable element of our Third World policy. To that end, he has sponsored seminar and workshop discussions of USOP at the University of Maryland.

J. William Middendorf II, United States representative to the European community, was appointed chairman of the Presidential Task Force on Project Economic Justice. The purpose of the task force was "to develop a plan for the expanded use of employee stock ownership plans (ESOPs) in development efforts of the United States in Latin America and the Caribbean."

In October of 1986, the task force issued its report, which was drafted by Jeff Gates, then a staff member of the Senate Finance Committee. Its 109 pages are packed with detailed information on Third World economies and how employee ownership could open the way for economic justice there. In the words of its executive summary:

Without economic justice, economic reforms cannot long endure, flight capital will not return, and fledgling democracies will remain ripe for revolution.

Economic justice requires widespread access to private property ownership of the means of production. Thus, the central theme of our Report concerns the widespread use of financing techniques designed to expand capital ownership — particularly through the privatization of state-

owned enterprises and through a new, more workable
model of land reform. (Middendorf, 1986)

In addition to privatization and land reform, the report sets
out detailed blueprints for swapping U.S. bank debt for shares
in Latin American businesses and then selling that equity to the
employees through ESOPs. This strategy was also recommended
by President Reagan's Commission on Privatization (Linowes,
1988, pp. 212–214).

On August 3, 1987, President Reagan formally accepted the
Middendorf report in a public ceremony during which he made
these remarks:

> The people of Central America — and, in a broader sense,
> the entire developing world — need to know first-hand that
> freedom and opportunity are not just for the elite but the
> birthright of every citizen; that property is not just some-
> thing enjoyed by a few, but can be owned by any individual
> who works hard and makes correct decisions; that free en-
> terprise is not just the province of the rich but a system of
> free choice in which everyone has rights; and that business,
> large or small, is something in which everyone can own a
> piece of the action.

President Reagan went on to praise Ambassador Middendorf
and the other authors of the Project Economic Justice Report,
saying that he had directed his staff to follow up on the recommendations for promotion of privatization, expanded employee
ownership, and land reform.

Jeff Gates, principal author of the report, feels that debt-to-
equity conversions without employee ownership provide modest short-term financial relief to Third World governments and
their foreign lenders, but only at the long-term cost of a missed
opportunity to convert this debt crisis into an opportunity to implement a more just and durable development strategy, one that
is essential to long-term democratic institution building. Gates
says of the use of ESOPs in the Third World:

> They offer a new economic model for the United States to
> advocate in its foreign relations, where concentrated own-

ership continues to be capitalism's geo-political Achilles heel. They also provide an exportable model of capitalism (something this nation has yet to offer) — demonstrating how capitalism can be structured to build capital for working people.

While our study of American ESOPs in Chapter Five noted that they bring benefits only to those who already have good jobs with strong companies, the weak non-industrialized economies of Third World nations are probably not ready for plans that go beyond ESOP to universal share ownership, since there simply is not enough of an industrial base to be shared. In our own economy we needed to take ESOP as the first step, and probably the same is true of the Third World nations. Therefore, Project Economic Justice is an important foundation stone, and its importance is not diminished by the fact that President Reagan supports it as a means of halting the spread of communism by giving workers an economic stake in the survival of democracy in Latin America.

Expanding Work and Ownership in Great Britain

As a member of a law firm that has offices in the United States and in London, I have observed at firsthand the similarities and differences between our economic systems. But I do not pretend to understand the British economy, particularly its performance during the successive Thatcher administrations. When Margaret Thatcher took office in 1979, there were 1.1 million unemployed people, constituting 4.3 percent of the workforce. In 1987, when she won her third straight election, there were 3 million people unemployed, representing 11 percent of the workforce. During her administrations, Britain grew poorer, to the point where the International Monetary Fund reported in 1985 that the average Briton was poorer than the average Italian. In spite of these grim statistics and business profits that would seem meager by American standards, prices on the London Stock Exchange in the 1980s zoomed even higher proportionately than did those on the New York Stock Exchange.

Britain has been able to keep the unemployed tranquilized by expanding welfare benefits, so that an unemployed person receiving welfare — living "on the social" as it is known in Britain — would need to earn at least £110 a week before any noticeable improvement over welfare. The great majority of the available jobs do not pay anything like £110 a week; for example, a watchman would receive about £49 per week.

This apparent acceptance of chronic unemployment and the welfare mentality is, in the opinion of qualified observers, making distressing changes in British life. A front-page article by Barry Newman in the *Wall Street Journal* of November 10, 1986, was headlined: "High Unemployment Wreaks Vast Changes on Life in Britain — Accustomed to a Jobless Life, Many Young Adults Live Like Eternal Adolescents." Newman noted:

> A new barrier has arisen on [British] society's landscape. In the eyes of Michael Banks, a social psychologist at Sheffield University, it overshadows even the class system. "There are two kinds of people: those with job security and those without it," he says. Those without it could number 10 million by some reckonings — more than a third of the work force.

Against this background of hopelessness, the American ability to create jobs seems like magic to those wrestling with the same problems in Great Britain. And although there are shortages of some skilled workers, nobody in Britain foresees an overall labor force shortage as is being predicted for the United States.

The progress of efforts to expand work and ownership in Great Britain can best be observed by examining the positions taken by the three major political parties in the June 1987 election, which returned the Thatcher government to office for the third time.

The Conservative Party

The Conservative governments of 1979–1987 have tried all of the usual formulas for creating jobs, with little success. As we have seen, the overall unemployment rate has risen dramatically during those years. But Thatcher has demonstrated that if the majority of voters feel themselves better off, they will return to power a party that continues to increase unemployment and continues to tolerate, if not create, a permanent underclass of unemployed and demoralized young people. Howell Raines reported in the *New York Times* for June 13, 1987, just after the Thatcher election victory: "A Middle-Class Mandate: Thatcher Victory Shows a Changed Britain, As Voters Support Own Economic Interest." Raines observed:

> What has buffaloed the opposition for three straight elections now has been Mrs. Thatcher's very un-British willingness to appeal to the voters' selfish interests. This [Conservative] vote represents the "haves" of British society, the people who in a nation of 3 million unemployed have jobs. These are also the people who own their own homes ... and who now own stock in companies, many of which were under government ownership when Mrs. Thatcher took office eight years ago. In pure arithmetical terms, these voters represent only a fraction of the 43 million people who are eligible to vote Thursday. But Mrs. Thatcher's program of "popular capitalism" has expanded their numbers and improved their political cohesion. Stockholders, for example, have increased from 2 million to 8 million during her tenure. Exit polls Thursday showed that almost 6 of 10 first-time stockholders voted Tory.

Thus, by appealing to a majority of those Britons who are better off than before and pacifying the swelling ranks of the unemployed with welfare money, Thatcher has managed to hold power. And she has also very cleverly moved toward fulfillment of Anthony Eden's earlier call for a "property-owning democracy." She has done this first by making it easier for people to own their own homes, including poor people who lived in public ("council") housing, by lowering interest rates, providing tax deductions for home mortgages, and making it easier for low-income people to get appropriate mortgages. About one million municipally owned council houses have been sold to former tenants since 1979, at favorable prices and on favorable terms, which has created a million or more property owners who were likely to become Tory sympathizers.

During her 1987 campaign, Thatcher hit on this theme again and again:

> Home ownership, second pensions, share ownership, and choice in education — all these were once the privileges of the few. They are now being extended to the many.

This program of "popular capitalism" shook the political loyalty of people who grew up in families of Labour supporters. While many working people still agree with Labour's social policies, they realize that personally they are better off under Thatcherism so long as they do not slip into the ranks of the jobless.

Thus, Mrs. Thatcher has demonstrated that expanded ownership is a powerful political weapon, a lesson that American politicians apparently have not yet learned. The Conservative Manifesto (party platform) for 1987 moves from home ownership to a separate section entitled "A Capital-Owning Democracy." The manifesto says:

> We were determined to make share-ownership available to the whole nation. Just as with cars, television sets, washing machines and foreign holidays, it would no longer be a privilege of the few; it would become the expectation of the many. We achieved this historic transformation in three ways:
>
> First, we introduced major tax incentives for employee share-ownership. Seven out of the last eight budgets have included measures to encourage people to purchase shares in the company in which they work.
>
> Second, starting this year, we brought in Personal Equity Plans, which enable people to invest in British industry entirely free of tax.
>
> Third, we embarked on a major programme of privatisation, insisting that small investors and employees of the privatised companies should have a fair chance to join in the buying.
>
> The results have been dramatic, and the direct consequence of government policy. Share ownership has trebled. Almost one in five of the adult population now own shares directly. And the figure will continue to rise.... This is

the first stage of a profound and progressive social transformation — popular capitalism. Owning a direct stake
in industry not only enhances personal independence; it
also gives a heightened sense of involvement and pride in
British business. More realistic attitudes to profit and investment take root. And the foundations of British economic achievement are further strengthened.

We will press on with the encouragement of popular
capitalism. In the next Parliament:

We will continue to extend share-ownership as we have
done with home-ownership.

We will reintroduce our proposed tax incentives for
profit-related pay.

We will privatise more state industries in ways that increase share-ownership, both for the employees and for the
public at large.

In the privatization program, the Thatcher government has
made special efforts to broaden employee share ownership. In
the British Aerospace privatization, each worker received approximately £150 worth of shares free of charge, and in the
Jaguar automobile privatization, each worker received £450
worth of free shares. In most of the other privatizations, the
government made it easy for workers to buy shares on the in-
stallment plan and sometimes they received discounts from the
public offering price.

But in a sobering note, the Wider Share Ownership Council
pointed out in its spring 1987 newsletter:

Whilst these figures are very encouraging, it must be re-
membered that the value of individual share ownership
(in money) has been declining for many years; shares have
been acquired massively by pension funds, institutional investors and overseas investors. There is still a long way
to go before we can be considered to be a share-owning
democracy.

Thus we see that there has been a minimal broadening of stock
ownership under the Thatcher administration, but it is wide
enough to support the slogan of "property-owning democracy."

No doubt Thatcher struck a popular chord, as the *Financial Times* pointed out on January 27, 1986:

> An unusual degree of political consensus has been developing over the past decade in support of employee share ownership. The Conservative Party and its backers in industry have abandoned their skepticism about the interest or willingness of workers to exercise their ownership and decision-making rights. ... The Liberal Party has long been an enthusiastic advocate and was responsible for the introduction of the first employee scheme with tax incentives in 1978. Even the Labour Party, which supported the 1978 scheme, has shed some of its traditional suspicion of such forms of collaboration with capital. For many on the right of the party, employee share schemes and cooperative ventures have replaced the centralized and monolithic nationalized industries as the model of industrial ownership.

Despite all the political mileage gained through British employee share ownership schemes, they have done little actually to democratize income or wealth distribution. Most of the shares have gone to people holding high-paying jobs. The shares made available to employees through the privatization scheme, for the most part, were paid for from savings and thus went to people who were pretty well off and did not necessarily increase their wealth or income since other assets had to be sold to pay for the shares. Nevertheless, under the Thatcher government, Great Britain has taken some long strides toward use of capital ownership as a political tool for income and wealth distribution. Later administrations may build on this foundation to create more equitable distribution.

The Writings of David Howell

David Howell has been a Conservative Member of Parliament since 1966. He held two cabinet posts in the first Thatcher administration, the last being Minister of Transport from 1981 to 1983. In that office, he presided over the privatization of the National Freight Consortium (NFC), which is one of the great success stories of employee ownership. NFC was bought from the government by a consortium of managers and employees in

February 1982. It employs 25,000 people in more than 700 locations and has annual revenue of over £600 million. 13,000 employees — more than half the workforce — participate in ownership of 83 percent of the common stock. The shares are widely dispersed, with senior managers together owning only 5 percent of the total equity. The buyout was highly leveraged, with £51 million out of the total cost of £62.5 million coming from long-term bank loans. The banks made their loans conditional upon a minimum amount of shareholding by the existing top management team.

NFC's operating plan does not require shareholding nor does it guarantee a job. The Transport and General Workers Union did not support the buyout, reasoning that it would mean layoffs and sales of equipment on which the workforce depends. They said that "the worker-shareholders would be a conscripted jury with no option but to pass their own death sentences." But the performance of National Freight did not bear out this gloomy prediction. Profits increased by 42 percent in its first year. Regular dividends have been paid since 1983 and the share prices have risen by 600 percent from the original buyout price. The average shareholding has risen from £500 to £3,000 and the average capital gain of senior management was about £100,000 in two years.

David Howell's economic philosophy extends beyond employee ownership to universal share ownership and its relationship to employment and the work of humanity, as expressed in his latest book, *Blind Victory* (Howell, 1986). Here are some key passages:

> The idea of a fully occupied society which is not fully employed is, as yet, too unfamiliar to be understood. The belief that if you are not in full-time work you must be on the scrapheap is so deeply rooted that it requires revolutionary persuasion to uproot it. (p. 14)

> How is everybody to be occupied in a society which does not require people to be all involved in full-time labour? How is income and wealth to be distributed, and the ownership of capital spread, in a world in which possibly only a minority have full-time remunerated employment and yet

people live longer, are more active, have higher expectations and want to be satisfyingly occupied throughout life?
(p. 17)

...the need is to move policy-thinking sideways out of
its overwhelming preoccupation with weekly incomes and
"wages", whether from the state or from the employer, and
to bring the concept of personal ownership to the centre
of the scene. A massive banking up of personal capital
resources for families in all income groups is a perfectly
feasible goal. If achieved on a sufficient scale it would provide precisely the same consequential and highly beneficial
effects as those claimed for the inordinately expensive idea
of a guaranteed basic income for all. (p. 108)

Attention will have to be increasingly turned to the wider
distribution of non-wage resources, notably capital and income from capital, if any conceivable sense of unity and
common purpose, embracing the whole of modern industrial society, is to be re-created. (p. 110)

Pursued to the full, the social aims of wider ownership become in fact the weapon by which the debilitating concept
of the labour scrapheap can finally be razed.
(pp. 129–130)

There is no need to be too restrictive about the initial form
which "capital" takes. All forms of experimentation should
be welcomed and encouraged — a sort of "capitalist Darwinism." One could be talking about shares in the local
firm, or redundancy money, or shares distributed by central government on a national basis as part of a sustained
and deliberate policy for widening ownership and placing
income producing assets in the hands of the vast majority
of the people. (This is the approach which Samuel Brittan
calls "citizen ownership." Something like it has been tried
in British Columbia, where shares in public utilities and
enterprises have been distributed to all adults.) (p. 136)

The principle with which we should be concerned is one
of "egalitarianism rightly understood," if one may borrow
from and adapt de Tocqueville's principle of "self-interest
rightly understood." It needs to be the widely appreciated aim that government, recognising its own changing
role in a more informed and dispersed society, is vigor-
ously committed to the spread of ownership (and its associated duties) and the dismantling of monopoly concentration of power, without the exceptions and qualifications
which erode the whole vision and make people question
whether anything is really changing at all. (p. 161)

Following the 1987 Thatcher election victory, Howell wrote an
Op-Ed piece for the *Wall Street Journal* of June 17, 1987. He
injected a sobering note into the victory of his own party, calling upon it to lead Great Britain into a new phase of popular
capitalism:

The old socialist morality, rooted in the virtues of a solid
and upright working class, in trade-union loyalty and in
the concentrated pattern of heavy industry, has probably
now at last subsided. But it has left a gaping hole. A new,
or reconstructed, capitalist morality now has to be pieced
together to take its place — and one that sits comfortably
with the totally different industrial and social structure the
electronic age permits and encourages.
    Once this great battle is won, and state socialism not
merely finally discredited and defeated but also convinc-
ingly replaced, the prospects for widely shared prosperity
and social progress in the last decade of the millennium
are unlimited. This applies not just to Britain but to the
global economy, and especially to areas such as Eastern
Europe, which has been most severely held back by collec-
tivist economics. What better place is there than Britain,
the oldest industrialized country and the worst scarred by
traditional industrial growth and welfare mentality, to be
the testing ground for working out this new, kinder and
more promising pattern of affairs?

The Labour Party

Clause IV, Section IV, of the Labour Party Constitution commits the party to work for "common ownership of the means of production." For more than half a century, this clause has caused friction and polarization within the party, since the only method to achieve common ownership that has been used is nationalization of privately owned businesses. As we have seen, nationalization has not met with notable success in Great Britain or other European nations. In fact, it has now gone out of style, and even the Socialist International, the descendant of Marx's First International, no longer advocates government ownership of the means of production. Since the framers of the Labour Party Constitution did not specify government ownership, why wouldn't universal share ownership achieve the aim of "common" ownership?

With its third consecutive resounding defeat at the hands of Margaret Thatcher in 1987, the Labour Party has begun to re-examine Clause IV and the whole question of nationalization. Even before the election, Unity Trust, the bank organized by British trade unions, had begun to supply financing for employee company buyouts. Then in 1987, Roy Hattersley, Deputy Leader of the Labour Party, publicly advocated a turn away from government ownership in the direction of employee share ownership, without departing from socialist principles or the Labour Party Constitution. In *Choose Freedom,* Hattersley says of employee share ownership:

> Ownership and wealth is being spread more evenly; the state is employed not to enhance its own power but to organise the distribution of power to the people — theoretical rights are changed into reality; the mechanisms of government, the tax system, the legislative process, are all being used to provide individuals with a greater influence over their daily lives. To fail to provide that process because of some half-digested notion about collective action, centralised planning or state ownership would be a denial both of the individual rights which ought to be at the heart of socialism and the long-held belief that the emancipation of the worker requires his relationship with his employer

(and his relationship with the capital which provides his employer with power) to change. (Hattersley, 1987, p. 205)

Hattersley limits this endorsement to employee share ownership that includes voting rights, which he describes as follows:

The worker owns some and controls more of the capital; his vote influences policy. And the more different schemes to extend worker control and influence proliferate — co-operatives, ESOPs, investment funds — the more the whole nature of society is changed. That is surely a more noble objective than the transformation of a few private monopolies into state monopolies.
(Hattersley, 1987, p. 206)

Hattersley writes an ending to the old socialist notion that nationalization of industry would achieve the equivalent of ownership by the nation in general and the employees in particular:

The practical answer is that any argument that suggests that the nationalised industry managements are anything other than remote from their employees is palpable nonsense. They are institutionally remote, forced, by the size of their industries, the bureaucracy of their organisation, the professional hierarchy in which they exist and the lower presence of their owners in Whitehall, to take the national decisions on which both their name is based and their special form of organisation is justified. It is as unreasonable to expect state monopolies to respond to the demands of real worker control as it would be to demand such a system be adopted by the armed forces of the crown.
(Hattersley, 1987, p. 188)

Neil Kinnock, leader of the Labour Party, took up the Hattersley proposal immediately after the 1987 election, announcing that the party must reappraise its attitude toward public ownership and that it would not be treachery or selling out if the party abandoned nationalization. This was followed by a resolution adopted by the Trades Union Congress in September of 1987, recognizing the need to take account of the growth in individual and worker share ownership schemes, and considering the incorporation of such schemes into the concept of "social ownership." Allan Tuffin, general secretary of the Union of Communications Workers, who led the call for such a change, argued that it was ludicrous to expect new share owners to support a compulsory renationalization by a future Labour government. He said such a nationalization policy was "unimaginative and unpopular, if not unworkable."

At the next Labour Party conference, Kinnock presented a report entitled "Moving Ahead," in which he urged his party to counter Thatcherism by arguing in the same terms of "individual self-interest and prosperity." And the *Financial Times* reported on September 30, 1987:

> In reshaping its policies for the next general election, Labour must be geared to the realities likely to dominate the 1990s — including wider share ownership — Mr. Neil Kinnock told the Labour Party conference at Brighton yesterday. . . .
>
> After the recent controversy over Labour's attitude to wider share ownership, Mr. Kinnock said that the party would be fooling itself if it did not accept that the increased ownership of shares had made a difference to their owners' personal economic perceptions.

These public reversals of established Labour positions herald a new era in British politics, in which all the major parties will be vying with each other to find new ways of broadening share ownership as the means to achieve socialist, capitalist, and democratic goals.

The SDP-Liberal Alliance

As we saw in Chapter Five, Dr. David Owen, leader of the Social Democratic Party, announced his support in 1984 for USOP (under the name of citizen share ownership) both as to companies that were being privatized and companies that were already privately owned. Unfortunately, Dr. Owen was not able to convince his colleagues, and so citizen share ownership was not included in the SDP-Liberal Alliance manifesto for the 1987

election. That manifesto did endorse expansion of cooperatives, employee share ownership and profit-sharing schemes,
and tax incentives for people to use their savings to become
small investors. But all of these measures were also supported
by the Conservatives, who had actually put them into practice.
Through its failure to endorse citizen share ownership, the SDP-
Liberal Alliance lost a golden opportunity to define the "social
market" which is at the core of its economic philosophy. This
is one reason why the Alliance was unsuccessful in the 1987
election, which led to an upheaval over the question of merging
the two parties. As the *Financial Times* noted on September
3, 1987, delegates to the SDP post-election conference agreed
that the social market economy was the cornerstone of Social
Democratic policies "but were in some confusion about what it
meant." One of the speakers, Ian Cundy, said that the motion
approved by the conference amounted to a statement that "we
strongly reaffirm our commitment to the idea of the social market economy but would be rather grateful if someone would tell
us what it means."

Perhaps the clearest statement about where the SDP and
the Liberal Party should stand on broadened share ownership
was made by Lord Grimond, former leader of the Liberal Party.
Writing in the *Independent* on July 15, 1987, in an Op-Ed piece,
he said:

> The main question in politics is no longer how we advance
> to a state socialist society while retaining our freedom. The
> questions now are how we make capitalism and the market
> work for the benefit of all and how we nurture our institu-
> tions. . . .
>
> On the left the ideals which inspired socialism persist.
> It is clear, however, that they cannot be realised by making
> everyone a client or employee of the state. . . .
>
> We must at once set about garnering the new ideas
> which have sprung up in universities, business and jour-
> nalism. We must then proclaim a third way in politics
> which is not a compromise but a new departure.

The soul-searching process of working toward merger of the
SDP and Liberal parties should produce some more definitive

statements on citizen share ownership, which is obviously an ideal vehicle for the social market "third way in politics." With the Conservatives and the Labour Party already committed to broader employee ownership, it would seem that the only way the middle-party alliance can distinguish itself is to come up with a definitive plan for citizen share ownership.

•

This study of the 1987 British election holds some important lessons for the United States. It shows, first of all, that broadened share ownership is a consensus issue that any American political party can embrace and advocate, since the Conservatives took the ball away from the center and left parties by themselves running with the issue of a share owning democracy. It demonstrates, I think, that the Democratic Party in the United States must develop some specific plans for broadening stock ownership beyond the ESOPs, which are supported as well by the Republicans. Otherwise, the "fairness" issue will be lost to the right wing, or will appear so vague as to become meaningless, as in the cases of the Labour platitude of "social ownership" and the SDP-Liberal Alliance's ethereal "social market."

The British experience also shows that even in a nation that is ostensibly less devoted to self-gratification than is the United States, most people are voting on the basis of self-interest — even people who come from families that were ideologically committed to socialism.

The Wider Share Ownership Council

The Wider Share Ownership Council (WSOC) was formed by a small group of politicians and City (financial) people in November 1958. Its prime mover was Toby Low, then a Conservative Member of Parliament and now Lord Aldington, who at that time was engaged in writing a book called *Every Man a Capitalist* for the Conservative Political Centre. The first chairman was Maurice MacMillan, M.P., son of Prime Minister Harold MacMillan. The council has four deputy chairmen, three of whom reflect its original resolve to be a non-party political organization, being chosen from the three main political parties.

It receives financial support from a few individuals and a distinguished list of public companies, among which Barclays Bank is a major contributor. It also enjoys the cooperation of the London Stock Exchange.

The WSOC has continuously worked for the extension of share ownership in general, and has also sought to promote employee share ownership plans within companies. This two-pronged approach gives it a much broader scope than the American ESOP organizations, both of which are devoted exclusively to employee share ownership.

Edgar Palamountain, who succeeded Maurice MacMillan as chairman of the WSOC in 1971 and has held that office since, summed up the WSOC's objectives succinctly in his 1985 annual report:

> In an ideal free capitalist society, just about everyone would own shares, and the stability of the system would be assured.

The WSOC has sponsored the Speiser British essay competitions, helping us to seek a workable plan of citizen share ownership that goes a step beyond employee share ownership to Type C ownership. The WSOC has extended its influence overseas, largely through the efforts of Harry Ball-Wilson, its honorary international liaison officer.

Implications for World Peace

As briefly noted in Chapter One, the power struggle between the United States and the Soviet Union, and the consequent nuclear arms race, are based at least partially upon the ideological differences between capitalism and communism. These ideological differences were highlighted by Pope John Paul II in his 1988 encyclical, *Sollicitudo Rei Socialis* (The Social Concerns of the Church):

> In the West there exists a system which is historically inspired by the principles of the liberal capitalism which developed with industrialization during the last century. In

the East there exists a system inspired by the Marxist collectivism which sprang from an interpretation of the condition of the proletarian classes made in the light of a particular reading of history. Each of the two ideologies, on the basis of two very different visions of man and of his freedom and social role, has proposed and still promotes on the economic level antithetical forms of the organization of labor and of the structures of ownership, especially with regard to the so-called means of production.

It was inevitable that by developing antagonistic systems and centers of power, each with its own forms of propaganda and indoctrination, the ideological opposition should evolve into a growing military opposition and give rise to two blocs of armed forces, each suspicious and fearful of the other's domination. (No. 20)

It has been my thesis that as the United States moves closer toward sharing ownership of the means of production by all citizens, and thereby dims Marx's scenario in which the nonowning workers are exploited by a tiny pinnacle class of capital owners, ideological tension with the Soviet Union will be reduced. I also believe that American adoption of USOPs as a form of capitalism based on higher moral principles should reduce the worldwide tensions that arise from pressures inherent in the present brand of capitalism. This thesis is spelled out in *How to End the Nuclear Nightmare* (Speiser, 1984), and in *Capitalism and the "Evil Empire": Reducing Superpower Conflict Through American Economic Reform* (Taylor, 1987).

As this is written, President Reagan and General Secretary Gorbachev have signed a treaty calling for removal and destruction of short range and intermediate range nuclear missiles and have stated that they are working toward an agreement to reduce the number of strategic missiles. This potentially monumental breakthrough coincides with economic developments in the Soviet Union that have forced Gorbachev to move further toward convergence with free market capitalist economics, under his *Perestroika* (restructuring) policy. The massive economic pressures of the arms race, which in the Soviet Union is carried on at the expense of civilian living standards, is beginning to take its toll. As we have seen, the Soviet Union, China, and other communist nations are now experimenting with market economics and incentives, realizing that in the age of the computer and the robot, communist societies cannot remain competitive and productive if they are shackled by huge government bureaucracies.

Thus, economic convergence is playing a part in our first opportunity to dampen the ideological warfare that fuels the nuclear arms race. In its cover story of July 27, 1987, *Time* magazine reported on "Gorbachev's revolution." *Time*'s editors felt that Gorbachev's admission of the need for economic reform at home has removed some of the thrust of international proletarianism. As a Soviet diplomat in Washington put it, "There is less of a temptation to enforce our own model on others, because we are questioning our own model." And on the effects of the lessening of ideological tensions across the board, *Time* reported:

> If, perchance, some of the ideological underpinnings of that struggle are beginning to fade away, the rivalry could become far more manageable. Unlike other great international rivals, the U.S. and the Soviets have little serious conflict over commercial markets. And despite the struggle for political influence, both sides share an interest in calming certain regional disputes, like the Iran-Iraq war.

In his speech of November 2, 1987, marking the seventieth anniversary of the Bolshevik Revolution, Gorbachev divorced the Soviet Union from the Trotsky specter of "hostile capitalist encirclement" and said that the inevitability of conflict between communism and capitalism was giving way to a new era of cooperation in a world that is now "interrelated, interdependent, and integral." And in his speech of December 8, 1987, on arrival at the White House for the treaty ceremony, Gorbachev said:

> We in the Soviet Union have made our choices. We realize that we are divided not only by the ocean but also by profound historical, ideological, socioeconomic, and cultural differences. But the wisdom of politics today lies in not using those differences as a pretext for confrontation, enmity, and the arms race.

Gorbachev struck the same note in his ground-breaking book, *Perestroika:*

> It is impossible to move toward more harmonious relations between the US and the USSR while being mesmerized by ideological myths. (Gorbachev, 1987, p. 211)

> We certainly do not need an "enemy image" of America, neither for domestic nor foreign policy interests. An imaginary or real enemy is needed only if one is bent on maintaining tension, on confrontation with far-reaching and, I might add, unpredictable consequences.
> (Gorbachev, 1987, pp. 216–217)

In that remarkable book, Gorbachev emphasized Lenin's flexible approach to achieving the goals of socialism, even if this meant discarding collective experiments in favor of policies that satisfied individual interests, such as Lenin's New Economic Policy, which revived some aspects of capitalism in the Soviet Union of the 1920s (Gorbachev, 1987, pp. 83, 96–98).

Once the preliminary disarmament agreements have been negotiated, I think the United States can go a long way toward ensuring world peace by demonstrating its dedication to economic justice in the form of universal capital ownership, thus moving the economic systems of the United States and the Soviet Union even closer to convergence. One of the planks in the platform supporting the Soviet-American nuclear confrontation is the retarded development of economic justice in both nations. The absence of economic justice within each nation, and between nations, is a festering sore that breeds the disease of aggression and threatens world peace. Pope John Paul II characterizes these injustices as "structures of sin" in his 1988 encyclical, *Sollicitudo Rei Socialis,* applying this term to "the all-consuming desire for profit" of the capitalist nations and the communist "thirst for power...at any price" (Nos. 36, 37).

As Martin Luther King, Jr., put it, "True peace is not merely the absence of tension; it is the presence of justice."

Chapter 8

Next Steps

THIS IS GOING TO BE A VERY SHORT CHAPTER. I think it would be presumptuous of me to suggest an agenda of religious social justice activity. There already exist hundreds of groups with millions of members who are dedicated to achieving economic and social justice, through religious activity and otherwise. Those organizations have the strength to move the mountain of economic inertia and bring us greater social justice through expanded work and ownership — provided that they realize the full definition and scope of their powers. I have just three suggestions to make as to next steps.

First, I hope that leaders and members of religious organizations will consider the Ten Principles outlined in this book and incorporate those that they consider valid into their own discussions. This may help to broaden those discussions to include such concepts as universal share ownership, Shareholders In America, Inc., and the work of humanity, which may not now be on their agendas.

Second, I hope that religious organizations will consider establishing a Subsidiarity Scoreboard, either within their own organizations or in cooperation with other organizations, so that we can determine the appropriate degree of government intervention without wasting effort on meaningless ideological arguments, and so that we can focus intelligently on the kinds of experiments needed to bring greater social justice.

Third, I hope that religious organizations will consider the results of the essay contests that I have sponsored, and establish their own essay contests. This will involve more people (particularly universities, faculties, students, peace and justice commissions, and social concerns committees) in the active search for ways of expanding work and ownership, especially the ideal plan of universal share ownership that is a key to economic democracy and social justice. We need to apply our best minds and strongest resources to the problem of finding new models and designing new experiments. Many of our best minds and strongest resources exist within religious organizations, where the climate is hospitable to the search for social justice.

All of this will lead eventually to the political action that is the final step. Seeking structural changes in the economic system is a lonely task. The years roll on without any semblance of political progress, even though intellectual progress is being made through development of more promising models and definitive experiments. Here we can take heart from the words of Milton Friedman, who wrote about the great patience needed to bring about such structural changes in his classic *Capitalism and Freedom:*

> There is enormous inertia — a tyranny of the status quo — in private and especially governmental arrangements. Only a crisis — actual or perceived — produces real change. When that crisis occurs, the actions that are taken depend on the ideas that are lying around. That, I believe, is our basic function: to develop alternatives to existing policies, to keep them alive and available until the politically impossible becomes politically inevitable.
>
> (Friedman, 1962, p. ix)

Chapter 9

Final Exam

THE FOLLOWING MULTIPLE CHOICE QUESTIONS will serve as a review of the main points discussed in the preceding chapters and may also be helpful to those using the book as a teaching or study guide. The questions relate mainly to the Ten Principles listed at the end of Chapter One.

The answers listed provide a spectrum of approaches. While there is only one answer to each question that I would support, there is no single "right" answer. Feel free to pick one or more answers to each question, according to your own lights.

1. Structural changes designed to make American capitalism a more moral and just system:

   a. are a waste of time, because any capitalist system is inherently unjust and immoral.

   b. cannot succeed because the system is built on immutable scientific principles, and changes designed by well-meaning moralists are likely to destroy its productivity.

   c. should be the subject of study and experimentation, since the system has been developed and improved by trial and error rather than through discovery of immutable scientific principles.

   d. can succeed only if they are based upon principles of welfare capitalism, which leaves the present systems of employment and ownership intact, and taxes productive people and companies to provide sustenance for those who do not otherwise participate in the economy.

2. Such structural changes:

   a. can be achieved even if they adversely affect personal incentives, economic growth and efficiency, living standards, individual freedom, or the self-interest of the middle class, because our need for a moral economic system transcends all these middle-class values.

   b. can be achieved only if they appeal to the self-interest of the middle class, whose support is essential to formation of the required consensus.

3. Such structural changes:

   a. should be enacted by federal legislation, because only the federal government has the power to make real structural changes in the economic system.

   b. should be enacted by state or local legislation.

   c. should be attempted through the private sector before turning to legislation, because it is easier and more efficient to test new ideas voluntarily in the private sector, and because most Americans regard governmental action as the least desirable choice.

4. Everyone who wants to work and is able to work:

   a. should go out and find a job, without any assistance.

   b. should be guaranteed a job by the government, regardless of need for their services.

   c. should be given a fair opportunity to work at a job that pays wages above the poverty level, with assistance in training, child care, and placement, if needed.

5. People receiving welfare payments:

   a. should instead receive "negative income-tax" payments to bring their income up to the poverty level, without incurring further expenses to support the bureaucracy needed to try to put them to work.

   b. should be required to work, even if the only jobs available pay minimum wages and offer no hope for advancement.

   c. should be deported.

   d. should receive assistance in training, child care, and placement in jobs that offer an opportunity for advancement beyond the levels of welfare, poverty, and minimum wages.

   e. should remain on welfare, without any work obligation.

6. Given the need for rebuilding our infrastructure and improving our society (the work of humanity):

   a. we should put millions of people on the public payroll and accomplish this work as it was done by the WPA in Depression days.

   b. we must let our infrastructure rot and our society disintegrate, because we can't afford to deal with these problems.

   c. we should study and experiment with ways of accomplishing this work with minimal use of tax funds and government facilities.

   d. we should accomplish this work through the U.S. Army.

   e. we should assign this work to prison inmates.

7. In the future, our main employment problem will be:

   a. an overall shortage of jobs.

  b. an overall shortage of workers.

  c. a shortage of workers possessing the skills needed for the new wave of jobs.

  d. a shortage of jobs that pay above-poverty-level wages and provide adequate work incentives through the prospect of advancement or wage increases.

8. The principle that economic justice requires participation in the economy by every person, through work and ownership:

  a. is a Jewish idea.

  b. is a Roman Catholic idea.

  c. is a Protestant idea.

  d. is consistent with the traditions of all the major religions.

9. The distribution of stock ownership, through which only 6 percent of Americans receive substantial capitalist income:

  a. is fair, because it is determined by free market forces, and ownership (as well as access to long-term credit) should be restricted to those who earn it according to the existing rules of the game.

  b. should be condemned as immoral and scrapped, because it enables a pinnacle class of owners to exploit the nonowners.

  c. can and should be made more equitable by providing more Americans access to long-term credit and other means of becoming stockholders.

10. Broadening of stock ownership to include all Americans:

  a. violates the established rules of capitalism, which cannot operate successfully unless ownership is restricted to those who have savings or access to long-term credit.

b. would make our economic system more just, more democratic, and less dependent on welfare state remedies.

c. is socialistic and therefore unacceptable.

d. is capitalistic and therefore unacceptable.

11. Employee Stock Ownership Plans (ESOPs):

    a. can and should be expanded, so that every American can become a stockholder in the enterprise that employs him or her.

    b. should be outlawed, because they are subsidized by tax breaks and they benefit only those people fortunate enough to have career jobs with our strongest private companies while doing no good for the unemployed and the majority of Americans.

    c. should be encouraged as useful experiments in the broadening of ownership that can serve as stepping-stones to the goal of universal share ownership.

12. Experiments in universal share ownership should use as reservoirs:

    a. capital additions of major companies.

    b. new stocks and bonds issued by businesses, as in the Albus National Mutual Fund plan.

    c. shares of local worker-owned companies organized to perform the work of humanity, such as Shareholders In America, Inc.

    d. Employee Stock Ownership Plans (ESOPs) and Employee Convertible Debentures (ECDs).

    e. the credit power of major companies, as in the Teddy Bear Principle (Figure 1) and leveraged buyouts.

    f. corporate profits.

    g. privatization of government-owned assets, including federal land.

    h. stock issued by companies in payment for government assistance.

    i. consumer payments to public utilities, as in Kelso's Consumer Stock Ownership Plan.

    j. assets other than corporate stock, such as real estate and art objects.

    k. some or all of the above potential reservoirs.

13. Government intervention in the economy:

    a. is a moral question.

    b. should be determined by political ideology, with liberals automatically choosing intervention to solve economic problems, and conservatives automatically opposing it.

    c. is a procedural question that should be decided after study of the alternatives according to the subsidiarity principle, rather than by resort to ideology.

14. The question of whether we can achieve greater social justice through increased employment, broader ownership, or both:

    a. must be determined according to long-established economic principles that cannot be altered without endangering our productivity and living standards.

    b. must be determined according to our hopes for a better world.

    c. must be determined by trial-and-error experimentation with carefully considered plans for broadening employment and ownership.

15. Income distribution and wealth distribution:

   a. must be determined by principles of economic science.

   b. must be determined by popular vote.

   c. must be determined by people familiar with details of the economic system, such as economists, business executives, and government officials.

   d. are political questions and value judgments, which religious organizations are at least as well qualified to decide as are economists, business executives, and government officials.

16. Full employment (reducing unemployment to 4 percent or less):

   a. cannot be achieved, because it requires government job-creation programs whose costs are unacceptable.

   b. must be achieved, regardless of cost.

   c. could be achieved through tackling the work of humanity, but to make such a program politically feasible, we must experiment with methods of paying for it without massive public funding.

17. Such a program for tackling the work of humanity:

   a. should offer unemployed people salaries above welfare levels, to be paid by the government.

   b. should be funded by contributions from charities and religious organizations.

   c. should conduct experiments that include in the compensation package shares of stock of corporations listed on major stock exchanges, or shares in new companies organized to do the work of humanity.

18. A program for tackling the work of humanity that includes the opportunity to own valuable shares of stock:

    a. is socialistic and therefore unacceptable.

    b. is capitalistic and therefore unacceptable.

    c. would offer stronger work incentives to the millions of Americans who now must choose between a poorly paid dead-end job or welfare.

19. The experience of religious organizations in performing some of the work of humanity:

    a. qualifies them to participate in experiments that may lead to broadening employment and to ownership through the work of humanity.

    b. demonstrates that this work can be achieved by contributions from charities and religious organizations, without need for any broader programs.

    c. is irrelevant and should be disregarded.

20. On issues of economic justice, religious organizations:

    a. should stick to religious matters and stay out of economics, since they do not have the specialized knowledge required to participate in discussions of income and wealth distribution with such experts as economists, business executives, and politicians.

    b. need not participate in the effort to make American capitalism a more moral and just system through structural changes, because such changes will be designed and implemented by other groups, such as academic, business, and political organizations.

    c. should take an active part in designing and implementing structural changes that will make American capitalism a more moral and just system, because the inertia of our economic and political systems is so strong that the moral energy of our religious organizations is indispensable to achievement of meaningful change.

Appendix

THE FOLLOWING MATERIAL IS REPRINTED from the "Scripture Guide to Justice" in *Building Economic Justice: The Bishops' Pastoral Letter and Tools for Action,* published in 1987 by the United States Catholic Conference, 1312 Massachusetts Avenue, N.W., Washington, DC 20005-4105.

Old Testament

Gn 4:9–10	Am I my brother's keeper?
Ex 3:1–20	God reveals himself as liberator; sends Moses to free his people from economic and political oppression.
Ex 6:2–13	God the liberator.
Ex 22:20–24	Justice and mercy toward stranger, orphan, widow.
Ex 22:25–27	Mercy and kindness toward neighbor.
Ex 23:9	Don't oppress strangers.
Lv 19:9–15	Treat your neighbor with justice and mercy.
Lv 19:23–24	Don't oppress strangers.
Lv 25:23–38	The land belongs to the Lord. You are strangers and guests.
Dt 10:16–20	Don't oppress strangers.
Dt 15:4	Let there be no poor among you.

Dt 24:17–22	Justice toward strangers, orphans, widows.
Dt 27:19	Don't oppress strangers.
Dt 30	Choose life. A nation that chooses the Lord chooses life.
1 Sm 15:22	Excessive formalism v. obedience to God.
Tb 4:16–17	Treat others as you would be treated.
Jb 1:21	"Naked I came from my mother's womb, naked I shall return."
Ps 9:9	Strength for the oppressed; justice toward all.
Ps 34:6–18	The Lord hears and protects the just.
Ps 41:1–3	Regard for the lowly and the poor.
Ps 72	God liberates and defends the poor and oppressed. Justice flourishes in his day.
Ps 82	No more mockery of justice.
Ps 103	"Yahweh is always on the side of the oppressed." We should be too.
Ps 146:6–9	The Lord gives justice and liberty.
Prv 21:3	Justice is more pleasing than sacrifice.
Prv 21:13	Listen to the poor.
Prv 22:22–23	Do not rob or injure the poor.
Prv 31:8–9	Be an advocate for the voiceless.
Eccl 4:1–3	The power of oppressors and the weak.
Sir 3:30; 4:11	Charity toward the poor.
Is 1:10–28	Religious hypocrisy; its punishment and cure.
Is 2:1–5	Turn swords into ploughshares.
Is 3:13–15	Grinding the face of the poor.
Is 5:1–7	God's people produce the bitter fruit of injustice.

Is 5:8–9	Woe to those who hoard riches.
Is 10:1–2	Bad legislators; denial of human rights.
Is 29:13	Change of heart requires more than lip service.
Is 32:16–17	Justice will bring peace.
Is 58:1–12	God doesn't want empty worship or meaningless religious exercises. He wants conversion of heart that produces justice, love, and mercy.
Is 61:1–2	Mission of Christ foretold, good news to the poor; liberation.
Jer 6:13–16	They cry, "Peace!" but there is none.
Jer 6:19–20	Worship is not acceptable without obedience.
Jer 7:1–11	The temple is no haven for evildoers.
Jer 22:3	Rescue the victim from the oppressor.
Jer 22:16	To know the Lord is to act justly.
Ez 34	Responsibilities of leaders and authorities — religious, civil, business, labor, etc.
Ez 37	The "dry bones" of the Church and our communities and nation can be renewed by the Holy Spirit.
Dn 9:1–19	The nation is called to repent.
Hos 6:6	Love, not empty worship.
Am 2:6–7	The unjust trample on the heads of ordinary people.
Am 5:14–15	Establish justice.
Am 5:21–24	God does not want empty, meaningless religious exercises, but rather worship that expresses true conversion and renewal that produces justice.

Am 6:1,3–6	Woe to the complacent and oppressive rich.
Am 8:4–7	The powerful trample on the poor and needy.
Mi 2:1–2	Woe to the oppressor.
Mi 6:8	Act justly.
Mi 6:9–14	Dishonesty condemned.
Hb 2:6–9	Trouble will come to those who exploit.
Zec 7:9–10	Justice and mercy.

New Testament

Mt 5:23–25	Forgiveness and reconciliation.
Mt 5:38–48	Give your coat. Walk the extra mile.
Mt 6:19–21	Your heart is where your treasure is.
Mt 6:25–34	Set your hearts on his kingdom first.
Mt 7:21; Lk 6:46–49	Combine prayer with action.
Mt 8:20	Christ lived in poverty.
Mt 10:37–39	Take up the cross daily; lose life to gain life.
Mt 11:2–6	The signs for recognizing the Messiah and his followers today.
Mt 12:46–50	Do God's will.
Mt 15:32	Compassion and a sense of responsibility.
Mt 20:26–28	Christians must be servants.
Mt 23:11	Be a servant.
Mt 23:23–24	Don't neglect justice and mercy.
Mt 25:31–46	Christ is identified with all people. Whatever we do to our neighbor, we do to Christ.
Mk 6:30–37	"Give them something to eat yourselves."

Mk 9:35; 10:41–45	To be first before God, be a servant.
Mk 10:17–31	The rich young man refuses invitation to voluntary poverty.
Lk 1:52–53	God exalts the poor and lowers the rich.
Lk 3:10–18	Sharing is the Christian way. John the Baptist's call to share extra clothing, food; for honesty in work (business, law enforcement).
Lk 4:16–30	Jesus announces that his mission is to liberate people and gets expelled from his hometown.
Lk 6:20–26	Beatitudes, condemnation of oppressive and complacent rich.
Lk 6:27–35	Make peace through nonviolence and love of enemies.
Lk 10:25–37	The Good Samaritan.
Lk 11:40–42	Pharisaism. We need justice and love.
Lk 12:13–21	A man's worth is not determined by how much he owns.
Lk 12:33	Sell your possessions and give alms.
Lk 14:7–14	Humility and hospitality.
Lk 15:1–3	Jesus associated with the outcasts of society.
Lk 16:19–31	The story of Lazarus and the rich man.
Lk 19:7–9	Conversion, repentance, and restitution.
Lk 19:41	Jesus weeps over Jerusalem. Does he weep over our cities?
Lk 22:24–27	Be a servant.
Lk 24:49	Christ empowers us to continue his work.
Jn 6:5–13	Christ feeds the hungry.
Jn 10:1–18	Jesus is the Good Shepherd. He laid down his life for us and calls us to lay down our lives for one another.

Jn 13:1–15	Jesus, the Suffering Servant, washes the feet of the Apostles. Invites us to do the same.
Jn 13:34–35	Love: the distinctive characteristic of the Christian.
Jn 14:10–17	You will do the same and greater works through the power of the Holy Spirit.
Jn 14:12	Christ empowers us to continue his mission.
Jn 16:33	Christ has overcome the world; through him we shall overcome.
Acts 1:4	The power we need to do Christ's work.
Acts 1:6–8	Our job is to be Christ's witness.
Acts 2:43–47; 5:12–16	The first parish shared everything. No one was in need.
Acts 4:18–22	Obey God rather than men.
Acts 4:32–35	True Christian community.
Acts 6:1–6	Deacons appointed for service.
Acts 10:34–35	God shows no favoritism.
Acts 16:16–24; 17:1–9	At times, being Christian means disturbing the status quo.
Rom 8:14–17	We have been given a spirit of freedom, not slavery.
Rom 12:10–18	Make hospitality your special care; make friends with the poor.
Rom 13:8–10	Our only debt is to love one another.
Rom 14:17–19	The kingdom is justice, peace, and joy.
1 Cor 12:7–11	The gifts of the Holy Spirit are tools for building Christian community.
1 Cor 12:24–26	If one suffers, all suffer.
1 Cor 13	Love as the Christian life style.

2 Cor 4:7	God's power working in and through us.
2 Cor 6:6	The qualities of a servant.
2 Cor 8:1–15	On sharing with the needy; Christ became poor to enrich us.
Gal 3:28	There are no distinctions. All are one in Christ.
Gal 5:1	You have been called to live in freedom.
Gal 5:13–15	Use your freedom to serve others. Love fulfills the law.
Gal 5:22–23	The fruits of the Holy Spirit.
Gal 6:2	Bear one another's burdens.
Eph 4:11–16	The base for ministry is the community. The individual alone is weak. The community has the power of Christ's Spirit.
Eph 4:23–24	Put aside old misdirected ways for a new, fresh way of thinking.
Phil 2:1–11	Unity and service; be a servant like Christ.
Col 3:10–12	On racial discrimination.
Col 3:17	Do all in Christ's name.
1 Thes 5:12–18	The demands of community life.
1 Tm 6:7–10	Love of money is the root of all evils.
1 Tm 6:17–19	Tell the rich not to be proud.
Heb 10:24–25	Concern in Christian community.
Jas 1:22–27	Be doers, not only hearers of the word.
Jas 2	We must practice what we believe and preach.
Jas 3:13–18	Peacemakers follow true wisdom.
Jas 5:1–6	Riches obtained unjustly bring misery.
1 Pt 4:7–11	Put your gifts at the service of others.
1 Jn 3:17	Selfishness precludes love.
1 Jn 4:19–21	We can't love God without loving neighbor.

Acronyms

BCRIC	British Columbia Resources Investment Corp.
CCC	Civilian Conservation Corps
CDC	Control Data Corporation
CETA	Comprehensive Employment & Training Act
CHD	Campaign for Human Development
CIPA	Council on International and Public Affairs
CSOP	Consumer Stock Ownership Plan
CWA	Civil Works Administration
ECD	Employee Convertible Debenture
ESOP	Employee Stock Ownership Plan
FCP	Financed Capitalist Plan
FHA	Federal Housing Administration
GAO	General Accounting Office
GJOP	Guaranteed Job Opportunity Program
GNP	Gross National Product
GSOP	General Stock Ownership Plan
ICOP	Individual Capital Ownership Plan
IRA	Individual Retirement Account
JEC	Joint Economic Committee of Congress
JTPA	Job Training Partnership Act

LBO	Leveraged Buyout
LISC	Local Initiatives Support Corp.
MOP	Means of Production
MUSOP	Mutual Stock Ownership Plan
NCCB	National Conference of Catholic Bishops
NDP	The National Dividend Plan
NMF	The National Mutual Fund
NMSDC	National Minority Supplier Development Council
PEP	Personal Equity Plan
PIC	Private Industry Council
PWA	Public Works Administration
RECOP	Residential Capital Ownership Plan
SEC	Securities and Exchange Commission
SIA	Shareholders In America, Inc.
USOP	Universal Share Ownership Plan
WEFA	Wharton Econometric Forecasting Associates
WPA	Works Progress Administration
WSOC	Wider Share Ownership Council

Bibliography

Albert, William. *The Turnpike Road System in England, 1663–1840.* Cambridge: Cambridge University Press, 1972.

Albus, James S. *Peoples' Capitalism: The Economics of the Robot Revolution.* Kensington, Md.: New World Books, 1976.

Aman, Kenneth, ed. *Border Regions of Faith: An Anthology of Religion and Social Change.* Maryknoll, N.Y.: Orbis Books, 1987.

Avery, Robert B., and Gregory E. Elliehausen. "Financial Characteristics of High-Income Families," *Federal Reserve Bulletin,* March 1986.

Azar, Edward E., and Joyce R. Starr, eds. "Development Diplomacy." In *A Shared Destiny.* New York: Praeger, 1983.

Batra, Ravi. *The Great Depression of 1990.* New York: Simon and Schuster, 1987.

Bazak Guide to Israel. New York: Harper & Row, 1985.

Bergmann, Frithjof. "The Future of Work," *Praxis International,* vol. 3, no. 3, October 1983.

————. "The Freedom of New Work," *Canadian Association of Mental Health,* October 1986.

Bezold, Clement, Rick J. Carlson, and Jonathan C. Peck. *The Future of Work and Health.* Dover, Mass.: Auburn House, 1986.

Blumberg, Barbara. *The New Deal and the Unemployed: The View from New York City.* Lewisburg, Pa.: Bucknell University Press, 1979.

Bovard, James. "Son of CETA," *The New Republic,* April 14, 1986.

Boyd, Julian P., ed. *The Papers of Thomas Jefferson,* vol. 8, February 25 to October 31, 1785. Princeton, N.J.: Princeton University Press, 1953.

Bradley, K., and A. Gelb. *Co-operation at Work: The Mondragon Experience.* London: Heinemann Educational Books, 1983.

————. *Share Ownership for Employees.* London: Public Policy Centre, 1986.

Brittan, Samuel. *The Role and Limits of Government: Essays in Political Economy.* London: Temple Smith, 1983.

———. *Jobs, Pay, Unions and the Ownership of Capital.* London: Financial Times, 1984a.

———. "The Case for Capital Ownership for All," *Financial Times* (London), September 20, 1984b.

———. "Thatcherism and Beyond," *Encounter,* April 1985a.

———. "Economic Viewpoint," *Financial Times* (London), July 4, 1985b.

Brown, Charles Reynolds. *The Social Message of the Modern Pulpit.* New York: Charles Scribner's Sons, 1912.

Burke, James E. "Reactions from Management." In Thomas M. Gannon, S.J., ed., *The Catholic Challenge to the American Economy.* New York: Macmillan, 1987.

Burress, David A. "The Spirit of St. Louis Model." In Stuart M. Speiser, ed., *Mainstreet Capitalism: Essays on Broadening Share Ownership in America and Britain.* New York: Council on International and Public Affairs, 1988.

Burton, John. *Would Workfare Work?* Buckingham, Eng.: The Employment Research Centre, University of Buckingham, 1987.

Butler, Stuart M. *Privatizing Federal Spending: A Strategy to Eliminate the Deficit.* New York: Universe Books, 1985.

Byers, David M., ed. *Justice in the Marketplace.* Washington, D.C.: United States Catholic Conference, 1985.

Campbell, A., C. Keen, G. Norman, and R. Oakeshott. *Worker Owners: The Mondragon Achievement.* London: Anglo-German Foundation, 1977.

Chambers, Ed. *Organizing for Family and Congregation.* Huntington, N.Y.: Industrial Areas Foundation, 1987.

Choate, Pat, and J. K. Linger. *The High-Flex Society: Shaping America's Economic Future.* New York: Alfred A. Knopf, 1986.

Choate, Pat, and Susan Walter. *America in Ruins: The Decaying Infrastructure.* Durham, N.C.: Duke Press Paperbacks, 1983.

Committee for Economic Development. *Jobs for the Hard-to-Employ: New Directions for a Public-Private Partnership.* New York: Committee for Economic Development, 1987.

Danziger, Sheldon H., and Daniel H. Weinberg. *Fighting Poverty: What Works and What Doesn't.* Cambridge, Mass.: Harvard University Press, 1987.

Davenport, Nicholas. *The Split Society.* London: Victor Gollancz, 1964.

———. *Memoirs of a City Radical*. London: Weidenfeld and Nicolson, 1974.

Davidson, Paul. "A Giant Step Back to the Preindustrial Age," *New York Times*, Sunday Business Section, April 7, 1985a.

———. "Symposium on Broadening Capital Ownership," *Journal of Post Keynesian Economics*, vol. 7, no. 3, 1985b.

DeAngelo, Yvonne, and Jean Heck. "Investing Your Conscience," *The Journal of Commerce and Finance*, Villanova College of Commerce and Finance, Spring 1987.

Dembo, David, and Ward Morehouse. *Joblessness and the Pauperization of Work in America*, Background Paper. New York: Council on International and Public Affairs, 1987.

Douglass, R. Bruce, ed. *The Deeper Meaning of Economic Life: Critical Essays on the U.S. Catholic Bishops' Pastoral Letter on the Economy.* Washington, D.C.: Georgetown University Press, 1986.

Drucker, Peter F. *The Unseen Revolution*. New York: Harper & Row, 1976.

Eaton, J. "The Basque Workers' Co-operatives," *Journal of Industrial Relations*, vol. 10, no. 3, 1979.

Ekins, Paul. *The Living Economy: A New Economics in the Making.* London: Routledge & Kegan Paul, 1986.

Ferm, Robert. *Issues in American Protestantism*. Garden City, N.Y.: Anchor, 1969.

Ferrara, Peter. *Social Security Reform*. Washington, D.C.: Heritage Foundation, 1982.

Fly, Richard. "Is Jack Kemp Fumbling His Presidential Bid?" *Business Week*, April 13, 1987.

Freeman, Richard B. "Create Jobs That Pay as Well as Crime," *New York Times*, July 20, 1986.

Frieden, Karl. *Workplace Democracy and Productivity.* Washington, D.C.: National Center for Economic Alternatives, 1980.

Friedman, Milton. *Capitalism and Freedom*. Chicago: University of Chicago Press, 1962.

Galbraith, John Kenneth. *Money: Whence It Came, Where It Went.* Boston: Houghton Mifflin, 1975.

Gannon, Thomas M., S.J., ed. *The Catholic Challenge to the American Economy.* New York: Macmillan, 1987.

General Accounting Office. "Employee Stock Ownership Plans: Benefits and Costs of ESOP Tax Incentives for Broadening Stock Ownership," Report No. GAO/PEMD-87-8, December 1986, Washington, D.C.: U.S. Government Printing Office, 1986.

Gingrich, Newt. *Window of Opportunity: A Blueprint for the Future.* New York: Tom Doherty Associates, 1984.

Godwin, William. *Enquiry Concerning Social Justice.* 1793. Reprint. Toronto: University of Toronto Press, 1969.

Gorbachev, Mikhail. *Perestroika.* New York: Harper & Row, 1987.

Grant, Jack B. "A Practical Experiment in Universal Share Ownership." In Stuart M. Speiser, ed., *Mainstreet Capitalism: Essays on Broadening Share Ownership in America and Britain.* New York: Council on International and Public Affairs, 1988.

Green, Ronald. "The Bishops' Letter — A Jewish Reading." In Thomas M. Gannon, S.J., ed., *The Catholic Challenge to the American Economy.* New York: Macmillan, 1987.

Gueron, Judith M. *Work Initiatives for Welfare Recipients.* New York: Manpower Demonstration Research Corporation, 1986.

———. *Reforming Welfare with Work.* New York: Manpower Demonstration Research Corporation, 1987.

Hamrin, Robert. "Broadening the Ownership of New Capital: ESOPs and Other Alternatives," Staff Study Prepared for the Use of the Joint Economic Committee, June 17, 1976. Washington, D.C.: Government Printing Office, 1976.

———. *Managing Growth in the 1980s: Toward a New Economics.* New York: Praeger, 1980.

Handy, Charles B. *The Future of Work: A Guide to a Changing Society.* New York: Basil Blackwell, 1984.

Harrington, Michael. *The Next Left: The History of a Future.* New York: Henry Holt, 1987.

Hart, Gary. *A New Democracy.* New York: William Morrow, 1983.

Hattersley, Roy. *Choose Freedom.* London: Penguin, 1987.

Hattersley, Roy, and Doug Jones, eds. *Economic Priorities for a Labour Government.* London: Macmillan, 1987.

Hayes, Edward. "From Rags to Riches," *American City & Country,* November 1986, pp. 64–72.

Heilbroner, Robert L., and Lester C. Thurow. *Economics Explained.* New York: Simon & Schuster, 1982.

Herbers, John. "Governors Vote a Plan Linking Welfare to Work," *New York Times,* February 25, 1987.

Hofstadter, Richard, ed. "Christianity and the Social Crisis." In *The Progressive Movement.* Englewood Cliffs, N.J.: Prentice-Hall, 1963.

Howell, David. *Blind Victory: A Study in Income, Wealth and Power.* London: Hamish Hamilton, 1986.

Jackall, Robert, and Henry M. Levin, eds. *Worker Cooperatives in America.* Berkeley: University of California Press, 1984.

Johannsen, Oscar B. "Land Based Shares." In Stuart M. Speiser, ed., *Mainstreet Capitalism: Essays on Broadening Share Ownership in America and Britain.* New York: Council on International and Public Affairs, 1988.

Johnson, A., and W. Whyte. "The Mondragon System of Worker Producer Co-operatives," *Industrial and Labor Relations Review,* vol. 31, no. 1, 1977.

Johnson, Clifford M. "Direct Federal Job Creation: Key Issues," Report No. 99-E, U.S. House of Representatives Committee on Education and Labor. Washington, D.C.: U.S. Government Printing Office, 1985.

Johnson, Paul. *A History of the Jews.* New York: Harper & Row, 1987.

Johnston, William B., and Arnold H. Packer. *Workforce 2000: Work and Workers for the 21st Century.* Indianapolis: Hudson Institute, 1987.

Joint Economic Committee of Congress. *1976 Joint Economic Report.* Washington, D.C.: Joint Economic Committee, 1976.

Jones, Derek, and Jan Svejnar, eds. *Participatory and Self-Managed Firms: Evaluating Economic Performance.* Lexington, Mass.: D.C. Heath, 1982.

Kelso, Louis O., and Mortimer J. Adler. *The Capitalist Manifesto.* New York: Random House, 1958.

———. *The New Capitalists.* New York: Random House, 1961.

Kelso, Louis O., and Patricia Hetter. *Two-factor Theory: The Economics of Reality.* New York: Vintage Books, 1968.

Kelso, Louis O., and Patricia Hetter Kelso. *Democracy and Economic Power: Extending the ESOP Revolution.* Cambridge, Mass.: Ballinger, 1986.

Keynes, John Maynard. *The General Theory of Employment, Interest and Money.* London: Macmillan. 1936. Reprint. Harbinger paperback, 1964.

———. *How to Pay for the War.* London: Macmillan, 1940.

Kissinger, Henry. "Saving the World Economy," *Newsweek,* January 24, 1983.

Klein, Lawrence R. "Economics, Morality and Justice for All," *The Journal of Commerce & Finance,* vol. 6, Spring 1987, pp. 7–11.

Krause, Kitry. "Hammers and Nails in Mt. Winans," *Washington Monthly,* April 1986.

Lay Commission on Catholic Social Teaching and the U.S. Economy. *Toward the Future: Catholic Social Thought and the U.S. Economy.* New York: Lay Commission on Catholic Social Teaching and the U.S. Economy, 1984.

Lekachman, Robert. "SuperStock: A Conservative Alternative to the Welfare State," *Journal of Post Keynesian Economics,* vol. 7, no. 3, 1985.

———. *Visions and Nightmares: America after Reagan.* New York: Macmillan, 1987.

Lindenfield, Frank, and Joyce Rothschild-Whitt, eds. *Workplace Democracy and Social Change.* Boston: Porter Sargent, 1982.

Linowes, David F. *Privatization: Toward More Effective Government.* Washington, D.C.: President's Commission on Privatization, 1988.

Louchheim, Katie, ed. *The Making of the New Deal: The Insiders Speak.* Cambridge, Mass.: Harvard University Press, 1983.

Low, Sir Toby (later Lord Aldington). *Every Man a Capitalist.* London: Conservative Research Centre, 1958.

Lydenberg, Steven D., Alice Tepper Marlin, and Sean O'Brien Strub. *Rating America's Corporate Conscience.* Reading, Mass.: Addison-Wesley, 1986.

Mackin, Christopher. *Strategies for Local Ownership and Control: A Policy Analysis,* Somerville, Mass.: Industrial Cooperative Association, 1983.

Marty, Martin E. *Pilgrims in Their Own Land: 500 Years of Religion in America.* New York: Penguin Books, 1985.

———. *Modern American Religion,* vol. 1, *The Irony of It All, 1893–1919.* Chicago: University of Chicago Press, 1986.

McClaughry, John, ed. *Expanded Ownership.* Fond du Lac, Wisc.: Sabre Foundation, 1972.

McClosky, Herbert, and John Zaller. *The American Ethos: Public Attitudes toward Capitalism and Democracy.* Cambridge, Mass.: Harvard University Press, 1984.

McConnell, Campbell R. *Economics.* 10th ed. New York: McGraw-Hill, 1987.

Meade, James E. "Full Employment, New Technologies and the Distribution of Income," *Journal of Social Policy* (Cambridge University Press), vol. 13, part 2, April 1984.

Middendorf, J. William, II. *High Road to Economic Justice: U.S. Encouragement of Employee Stock Ownership Plans in Central America and the Caribbean.* Washington, D.C.: Center for Economic and Social Justice, 1986.

Mill, John Stuart. *Principles of Political Economy: With Some of Their Applications to Social Philosophy.* 1848. Reprint. New York: Augustus M. Kelley, reprinted 1969.

Mollner, Terry. *Mondragon: A Third Way.* Shutesbury, Mass.: Trusteeship Institute, 1984.

Nader, Ralph, and William Taylor. *The Big Boys.* New York: Pantheon, 1986.

National Conference of Catholic Bishops. "Economic Justice for All: Catholic Social Teaching and the U.S. Economy," *Origins* (National Catholic News Service), vol. 16, no. 24, November 27, 1986.

Newman, Barry. "Change of Heart: Yugoslavia's Workers Find Self-Management Doesn't Make Paradise," *Wall Street Journal,* March 25, 1987.

Niebuhr, Reinhold. *The Children of Light and the Children of Darkness.* New York: Charles Scribner's Sons, 1944.

Nixon, Russell A. "The Historical Development of the Conception and Implementation of Full Employment as Economic Policy." In David C. Colander, ed.*Solutions to Unemployment.* San Diego: Harcourt, Brace, Jovanovich, 1981.

Norris, William C. *New Frontiers for Business Leadership.* Minneapolis: Dorn Books, 1983.

Novak, Michael. *Freedom with Justice: Catholic Social Thought and Liberal Institutions.* San Francisco: Harper & Row, 1984.

Novak, Michael, and William E. Simon. *Report of the U.S. Catholic Bishops' Pastoral Letter on the American Economy.* New York: Lay Commission on Catholic Social Teaching and the U.S. Economy, 1986.

Oakeshott, R. *The Case for Workers' Co-ops.* London: Routledge and Kegan Paul, 1978.

Pawlikowski, John, and Donald Senior, eds. *Economic Justice: CTU's Pastoral Commentary on the Bishops' Letter on the Economy.* Washington, D.C.: Pastoral Press, 1988.

Pemberton, Prentiss, and Daniel Rush Finn. *Toward a Christian Economic Ethic: Stewardship & Social Power.* Minneapolis: Winston, 1985.

Perry, John H., Jr. *The National Dividend.* New York: Ivan Obolensky, 1964.

Peters, Thomas J., and Robert H. Waterman, Jr. *In Search of Excellence: Lessons from America's Best-Run Companies.* New York: Warner, 1982.

Phillips, Kevin P. *Staying on Top: Winning the Trade War.* New York: Vintage Books, 1986.

Potterton, Susan. "Towards Wider Share Ownership: The National Work Scheme." In Stuart M. Speiser, ed., *Mainstreet Capitalism: Essays on Broadening Share Ownership in America and Britain.* New York: Council on International and Public Affairs, 1988.

Rawls, John. *A Theory of Justice.* Cambridge, Mass.: Harvard University Press, 1971.

Reich, Robert B. *Tales of a New America.* New York: Times Books, 1987.

Robertson, James. *Future Work: Jobs, Self-Employment and Leisure after the Industrial Age.* New York: Universe Books, 1985.

Robison, David. *Training and Jobs Programs in Action: Case Studies in Private-Sector Initiatives for the Hard-to-Employ.* Work in America Institute, Inc., 1978.

Rohatyn, Felix G. "Ethics in America's Money Culture," *New York Times,* June 3, 1987, Op Ed piece.

Rosen, Corey, Katherine J. Klein, and Karen M. Young. *Employee Ownership in America: The Equity Solution.* Lexington, Mass.: Lexington Books, 1986.

Samuelson, Paul A. *Economics.* 11th ed. New York: McGraw-Hill, 1980.

Samuelson, Paul A., and William D. Nordhaus. *Economics.* New York: McGraw-Hill, 1985.

Schlesinger, Arthur M., Jr. *The Coming of the New Deal.* Boston: Houghton Mifflin, 1958.

Sedlak, John A. "Guaranteed Work-Ownership Opportunity as an Alternative to Social Security and Certain Other Social Programs." In Stuart M. Speiser, ed., *Mainstreet Capitalism: Essays on Broadening Share Ownership in America and Britain.* New York: Council on International and Public Affairs, 1988.

Shad, John S. R. "Business's Bottom Line: Ethics," *New York Times,* July 27, 1987, Op Ed piece.

Simmons, John, and William Mares. *Working Together.* New York: Alfred A. Knopf, 1983.

Simon, Senator Paul. *Let's Put America Back to Work.* Chicago: Bonus Books, 1987.

Smith, Adam. *An Inquiry into the Nature and Causes of the Wealth of Nations.* 1776. Reprint. New York: Modern Library, 1937.

Solomon, Anthony. "Economics, Ideology, and Public Policy," *Challenge,* July/August 1986.

Sowell, Thomas. *A Conflict of Visions.* New York: Morrow, 1987.

Speiser, Stuart M. *A Piece of the Action.* New York: Van Nostrand Reinhold, 1977.

———. *SuperStock.* New York: Everest House, 1982.

———. *How to End the Nuclear Nightmare.* Croton-on-Hudson, N.Y.: North River Press, 1984.

———. "Symposium on Broadening Capital Ownership," *Journal of Post Keynesian Economics,* vol. 7, no., 3, 1985.

———. *The USOP Handbook: A Guide to Designing Universal Share Ownership Plans for the United States and Great Britain.* New York: Council on International and Public Affairs, 1986a.

———. "Shareholders In America, Inc." Supp. to *The USOP Handbook.* New York: Council on International and Public Affairs, 1986b.

———. ed. *Mainstreet Capitalism: Essays on Broadening Share Ownership in America and Britain.* New York: Council on International and Public Affairs, 1988.

Stein, Herbert. *Washington Bedtime Stories: The Politics of Money and Jobs.* New York: Free Press, 1986.

Tamari, Meir. *With All Your Possessions: Jewish Ethics and Economic Life.* New York: Free Press, 1987.

Taylor, Kenneth B., ed. *Capitalism and the "Evil Empire": Reducing Superpower Conflict through American Economic Reform.* New York: Council on International and Public Affairs, 1987.

Taylor, Kenneth B. "The Common Fund." In Stuart M. Speiser, ed., *Mainstreet Capitalism: Essays on Broadening Share Ownership in America and Britain.* New York: Council on International and Public Affairs, 1988.

Taylor, Robert J., ed. *The Papers of John Adams,* vol. 4, February–August 1776. Cambridge, Mass.: The Belknap Press of Harvard University Press, 1979.

Thomas, H., and C. Logan. *Mondragon: An Economic Analysis.* London: Allen and Unwin, 1982.

Thurow, Lester C. "The Leverage of our Wealthiest 400," *New York Times,* October 11, 1984.

————. *The Zero-Sum Solution: Building a World-Class American Economy.* New York: Simon and Schuster, 1985.

————. "Ethics Doesn't Start in Business Schools," *New York Times,* June 14, 1987, Op Ed piece.

Toffler, Alvin. *The Third Wave.* New York: William Morrow, 1980.

Turnbull, Shann. *Democratising the Wealth of Nations.* Sydney, Australia: Company Directors Association of Australia, 1975.

————. "Another America." In Stuart M. Speiser, ed., *Mainstreet Capitalism: Essays on Broadening Share Ownership in America and Britain.* New York: Council on International and Public Affairs, 1988.

U.S. House of Representatives. *Direct Federal Job Creation: Key Issues,* Serial No. 99-E. Washington: U.S. Government Printing Office, 1985, p. iii.

Vidal, Avis C., Mark H. Moore, Arnold M. Howitt, and Herman B. Leonard. "Discussion Paper D85-1." *The Local Initiatives Support Corporation — Preliminary Findings of an Evaluation in Progress.* Cambridge, Mass.: Harvard University State, Local and Intergovernmental Center, 1985.

Von Thunen, Johann Heinrich. *The Isolated State.* Abridged and trans. from the 2nd German ed. Oxford, England: Pergamon Press, 1966.

Wattenberg, Ben J. *The Birth Dearth.* New York: Pharos Books, 1987.

Weber, Max. *The Protestant Ethic and the Spirit of Capitalism.* Reprint. New York: Charles Scribner's Sons, 1980.

Weitzman, Martin L. *The Share Economy: Conquering Stagflation.* Cambridge, Mass.: Harvard University Press, 1984.

Whyte, William Foote, and Kathleen King Whyte. *Making Mondragon: The Growth and Dynamics of the Worker Cooperative Complex.* Ithaca, N.Y.: ILR Press NYSSILR, 1988.

Wisman, Jon. *Economic Reform for Humanity's Greatest Struggle.* New York: Council on International and Public Affairs, 1986.

Wogaman, J. Philip. *The Great Economic Debate: An Ethical Analysis.* Philadelphia: Westminster, 1977.

Woodson, Robert L., ed. *On the Road to Economic Freedom: An Agenda for Black Progress.* Washington, D.C.: Regnery Gateway, 1987.

Yeager, Diane. "The Bishops and the Kingdom." In R. Bruce Douglass, ed., *The Deeper Meaning of Economic Life: Critical Essays on the U.S. Catholic Bishops' Pastoral Letter on the Economy.* Washington, D.C.: Georgetown University Press, 1986.

Index

United Jewish Appeal, 62
United Nations General Assembly, 216
United States Catholic Conference, 21
United States Travel and Tourism Administration, 139
United States Supreme Court, 2, 177
Unity Trust, 229
Universal Share Ownership Plan (USOP), 23–24, 164, 165, 171–200, 209, 215–218, 231
Valley Nitrogen Producers Inc., 191
Vatican, 97
Veterans Administration, 139
Vidal, Avis C., 113
VISTA, 122
von Thunen, Johann Heinrich, 157, 158
Walker, Jay L., 201
Wallace, Mike, 2
Walter, Susan, 41
Watergate, 3
Waterman, Robert H., Jr., 50
Wattenberg, Ben J., 136
Weakland, Archbishop Rembert G., O.S.B., 20, 71
Weber, Max, 90
Weigand, Bishop William, 71
Weinberg, Daniel H., 145
Weintraub, Sidney, 15, 16
Weirton Steel Company, 168
Weitzman, Martin, 158–160, 178, 199

Wharton Econometric Forecasting Associates (WEFA), 6, 13
White, Erskine, 142
Whitfield, Alphonso, Jr., 116
Wholey, Dennis, 18
Whyte, William and Kathleen, 167
Wider Share Ownership Council (WSOC), 9, 23, 184, 185, 224, 233, 234
Wisman, Jon D., 18, 160, 182
Wogaman, J. Philip, 91
Wolfe, Art, 204
Woodson, Robert L., 116, 117
Working Assets Money Fund, 210
Works Progress Administration (WPA), 19, 20, 49, 51, 118, 119, 133, 150, 197, 242
World Council of Churches (WCC), 97
World War II, 96
Wright Brothers, 198
Xerox, 176
Yankelovich Clancy Shulman, 201
Yeager, Diane, 82, 95
Young, Andrew J., 111
Young Americans for Freedom, 44
Youth Employment Demonstration Projects Act, 123
Zaller, John, 29, 30, 38, 40, 42, 45, 49, 91, 92
Zedakah, 61
Zion Investment Corporation (ZIC), 117